Critical Sociology

Critical Sociology

Steven M. Buechler

Paradigm Publishers
Boulder • London

Copyright © 2008 Steven M. Buechler

Published in the United States by Paradigm Publishers, 3360 Mitchell Lane Suite E, Boulder, CO 80301 USA.

Paradigm Publishers is the trade name of Birkenkamp & Company, LLC, Dean Birkenkamp, President and Publisher.

Library of Congress Cataloging-in-Publication Data

Buechler, Steven M., 1951–
  Critical sociology / Steven M. Buechler.
    p. cm.
  Includes bibliographical references and index.
  ISBN-13: 978-1-59451-430-2 (hardcover : alk. paper)
  1. Sociology—Philosophy. 2. Critical theory. I. Title.
  HM585.B84 2008
  301—dc22
2007052291

Printed and bound in the United States of America on acid-free paper that meets the standards of the American National Standard for Permanence of Paper for Printed Library Materials.

Designed and typeset by Straight Creek Bookmakers.

12 11 10 09 08   1 2 3 4 5

Contents

Preface

The title *Critical Sociology* has three meanings.

First, it means that the sociological perspective is increasingly critical to human survival. The good news is that we have developed the material, intellectual, and technological capacity to address problems that were previously unsolvable. The bad news is that we have created new problems that will tax these capacities to their limits. These include, to name a few, thermonuclear annihilation, global warming, terrorist anarchy, global poverty, environmental devastation, and ethnic cleansing. Whether our new capacities can meet these challenges is an open question. Given this, the sociological perspective is increasingly critical if we are to understand clearly, decide rationally, and act wisely. It is simply the best angle of vision that we have to capture life's complexity, to interpret its history, to anticipate its future, and to guide reasoned action.

A second meaning of critical sociology is that thinking sociologically inevitably involves thinking critically. It is inherent in the very nature of the sociological perspective that all familiar "truths" and established "facts" come under scrutiny. Sociology requires a skeptical and restless quality of mind. It continually questions the self-proclaimed reasons for any social arrangement. To be a sociologist is to assume that things are not what they appear to be, that hidden interests are at work, and that no claims can be taken at face value. In this second meaning, the phrase critical sociology is almost redundant, because even the most generic versions of the sociological perspective inevitably lead the sociological thinker to adopt a critical stance toward the world around them.

The third meaning of critical sociology refers to one type of sociology among others. This type is explicitly based on the values of freedom, equality, and justice. These values shape both the questions and the answers sought by this sociology.

This sociology examines how social structures create relations of domination among various social groups. It is committed to exposing their operation and undermining their stability. This type of sociology is dedicated to progressive social change. The point of seeking sociological knowledge is to foster change while being as inclusive as possible about who participates in the process. To promote such change means that sociology must have a vision of a better society. It must also have the conviction that such a world is within our grasp.

In sum, critical sociology means that a sociological perspective is increasingly critical to our survival, that sociology is an inherently critical angle of vision, and that one type of sociology is explicitly dedicated to progressive change. All three meanings are in play throughout this book.

Critical sociology is relevant to many historical periods and social forms. But it began in nineteenth-century Europe and subsequently migrated to societies like the United States. Given this history and my own knowledge base, this book primarily applies critical sociology to the United States. By the same token, the United States exists in a globalizing world alongside other societies, and this analysis addresses these relationships as well.

The book is organized into five sections.

The first section describes the sociological perspective. Chapter one traces the origins of sociology and its relationship to the modern world. It then explores how to think sociologically and the role of critique in that process. Chapter two sketches the history of sociological theory by grouping classical and contemporary thinkers into scientific, humanistic, and critical schools. Chapter three expands on the critical school as a prelude to its application throughout the remainder of the book.

The second section addresses power and domination. Chapter four analyzes modern capitalism as a source of inequality and an impediment to democracy. Chapter five examines the political system, the relationships between economic and political power, and how a formally democratic process is turned against the interests of a majority of its citizens. Chapter six explores mass media, its role as a handmaiden to economic and political power, and its contradictory effects on information flows and the prospects for a vibrant civil society.

The third section analyzes inequality and difference. Chapter seven examines social class in modern society with an eye toward how class dynamics have both persisted and changed in our times. Chapter eight takes a parallel look at race and reviews sociological ways of looking at racial differences and inequality. Chapter nine traces a third story of inequality with a focus on gender as the oldest, most intimate, and most pervasive basis of inequality and difference.

The fourth section examines self and society. Chapter ten traces the historical emergence of the individual, leading to the contemporary glorification of individuality. Chapter eleven sketches a dialectical view of the relationship between self and society as they shape identity. Chapter twelve explores the delicate construction of everyday life, including the presentation of self in the routine dramas that compose our lives.

The fifth section explores social change. Chapter thirteen offers a critical analysis of globalization that situates it relative to earlier historical change and development. Chapter fourteen discusses social movements as increasingly important change agents in the world. Chapter fifteen advocates the democratization of society and discusses how the sociological perspective can cultivate the citizenship required for this development.

As you read this book, I hope you enjoy the journey. I also hope the book helps you become a better traveler who is more attuned to your surroundings and more capable of assessing and responding to the worlds you discover. Such is the promise of the sociological perspective.

PART ONE
SOCIOLOGICAL PERSPECTIVES

Chapter 1

How to Think Sociologically

People have always tried to make sense of the world around them. Myths, fables, and religion provided traditional ways of making sense. More recently, science has provided additional ways of understanding the world. Sociology is part of the rise of science as a means of making sense of the world.

As we know in our own time, there can be tension between religious and scientific views. Contemporary disputes over evolution, sexuality, and the family often pit religious values against scientific interpretations. More broadly speaking, both at home and abroad, religious fundamentalisms rest uneasily alongside modern, secular worldviews. These familiar tensions have a history that takes us back to the origins of sociology itself.

SOCIOLOGY AND MODERNITY

The rise of sociology is part of a much larger story about the emergence of the modern world itself. Modernity emerged in European societies through a long process of social change that unfolded from the sixteenth to the nineteenth centuries. During this time, virtually everything about organized social life in Europe was fundamentally transformed. In our day, we speak of globalization as a force that is changing the world in the most basic ways. But current patterns of globalization can be traced back to the rise of modernity itself; in many respects, they are a continuation of the changes that ushered in the modern world.

Economically, modernity transformed most people from peasants to workers in a complex division of labor. Politically, modernity created distinct nation-states with clear boundaries. Technologically, modernity applied scientific knowledge to producing everything from consumer goods to lethal weapons. Demographically, modernity triggered population growth and massive migration from small, familiar, rural communities to large, urban, anonymous cities.

3

When social worlds change like this, some people benefit while others are harmed. In addition, most people find rapid change and its inevitable conflict to be unsettling, and they seek to understand what is happening. It was this moment that give rise to sociology. Explaining modernity became sociology's task at the same time that modernity was making sociology possible in the first place.

The link between modernity and sociology was the Enlightenment. This intellectual revolution accompanied other revolutionary changes occurring throughout Europe. In the broadest terms, the Enlightenment challenged religious belief, dogma, and authority. It sought to replace them with scientific reason, logic, and knowledge.

Four basic themes pervaded Enlightenment thought (Zeitlin 1987). First, human reason was the best guide to knowledge, even if it meant that scientific skepticism displaced religious certainty. Second, reason must be paired with careful, scientific observation. Third, Enlightenment thought insisted that social arrangements be rationally justified; if not, they must be changed until they could be rationally defended. Finally, Enlightenment thought assumed that with the systematic application of reason, the perfectibility of people and progress of society were all but inevitable.

Enlightenment thought contained some potentially fatal flaws. It was a Eurocentric worldview, created by privileged, white men, that made universal pronouncements about all people in all times and places. While applauding Europe's progress, it ignored the colonial domination of the rest of the world that provided the labor, goods, and wealth that underwrote that progress. Generalizations about "humanity," meant "males," to the exclusion of women, and pronouncements on the "human race" meant white Europeans, to the exclusion of darker people who were viewed as subhuman.

The Enlightenment was much more than a justification of imperialism, sexism, and racism, but it could become that as well. More than two centuries later, the jury is still out on whether Enlightenment biases can be overcome and its promises be fulfilled. Some postmodernists see little hope for this to happen. Others, myself included, think that the critical spirit of the Enlightenment can help uproot its biases. The project is already under way as feminists, people of color, and postcolonial writers find their way into contemporary sociological discourses (Lemert 2004).

In its own day, the Enlightenment provoked a "romantic conservative reaction" (Zeitlin 1987) that rejected the elevation of reason and science over faith and tradition. It defended traditional customs, institutions, and ways of life from the new standard of critical reason. The debate between Enlightenment progress and conservative reaction set the agenda for sociology as the social science of modernity. Progress or order? Change or stability? Reason or tradition? Science or religion? Individual or group? Innovation or authority? Such dichotomies framed the subject matter of the new science of sociology.

The classical era of sociology refers to European thinkers whose ideas brought this new discipline to maturity from the late eighteenth to the early twentieth centuries. The very different sociologies of Auguste Comte, Herbert Spencer, Ferdinand

Toennies, Karl Marx, Max Weber, Georg Simmel, Emile Durkheim, and others are variations on sociology's main theme: How do we understand modern society? Given these efforts, we might think of sociology as the ongoing effort of human beings to understand the worlds they are simultaneously inheriting from earlier generations and maintaining and transforming for future generations.

This approach has been described as the "sociological imagination." It arises when people realize that they can only know themselves by understanding their historical period and by examining others in the same situation as themselves. We think sociologically when we grasp how our historical moment differs from previous ones and how the situations of various groups of people differ from each other (Mills 1959).

The sociological imagination is guided by three related questions. The first concerns the social structure of society. How is it organized, what are its major institutions, and how are they linked together? The second concerns the historical location of society. How has it emerged from past social forms, what mechanisms promote change, and what futures are possible based on this historical path? The third concerns individual biography within society. What kinds of character traits are called forth by this society, and what kinds of people come to prevail? The sociological imagination is thus about grasping the relations between history and biography within society.

The sociological imagination sensitizes us to the difference between "personal troubles" and "public issues." A personal trouble is a difficulty in someone's life that is largely a result of individual circumstances. A public issue is a difficulty that is largely owing to social arrangements beyond the individual's control. The distinction is crucial because common sense often interprets events as personal troubles; we explain someone's difficulties as springing from individual shortcomings. The sociological imagination recognizes that such difficulties are rarely unique to one person; they rather happen to many people in similar situations. The underlying causes derive more from social structures and historical developments than the individual alone. If our goal is "diagnosis," the sociological imagination locates problems in a larger social context. If our goal is "treatment," it implies changing the structure of society rather than the behavior of individuals.

This applies to success as well. Common sense often attributes success to individual qualities. The sociological imagination asks what social and historical preconditions were necessary for an individual to become a success. Many successful people, in Jim Hightower's memorable phrase, "were born on third base but thought they hit a triple." The point is that whereas common sense sees the r in individual terms, sociological thinking sees it in structural terms. Only by the connections between structure, history, and biography can we under world in a sociological way.

This discussion implies that professional sociologists and ordir the world differently. This is often true, but the issue is more compli has also led ordinary people to develop a practical sociology in ' Think about it this way. Sociology sees the world as a social c follow various blueprints. Indeed, social worlds *are* constructed in very different ways in different times and places.

In our time, an awareness of the socially constructed nature of social worlds is no longer the privileged insight of scholars but has become part of everyday understanding. Whether owing to rapid change, frequent travel, cultural diffusion, or media images, many people understand that we live in socially constructed worlds. Some people are distressed by this fact, and others rejoice in it, but few can escape it. Thus, an idea that was initially associated with professional sociology has become part of the everyday consciousness of ordinary people today.

The result is that many people without formal sociological training understand social processes quite well. Put differently, the objects of sociological analysis are people who are quite capable of becoming the subjects of the sociological knowledge created by that analysis. Although few people can explain how quantum mechanics governs the physical world, many can describe sociological processes that shape the social world.

Certain circumstances prompt people to think sociologically. Perhaps the key stimulant is when familiar ways of doing and thinking no longer work. It is when people are surprised, puzzled, challenged, or damaged that they are most likely to think sociologically (Lemert 1997). People then develop sociological competence as they try to make sense out of specific, individual circumstances by linking them to broader social patterns. In this way, sociological awareness begins to understand bigger things as a byproduct of wrestling with the practical challenges of everyday life.

Circumstances do not inevitably provoke sociological consciousness. Some people redouble their faith or retreat into ritualism. So perhaps we can conclude this way. Societies confront people with problems. These problems have always had the potential to promote a sociological awareness. In our times, there is a greater awareness of the socially constructed nature of the world. This makes it even more likely that when people in this society are confronted with practical challenges, they will develop sociological competence as a practical life skill. In late modernity, everyone can become a practical sociologist.

THINKING SOCIOLOGICALLY

The sociological perspective involves several themes. They overlap with one another, and some may be found in other social sciences as well as everyday consciousness. Taken together, they comprise a distinctive lens for viewing the social world. Here are some of those themes.

Society Is a Social Construction

Social order is constructed by people. Sociology does not see society as God-given, biologically determined, or as following any predetermined plan beyond human intervention. At the same time, this does not mean that everyone plays an equal role in the process or that the final product looks like what people intended.

Social construction begins with intentions that motivate people to act in certain ways. When many people have similar goals and act in concert, larger social patterns or institutions are created. Goal-driven action is essential to the creation of institutions, and it remains equally important to their maintenance and transformation over time. Put succinctly, society is a human product (Berger and Luckmann 1966).

Basic human needs ensure some similarities in the goals that people pursue in all times and places. But these pursuits also unfold in specific historical circumstances and cultural contexts that have led to a dazzling variety of social worlds. This variety is itself the best evidence of the socially constructed nature of social worlds. If biology or genetics were the determining force behind social worlds, wouldn't they look a lot more similar than what we actually see around the globe?

Social constructionists thus insist that society arises from the goal-driven action of people. But they also recognize that the institutions created by such actions take on a life of their own. They appear to exist independently of the people who create and sustain them. They are experienced by people as a powerful external force that weighs down on them. When this external force becomes severe enough, people are likely to lose sight of the fact that society is a social product in the first place.

The value of the social constructionist premise is this dual recognition. On the one hand, society is a subjective reality originating in the intentions of social actors. On the other hand, it becomes an objective reality that confronts subsequent generations as a social fact that inevitably shapes *their* intentional actions—and so it goes. Understood this way, the idea that society is a social construction is at the heart of the sociological perspective.

Society Is an Emergent Reality

Another premise of sociology is emergentism. This reveals sociology's distinctive level of analysis. For psychology, the level of analysis is the individual, even if it is acknowledged that individuals belong to groups. For sociology, the level of analysis is social ties rather than individual elements. Emergentism recognizes that certain realities only appear when individual elements are combined in particular ways. When they are, qualitatively new realities emerge through these combinations.

Take a simple example. Imagine a random pile of ten paper clips. Now imagine linking these paper clips together to form a chain. There are still ten paper clips, but a new emergent reality has appeared that is qualitatively different from the random pile because of how the elements are related to one another. Or consider human reproduction. Neither sperm nor egg are capable of producing human life on their own; in combination, qualitatively new life begins to emerge from a particular combination of elements.

Sociology specializes in the social level of analysis that emerges when elements are combined to create new, emergent realities. Emergentism also implies that when we try to understand elements outside of their context, it is at best a simplification and at worst a distortion. The parts derive meaning from their relationship with other parts, and the sociological perspective is fundamentally attuned to such relationships.

Society Is a Historical Product

Thinking historically is a crucial part of the sociological imagination (C. Wright Mills 1959). Classical sociologists thought historically because they lived in times of rapid social change and it was a major challenge to understand such change. Modern sociology tends to be more static, and modern people tend to be very present-oriented. Both professional and practical sociologists would benefit from a more historical perspective on the social world.

Seeing society as a historical product means recognizing that we cannot understand the present without understanding the past. Historical knowledge of past social conditions provides crucial comparisons. Without such benchmarks, it is impossible to understand what is genuinely new in the present day. Without a historical referent for comparison, sociology is clueless when it comes to understanding social change. Historical knowledge also provides the raw material for categories, comparisons, typologies, and analogies that are crucial to understanding both the present and possible future worlds.

The concept of emergentism applies here because the importance of seeing relationships between elements also works chronologically. If we look at society at only one point in time, we sever it from its past and its potential futures. Its very meaning arises from these relationships; to ignore them is to distort even the static understanding of society at one point in time. Consider the difference between a photograph and a film that presents a succession of images. We can learn something from the still photo, but its meaning often changes dramatically when we see it as one of a series of interrelated images.

Society Consists of Social Structures

Sociologists use the term *structure* to refer to the emergent products of individual elements. Structure implies that the social world has certain patterns or regularities that recur over time. Put differently, sociologists are keenly interested in social organization.

Structures are products of human purposes, but they acquire an objective reality and become a powerful influence on human action. Think about how physical structures like buildings shape action. We almost always enter buildings through doors; in rare cases we might do so through windows, but walking through walls is not an option. Social structures are less visible and more flexible than buildings, but they also channel people's actions, because they make some actions routine and expected, others possible but unlikely, and still others all but impossible.

Like buildings, social structures often have a vertical dimension. Social structures ensure that some people are better off than others and that some are not very well off at all. Some residential buildings have penthouses at the top, premium suites near the top, standard accommodations below them, and housekeeping staff in the basement. Social structures are also stratified, granting power, privilege, and opportunity to some while limiting or denying them to others. Sociologists are especially interested in the hierarchical dimension of social structures.

Sociologists traditionally thought of social structures as powerful forces weighing down upon the individual. In this image, structures constrain freedom of choice and behavior. But this is a one-sided view. Structures are constraining, but they are also enabling. These established patterns of social organization also make many actions possible in the first place or easier in the second place. Without preexisting social structures, we would have to do everything "from scratch," and the challenge of sheer survival might overwhelm us. The trick is thus to see social structures as simultaneously constraining and enabling social action (Giddens 1984).

Society Consists of Reflexive Actors

People in society are aware of themselves, of others, and of their relationships with others. As reflexive actors, we monitor our action and its effects on others. We continue, modify, or halt actions, depending on whether they are achieving their intended effects. According to one school of thought, we are literally actors, because social life is like a theatrical performance in which we try to convince others that we are a certain kind of person (Goffman 1959). To stage effective performances, we must constantly be our own critic, judging and refining our performances. Reflexivity thus means that when we act, we are conscious of our action, we monitor its course, and we make adjustments over time.

To stage such performances, we must undergo socialization. Along the way, we acquire a language that provides us with tools for reflexive thinking. We also acquire a self. Oddly enough, to have a self requires that we first have relationships with others. Through those relationships, we imaginatively see the world from their perspective, which includes seeing ourselves as we imagine we appear to them. It is this ability to see ourselves through the perspective of others—to see ourselves as an object—that defines the self. Reflexive action only becomes possible with a self.

Reflexivity makes ordinary people into practical sociologists. To be a competent person is to be a practical sociologist. We cannot help being sociologists every time we ponder a potential relationship, reconsider a hasty action, or adopt someone else's viewpoint. All such situations call upon and refine the reflexivity that is the hallmark of social action as well as a defining characteristic of the sociological perspective.

Society Is an Interaction of Agency and Structure

Social structures and reflexive actors are intimately connected. Unfortunately, much sociology emphasizes one side of this connection at the expense of the other. Agency-centered views stress the ability of people to make choices out of a range of alternatives in almost any situation. The emphasis on choice implies that people control their own destiny, at least within broad limits. Structure-centered views stress the extent to which people's choices are limited by social structures. The emphasis on structures implies that people's options—if not their lives—are essentially determined by larger social forces over which they have little control. Both approaches have merit, but the challenge is to see structure and agency in a more interconnected way.

Marx once said that people make their own history (acknowledging agency), but under circumstances they do not choose but rather inherit from the past (acknowledging structure). Here's an analogy from the game of pool. Each time you approach the table, you "inherit" a structure left by your opponent when they missed their last shot. Yet, for every layout of balls on the table, there is always a shot that you can attempt, and that action will alter the structure of the table for subsequent shots. In this analogy, structure (the position of balls on the table) both limits and creates opportunities for agency (taking a shot), which in turn alters the structure for the next round of shooting. If pool is not your game, chess is also a good analogy. The point is that agency and structure are two sides of the same coin; each conditions the possibilities of the other as we make our own history in circumstances we don't choose.

The close connection between structure and agency has led one theorist to reject the notion of structure altogether, because it implies something that exists apart from agency. Anthony Giddens (1984) talks about a *process* of structuration. In this view, actors use preexisting structures to accomplish their goals, but they also recreate them as a by-product of their actions. Consider a wedding ceremony. It is a preexisting cultural ritual people use to accomplish the goal of getting married. The by-product of all these individual marriages is the perpetuation of the cultural ritual itself. Generalize this to any situation in which we draw upon an established part of our social world to achieve a goal; in using this part we also sustain (and perhaps transform) it as a part of social structure.

Society Has Multiple Levels

Although society has multiple levels, sociologists often focus on one level at a time. Imagine a telescope. You can focus widely to get the big picture at the expense of not seeing some important details. Alternatively, you can zoom in on some key details at the expense of not seeing the big picture. Such choices might be necessary as a starting point in understanding the social world, but we must remember it is ultimately all one interconnected landscape.

Sociologists nevertheless distinguish between macro- and micro-levels of society. When we look at the macro-level, we typically include millions of people organized into large categories, groups, or institutions. The macro-level is the "big picture" or "high altitude" perspective in which society's largest patterns are evident and individuals are invisible. When we look at the micro-level, we might inspect no more than a dozen people interacting in a small group setting. Here, the role of particular individuals is very prominent, and larger social patterns fade into the background.

Some of the best sociology involves understanding not only structure-agency connections but micro-macro links. Every macro-structure rests on micro-interaction, and every micro-interaction is shaped by macro-structures. The previous example of a wedding also illustrates this point. On the macro-level, weddings are a cultural ritual that inducts people into the institution of marriage and the family. However, weddings, marriage, and the family would not exist on the macro-level without countless, micro-level interactions. The macro-level institution depends on micro-level actions to sustain it. At the same time, anyone who has ever gotten married will tell you that macro-level, cultural expectations about weddings impose themselves on people as they plan for this supposedly personal event. Every micro-level wedding depends on a macro-level, cultural blueprint for its social significance. The micro- and macro- levels of society are one interdependent reality rather than two separate things.

Society Involves Unintended Consequences

One of the more profound insights of the sociological perspective concerns unintended and unanticipated consequences of action. Much human action is purposive or goal-directed. People act because they want to accomplish something. Despite this, they sometimes fail to achieve their goals. But whether people achieve their goals or not, their actions always create other consequences that they don't intend or even anticipate. Shakespeare made a profoundly sociological point when he had Juliet fake her own suicide to dramatize her love for Romeo. Unfortunately, the plan never reached Romeo. Juliet neither intended nor anticipated that Romeo would find her unconscious, believe that she was really dead, and take his own life in response. Nor did he intend (or even realize) that she would awaken, discover his real death, and really take her life in response. Talk about unintended consequences!

This principle acknowledges the complexity of the social world and the limits on our ability to control it. It says that despite our best efforts, the effects of social action cannot be confined to one intended path; they always spill over into unexpected areas. The principle is also a cautionary message for those seeking to solve social problems. Such efforts might succeed, but they often bring other consequences that are neither positive nor intended.

Efforts to control crime provide an example. Consider policies to "get tough" on crime through harsher treatment like capital punishment and mandatory sentencing. Because the human beings who serve as judges and juries are reflexive actors who take these facts into account, they are often less likely to convict suspects without overwhelming evidence because of the harshness of the sentence. Thus, the unintended consequence of an attempt to "get tough" on crime might be the opposite, because fewer suspects are convicted than before.

A related idea is the distinction between manifest and latent functions. A manifest function is an outcome that people intend. A latent function is an outcome that people are not aware of; it can complement, but it often contradicts, the manifest function. Crime and punishment provide yet another example. The manifest function of imprisonment is punishment or rehabilitation. The latent function is to bring criminals together where they can meet one another, exchange crime techniques, and become better criminals upon their return to society.

The concept of latent functions is crucial to sociological analysis. Sometimes we observe behavior or rituals that seem irrational, pointless, or self-defeating. This is the time to begin looking for latent functions. What we will often find is that such "irrational" behavior reinforces the identity and sustains the cohesion of the group that performs it. Thus, before we dismiss the tribal rain dance (because "rain gods" don't exist), we must explore its latent function. Even when people don't (manifestly) know what they are (latently) doing, their behavior can be crucial to group cohesion.

Recognizing unintended consequences and latent functions is not just for professional sociologists. Daily living requires managing risk, and ordinary people in everyday life recognize the tricky nature of goal-directed action. The folk wisdom that "the road to hell is paved with good intentions" acknowledges the potential disconnect between goals and outcomes. Such recognition, however, never completely prevents outcomes we neither intend nor expect. These principles give social life some of its most surprising twists, and sociology some of its most fascinating challenges.

No attempt to capture the sociological perspective in a small number of themes can be complete. Other sociologists would doubtless modify this list. But most would recognize these themes as central to thinking sociologically. As such, they provide a foundation for the more detailed investigations to follow.

SOCIOLOGY'S DOUBLE CRITIQUE

This final theme deserves special emphasis as the foundation of this book. Last but not least, thinking sociologically means looking at the social world in a critical way.

In everyday language, *critical* implies something negative. To be critical is often seen as being harsh, unfair, or judgmental. When we say someone is "critical," we often mean that their behavior is inappropriately mean-spirited. This is a perfectly reasonable use of everyday language, and the point it makes about how people should treat one another is also perfectly reasonable.

In sociological language, *critical* means something else. Doing sociology in a critical way means looking beyond appearances, understanding root causes, and asking who benefits. Being critical is what links knowledge to action and the potential of building a better society. Being critical in the sociological sense rests on the profoundly *positive* belief that we can use knowledge to understand the flaws of the world and act to correct them.

The sociological perspective contains a double critique. First, mainstream sociology brings an inherently critical angle of vision to its subject. Second, some particular approaches in sociology carry this critique further by building on values that make sociological analysis especially critical of power and domination.

The critical dimension of mainstream sociology derives from the Enlightenment. Despite the flaws noted earlier, the Enlightenment advocated the use of reason, science, and evidence to critically examine religious truth, established doctrine, and political authority. Given its Enlightenment roots, sociology has always cast a critical eye on all types of claims, forms of knowledge, and exercises of power.

It is this quality that Peter Berger (1963) called the "debunking" tendency of sociological consciousness. Debunking means that the sociological perspective never takes the social world at face value and never assumes that it is what it appears to be.

The sociological perspective rather looks at familiar phenomena in new ways to get beyond the immediately obvious, publicly approved, or officially sanctioned view. In this way, sociology sees through the facades of social structures to their unintended consequences and latent functions. Sociologically speaking, the problem might not be crime but laws, not revolution but government. Berger concludes that sociology is not compatible with totalitarianism, because the debunking quality of sociology will always be in tension with authoritarian claims to knowledge and power.

Although the world has changed since Berger wrote, the need for debunking is greater than ever. The political fundamentalisms of Cold War and rival super-powers have been replaced by other fundamentalisms that are logical targets for sociology's debunking insights. A world in which more and more people feel they know things with absolute certainty is a world that drastically needs the sociological perspective.

At the same time that some people embrace fundamentalist beliefs, others become suspicious and cynical about everything. This pose ("debunking on steroids") is too much of a good thing. For the ultra-cynical poser, all ideas, values, and beliefs are suspect, and none deserve support. Against this stance, sociology offers nuance and judgment. The sociological perspective recognizes that some ideas, values, and beliefs have more merit, logic, or evidence than others. Careful sociological thinkers make such distinctions. Indeed, the ultra-cynical mind-set itself needs debunking. Cynicism helps people avoid action or evade responsibility. A sociological perspective suggests that such inaction, or evasion, is action that tacitly supports dominant powers by refusing to challenge them in any way.

Mainstream sociology does not take the world for granted. Just when we think we have the answers, it poses another level of questions. For all these reasons, sociology in its most generic form has always included a critical angle of vision.

Although mainstream sociology is inherently critical, some versions of sociology take critique to another level, by adopting certain values as the basis for their critique. In contrast to mainstream sociology, these approaches are devoted to a critical analysis of how social structures create relations of domination.

This fully critical sociology is best understood in contrast to mainstream sociology. Although mainstream sociology is critical because of its debunking tendency, it also follows a scientific posture of detachment. Mainstream sociology seeks to be value-free, value-neutral, or objective. Put differently, mainstream sociology deliberately refrains from taking sides that would jeopardize its scientific neutrality. Mainstream sociology recognizes that *as citizens,* sociologists can be political actors. But it insists that in their role as scientific sociologists, they must maintain their objectivity.

Critical sociology differs from mainstream sociology on these issues. It emphasizes that in social science, humans are both the subjects and the objects of study. Notions of objectivity derived from the natural sciences don't necessarily translate into social science. But even if sociology could approximate objectivity, critical sociologists reject such a stance. It is not desirable, because the quest for objectivity diverts sociologists from asking the most important questions and from taking a more active role in the resolution of social problems.

Think of the contrast in this way. Mainstream sociology is primarily committed to one set of Enlightenment values having to do with science and objectivity. Critical sociology is primarily committed to another set of Enlightenment values having to do with freedom and equality. The latter values demand critical scrutiny of any social order that imposes unnecessary inequalities or restrictions on people's ability to organize their lives as they wish. These values require critical analysis of social arrangements that create conflicting interests between people and allow one group to benefit at the expense of another.

Critical sociologists deliberately focus on relations of domination, oppression, or exploitation, because these actions so obviously violate the values of freedom and equality. Critical sociologists are willing to advocate for groups who are victimized by such arrangements. Good critical sociologists realize they cannot speak for such groups. But they can explore how social arrangements make it difficult for some to speak for themselves, and they can underscore the importance of changing those arrangements.

Other issues distinguish mainstream from critical sociology. Mainstream sociology's commitment to science means it maintains a strict divide between scientific questions of what *is* and normative questions of what *ought* to be. Critical sociology wants to transcend this divide by linking critical analysis of how the world is organized now with normative arguments for how the world should be organized in the future. Behind such arguments are hopeful, or even utopian assumptions about alternative worlds that might be constructed. Critical sociology is simultaneously pessimistic about the current state of the world and optimistic about its possible futures. It examines our potential for living humanely, the social obstacles that block this potential, and the means to change from a problematic present to a preferable future.

The debate between mainstream and critical sociology is important and complex, and it will not be resolved by anything said here. But what can be said is that sociology is better because of the debate. Each side provides a corrective to the faults of the other. At the extreme, mainstream sociology becomes an inhumane, sterile approach that reduces human beings to objects of scientific curiosity; it needs a course correction through the humane values of critical sociology. At the extreme, critical sociology becomes an empty, ideological stance that denies the complexities of its own value commitments; it needs a course correction through the scientific caution of mainstream sociology.

Sociology's double critique thus derives from mainstream and critical sociology, respectively. My primary goal in this book is to illustrate critical sociology, but I also include the critical insights of mainstream sociology. I do so because these approaches sometimes speak to different issues, because neither seems adequate on its own, because they are often complementary, and because this best conveys the richness of our discipline itself. In the end, it is less important which side is "right" than that both sides coexist and continually provoke us to be reflexive about our role as sociologists and as actors in the world.

Sociology's double critique is also crucial to rethinking the flaws of the Enlightenment itself. Mainstream sociology's notion of debunking accepted truths grew out of the Enlightenment struggle against religion, but there is no reason it can't also foster critical examination of the Enlightenment itself. Critical sociology's challenge to domination also seems tailor-made to examining and overturning those forms of domination that the Enlightenment ignored, accepted, or promoted. Thus, for all its flaws, the Enlightenment provides tools for its own examination, critique, and transformation.

Chapter 2

The Legacy of the Discipline

For more than two centuries, sociology has developed a rich legacy of theoretical approaches that help make sense out of the world. This chapter describes three basic types of sociology (Habermas 1969). Scientific sociology applies the scientific method of the natural sciences to the social world. Humanistic sociology emphasizes how consciousness and reflexivity distinguish people from other topics of scientific study. Critical sociology examines and challenges relations of domination while promoting more egalitarian relations. Good (and bad) sociology has been done within each of these traditions.

SCIENTIFIC SOCIOLOGY

Auguste Comte (the "father" of sociology) was among the first to argue that sociology should model itself on the natural sciences. From Comte to the present, the premise of scientific sociology is that there is a single, universal, scientific approach to knowledge that applies to both the natural and the social worlds. This approach involves systematic testing of hypotheses through experimental methods to discover the most general laws that govern the world around us. Whether one is a physicist, botanist, economist, or sociologist, the differences in subject matter are less important than the similarities in how all these subjects are handled by the scientific method.

Durkheim's Sociology
The best classical spokesperson for scientific sociology was the French sociologist Emile Durkheim (1858–1917). He was a strong advocate for sociology and the idea of emergentism. For Durkheim, society was more than the sum of its parts; it was a reality *sui generis,* or unto itself. Society consists of social facts, which must be explained by other social facts. Durkheim relentlessly argued for the superiority of sociological explanations over individual, biological, or physiological ones. His

argument was strengthened when he advocated a scientific sociology, linking this new discipline to established sciences.

Durkheim's early work on the division of labor (1895) contrasted traditional and modern societies. In traditional societies, people are very similar to one another. In these small-scale societies, everybody does everything. What unites people is a common set of cultural beliefs known as the collective conscience. As societies become larger and more differentiated, the bond of common beliefs weakens and conflict over scarce resources intensifies. Some societies disintegrate, but others survive because they find a new method of integration. In modern societies, the division of labor provides the social glue that holds things together. In these societies, people are different from one another and do different things. These differences create interdependency among people. Social evolution involves a transition from worlds united by common beliefs to ones united by functional differences. This social evolution is best understood through the same scientific method used to understand biological evolution.

In subsequent work on suicide (1897), Durkheim strengthened the case for a scientific sociology. He chose suicide because the decision to end one's life seems intensely personal. Durkheim, however, sought sociological explanations of this seemingly individual act. He de-emphasized individual suicides and focused on variations in suicide rates between different groups of people. Group suicide rates are social facts that need to be explained by other social facts rather than individual predispositions. The most important social fact in the explanation of suicide rates is the degree of social integration. Whenever people become less integrated into a group, suicide rates are likely to increase. People become "unplugged" in two ways. *Egoism* means the bonds linking people to the group are broken. *Anomie* means the norms guiding people's lives are weakened or irrelevant. Egoistic and anomic suicide are thus extreme expressions of much broader social problems that occur whenever individuals are disconnected and set adrift from their normal social anchors. Social facts like suicide rates are thus best explained by other social facts like changing degrees of social integration.

Durkheim's sociology of religion (1912) also illustrates his scientific sociology. He argued that some form of religion is virtually universal in human societies but that specific beliefs are highly variable. He claimed that the single common thread in all religions is a distinction between the sacred and the profane. That which is sacred is seen as external, powerful, constraining, and eternal in relation to the individual. Durkheim concluded that there is one reality that has the qualities that religion attributes to the sacred realm. That reality is society itself. When people worship their respective gods, they are recognizing a genuinely higher power. What they are not recognizing is that power is society itself.

Whether addressing evolution, suicide, or religion, Durkheim advocated a scientific sociology that analyzed society as an emergent reality of social facts that could be explained through the scientific method.

Functionalist Analysis

Many of Durkheim's concerns were revived in Talcott Parsons's functionalist theory in the mid-twentieth century. Parsons sought a general theory applicable to all times and places; this quest for generality is another hallmark of scientific sociology. Parsons's early focus was the structure of social action (1937). He saw people as selecting means to pursue goals. Such choices are shaped by situational conditions and cultural values. Parsons stressed that actors make choices; at the same time, their choices are guided by common values that predispose them to conform. Having analyzed these "unit acts," Parsons then became interested in how these unit acts were linked together.

The new problem was *interaction*; the new answer was the social system (1951). A social system is an ongoing, patterned relationship between social actors. Systems provide actors with status-roles; these are positions in the system along with guidelines for how to act. Roles are reciprocal and complementary. In Parsons's language, imagine two actors: Ego and Alter. Ego's role obligates her to do certain things that are identical to Alter's role expectations. In reverse order, Alter's role obligations match Ego's role expectations. Integrated social interaction occurs whenever people meet their role obligations because they are simultaneously meeting the role expectations of others.

Consider this example. If teachers are knowledgeable in their subject and fair in their grading, they are meeting not only their role obligations as teachers but also the expectations of students, because "teacher's obligations = student's expectations." By a similar logic, if students study hard and participate in class, they meet not only their role obligations but also the expectations of teachers, because "student's obligations = teacher's expectations." Integrated social systems thus arise whenever people learn their roles and are motivated to play them. Learning occurs through socialization that links the personality system (people) to the social system; motivation is provided by the cultural system and its core values. Parsons thus proposed a highly general and abstract model of how social order was possible.

If a social system is to survive over time, it must fulfill certain functions. Adaptation means systems must get resources from outside the system and distribute them throughout the system. Goal attainment means that systems must set priorities and allocate resources to them. Integration means that systems must maintain cohesion and connections among various parts of the system. Latency means that systems must motivate people to meet their obligations and smooth over tensions that might arise. Healthy societies develop social institutions that meet these functions on a regular basis. Parsons thus continued the quest for a scientific sociology through a theory of systems and functions that could be applied to any ongoing social system.

Consider another example. The United States is a social system with various institutions that meet functional needs. The economy accomplishes adaptation by producing and distributing resources. The political system achieves goal attainment by setting priorities and allocating resources. The need for integration is met both by informal community norms and formal legal procedures. Finally, the latency function of providing motivation to people is met by family, religion, and education.

By the 1950s, Parsons's functionalism dominated sociology. It then attracted much criticism. Robert Merton (1968) thought sociology should develop more modest, middle-range theories. C. Wright Mills (1959) accused Parsons of a hopelessly abstract "grand theory" that obscured more than it revealed. Many claimed that functionalism exaggerated social integration and ignored social conflict. These criticisms redirected sociology toward conflict while maintaining the quest for a scientific sociology.

Conflict Theory

Lewis Coser (1956) used functionalist logic to provide a novel understanding of conflict. He argued that conflict was a constant element in social life. On the other hand, conflict can have beneficial consequences. It can be a source of creativity, innovation, and healthy social change. Moreover, conflict actually causes much of the integration in society. When conflict occurs within groups, it is often a healthy release that resolves tensions and solidifies the group. When conflict occurs between groups, it increases integration within each group as they conduct the conflict. When conflict occurs in society, it clarifies group boundaries and identities by forcing people to commit to a side. In all these ways, conflict creates order that might not otherwise be there.

When societies have cross-cutting conflicts, opponents on one issue are allies on another issue. This reduces the violence and intensity of conflict and promotes smoother resolution of conflict. As a final example, imagine two groups who share a common enemy. Because "the enemy of my enemy is my friend," new alliances often emerge between previously unconnected groups. Although not all conflict is beneficial, much conflict has functional consequences. Conflict and order are intimately connected. We cannot explain order without acknowledging how conflict helps create it.

Other conflict theorists focused on how modern society is dominated by large bureaucratic organizations that rest on a hierarchical and unequal distribution of authority (Dahrendorf 1959). In any such organization, there are a small number of positions at the top that have authority and a larger number of positions below them that do not. This structure creates conflicting interests. Those with authority will seek to maintain the organization and their position within it. Those without authority will seek to change both the organization and their positions within it. Such conflicts are built into the very structure of authority; they are endemic to bureaucracy. Under the right conditions, such latent conflicts become overt battles between political parties, labor and management, students and administration, or soldiers and officers. Because bureaucratic authority is so widespread in modern society, this form of conflict will also be common.

The social conflicts of the 1960s promoted conflict theory in sociology. Randall Collins (1975) revived the call for a scientific sociology of conflict. His logic went like this. Coercion is always a potential resource in social life. Some people are better at threatening or using coercion than others. When coercion is directed at people, they resist in whatever ways they can. People compete for scarce and valued resources like wealth, status, and power. On the basis of these plausible principles, Collins concluded that conflict is the central social process in modern life. At the same time, he recognized that the form of conflict varies tremendously. It can involve subtle battles for strategic advantage, competition for educational credentials, claims to moral high ground, or overt, violent, and even deadly struggles.

Collins sought to synthesize sociology around conflict by linking macro-level institutions with micro-level interaction. On the macro level, social stratification and complex organizations are the outcome of past conflicts and the seeds of future ones. But macro-institutions don't exist on their own; they always have micro-level foundations in everyday interaction. This "micro-conflict" is evident in conversational strategies people use to manipulate others so they can achieve their goals. Conflict sociology would thus link micro and macro levels through a scientific approach.

Rational Choice

A final example of scientific sociology is rational choice, or exchange theory. It borrows from economic theory and behavioristic psychology. The challenge is to take premises from other disciplines and make them sociological. This means recognizing that people seek symbolic as well as material rewards, that social norms limit self-interested behavior, and that people are not always or fully rational in their behavior. With such adjustments, rational choice theorists argue that scientific explanations of human behavior become possible.

George Homans (1974) followed the psychological behaviorism of B. F. Skinner to identify a small number of general laws to explain a wide range of behavior. These laws are straightforward: Rewarded actions will be repeated; the more valuable the result, the more likely the action that leads to it; frequent rewards have declining value; and the like. Homans argued that when sufficiently tested, refined, and combined, these laws could scientifically explain human behavior. Many sociologists criticized this work. With its strong focus on individual behavior, it seemed to deny the emergent level of social reality and to reduce macro-level sociology to micro-level psychology.

Peter Blau's (1964) version of exchange theory recognized emergentism and the need to explain exchange on both micro and macro levels. Blau argued that all social exchange rests on a social norm of reciprocity: In order to get something, we must give something. It is even in our self-interest to give something, because that is how we get something back. When exchanges are satisfactory to both parties, they foster trust. It is the trust established through small exchanges that makes people willing to risk larger exchanges; by this logic, the sequence from casual dating to serious commitment to formal marriage is a spiral of increasing trust born of successful exchanges.

Micro-level exchange includes situations where coworkers exchange favors, knowledge, or status, as long as it serves their interests. In contrast, macro-level exchange is long term, indirect, and involves multiple parties. A nice example is the Social Security system, in which younger workers support older retirees, with the expectation that they will get the same deal when they retire. When exchanges succeed, order results. Whey they don't, conflict occurs. In this way, rational choice principles can explain both order and conflict.

The connections between exchange and power are most interesting. Consider the principle of lesser interest: In any relationship, the side with less interest in maintaining the relationship has more power. This principle applies to everything from romantic involvements to labor negotiations to international alliances. More generally, power arises whenever one side is dependent on the other for a needed resource. In its emphasis on power and micro-macro linkages, Blau's rational choice theory resembles Collins's conflict theory.

Scientific sociology analyzes a wide variety of topics. What links them is not the subject matter but the approach. The common thread is the quest for a genuinely scientific sociology modeled on the natural sciences. This thread distinguishes scientific from both humanistic and critical sociology.

HUMANISTIC SOCIOLOGY

When scientific sociologists do social science, they emphasize the word *science,* linking it to other sciences. When humanistic sociologists do social science, they emphasize the word *social,* separating it from other sciences. For humanistic sociology, people have unique traits like reflexivity and self-consciousness that require a different approach. As a result, humanistic sociology is less interested in general theories with universal applicability and more interested in how people create meanings that shape their actions. These distinctive human traits must be at the center of any worthwhile sociology. As a result, the best humanistic sociology can be more like a good novel exploring people's motivation than an analytical research report documenting human behavior.

Weber's Sociology

The classical theorist Max Weber (1864–1920) was a complex thinker whose work crossed the categories of scientific, humanistic, and critical sociology. Nonetheless, one dimension of his work nicely typifies humanistic sociology: his emphasis on the role of subjective meanings in human actions. Indeed, Weber argued sociology must begin with an interpretive understanding of social action in order to arrive at causal explanations. Without subjective meaning, we have mere behavior that hardly merits sociological study.

Because people attach different meanings to actions, Weber distinguished different types of social action. Purposive-rational action pursues goals efficiently; think of economic behavior. Value-rational action embodies commitment to a transcendent value; think of religious worship. Affectual action expresses an emotional state; think of maternal love. Traditional action repeats social customs; think of sheer habits. In each case, the action means something to the actor, and that meaning must be part of any worthwhile sociological explanation.

Sociological analysis needs a unique method Weber called *Verstehen.* This requires researchers to empathetically understand the meanings motivating someone's action. Consider Weber's study *The Protestant Ethic and the Spirit of Capitalism*

(1904). He wanted to understand why Protestants were so prominent among early entrepreneurs. His explanation required understanding how the Calvinist belief in predestination created anxiety among true believers. They responded by throwing themselves into productive activity. Their religious beliefs made this activity into a moral imperative. Capitalism thus arose less from material greed than from a spiritual incentive to demonstrate one's worth and salvation through productive activity. The rise of capitalism was, in part, an unintended consequence of religious motivations. But it could not be explained without first grasping the subjective meaning of these actions to the people doing them.

Weber's sociology ranged far and wide but was always rooted in this principle. Consider his analysis of authority. Power is the ability to achieve one's will against resistance; although effective, it is often unstable. Hence, power holders try to convert power into authority by seeking legitimacy. This can be done in several ways: by appealing to traditional customs, to charismatic leaders, or to rational-legal rules. What is crucial is that legitimacy cannot be created by leaders. It can only be granted by followers, when they attach a subjective meaning to the power being exercised over them. If they see it as legitimate, they will obey, and social order will be stable. If they don't, they might disobey and undermine social order. Even when analyzing macro-level issues in political sociology, social action involves subjective meanings.

Weber saw rationalization as the master trend of Western society. Rationalization meant that in all human activity, the emphasis was on maximizing efficiency, calculability, predictability, and control. George Ritzer's (2000) analysis of how the cultural experience of eating has been reduced to the industrial production of fast food is one example of rationalization. Although it brings the efficiency of abstract technique, rationalization sacrifices the sensuality of direct experience. This is why Weber took a dim view of this trend. He was especially troubled by the rise of giant bureaucracies, seeing them as "iron cages" from which we could not escape. Rationalization threatened human qualities like spontaneity, creativity, sensuality, and myth-making. Weber's humanistic approach is evident in his distress over modern trends that threatened the very qualities that make us human.

Symbolic Interactionism

Among contemporary approaches, symbolic interactionism is the best example of humanistic sociology. George Herbert Mead (1934) is the founder of this approach, which reveals how people literally become human through socialization. Only when we are immersed in social relations with others do we develop the seemingly individual traits of mind and self that allow us to become fully human. In rare cases of children reared in extreme isolation, they fail to develop a mind and a self because they are deprived of the social interactions that create our humanity.

Although behaviorism speaks of stimulus and response as if they are transparently obvious and similar for all social actors, Mead argues that stimuli and responses involve symbolic interpretation. They are not objectively meaningful; they become intersubjectively meaningful when people relate to them in certain kinds of ways.

It is interaction that creates, sustains, and transforms the meanings that are crucial to human action and that distinguish it from the instinctive responses of other organisms.

It is this meaningful interaction that triggers the development of minds and selves. To have a mind is to engage in thinking and reflection. This process is like having a conversation with oneself. Mead's point is that we first must have conversations with others before we can have conversations with ourselves. It is the others in our environment who provide the conversational and interactional tools that we need to engage in thinking. Infants begin with random babbling and untutored impulses. Through interaction with others, we gradually move from babbling to meaningful speech and from impulses to purposive action. Having learned through others, we can then internalize these lessons, talk to ourselves, and have a mind.

We are born with a brain but must develop a mind. In a parallel way, we are born with a body but must develop a self. Just as social interaction is necessary to develop a mind, it is also necessary to develop a self. Having a self means the ability to take oneself as an object. We only develop a self through interaction with others. What such interaction provides is the opportunity to "take the role of the other," or imaginatively adopt someone else's viewpoint. Their viewpoint helps us learn to see ourselves as an object. Children start by imitating particular people; they end up with a more generalized notion of how others see them. Once again, society comes first because it provides the others whose roles we need to take in order to develop a self. The social world is thus the mechanism by which we become human.

The development of mind and self is a generic process making us human. It is the foundation for the more specific process of acquiring an individual identity. Identity refers to the symbolic meanings attached to our self-object. Like our generic self, our individual identity is a product of what others reflect back to us about who we are. When we detect consistent messages from other people about who we are, that gradually becomes internalized as our identity. If the messages are largely positive, we develop an equally positive identity; if they are negative, our self-image is likely to suffer. In this way, our perceptions of the perceptions of others become a self-fulfilling prophecy producing our identity.

By emphasizing symbolic meanings, this approach focuses on the distinctive processes and properties that make us human. As such, it is central to humanistic sociology.

✗ *Phenomenological Sociology*

A similar emphasis is evident in phenomenological sociology, which studies the lifeworld of immediate experience. This lifeworld involves a "here and now" that rests on many taken-for-granted assumptions. We assume that our "here and now" is part of a larger, objective world that is shared with others. Phenomenological sociologists are less interested in whether these beliefs are true than in how we sustain them.

One way we do this is by routinely assuming that our perspective is the same as others (Schutz 1932). In other words, we assume the world we experience is the same one they experience. We also rely on culturally learned techniques to sustain belief in an orderly world. These techniques are learned through socialization, but then they become second nature. We forget that we had to learn them and instead believe that they reflect the natural order of things. It would be too simple to say "believing makes it so." But phenomenological sociologists argue that when deeply rooted, taken-for-granted beliefs motivate our actions, and when interaction proceeds smoothly, we convince ourselves that our world is objectively real. In so doing, we deny our own role in creating whatever order exists around us.

Ethnomethodology refers to methods people use in everyday life to make sense of their world (Garfinkel 1967). Through such methods, people create their social worlds. Thus, when we interpret words or actions, we begin with what people say or do but we "fill in" a great deal of other information as well. It is only by adding what we know about people's biographies, the context of the situation, or our history with them that we fully know what their words or actions mean. Whatever order we experience is less "out there" than a projection of our methods of making sense of the world.

Another way we assign meaning is by using mental categories to make sense. When we experience a situation—especially if it contains novel or unexpected elements—we search our categories to find one that best fits the moment. Once we do, our understanding of "what is going on" is as much a function of the category we bring to it as the raw experience. Again, the order we presume to be "out there" is inseparable from our own efforts to find it. We don't just live in society; we *accomplish* it through such methods.

These techniques sustain our belief in an orderly, objective, shared world. Despite our best efforts, however, such beliefs can unravel quite easily. You can unravel them by entering a familiar situation and doing things that contradict the expectations of others. But you'd best be prepared for unpleasant consequences. People might become angry, question your sanity, or quickly withdraw because they find things too disorienting. So here's the point. If "social order" can be disrupted this easily, doesn't this show that it is not objectively real but rather a collaboration sustained by people's beliefs and actions?

Phenomenological sociology is thus about the social construction of reality (Berger and Luckmann 1966). It reveals that the world we assume to be real is relative and arbitrary. It "feels" real because of the sense-making techniques we employ. A final example is a relevance structure. This is a purpose, goal, or intention that focuses attention and motivates action. It is through relevance structures that individuals come to experience the world as a meaningful, orderly place, and to act accordingly. Once they act, the outcomes of their actions take on a life of their own and seem to exist independently of the people who created them. We thereby trick ourselves into thinking that we live in an objective, orderly, and shared social world.

Like scientific sociology, humanistic sociology addresses many topics. The thread that connects them is the premise that people create, interpret, and act on meanings. For humanistic sociology, this fundamental fact must be at the center of sociological analysis. Because these qualities distinguish humans from other objects of scientific study, a *social* science must be quite different from natural science.

CRITICAL SOCIOLOGY

Critical sociology shares some concepts, approaches, and techniques with both scientific and humanistic sociology. What distinguishes it is a value commitment to create and use knowledge to promote emancipation. To paraphrase Marx, the point is not merely to understand the world; the point is to change it. Critical sociology analyzes social forces that limit human potential, narrow people's freedom, and sustain social domination. Critically understanding such forces can help move society in more egalitarian directions. Good critical sociologists know that the application of knowledge is fraught with dangers and unintended consequences. But they nonetheless remain committed to doing sociology to promote emancipation.

Marx's Sociology

Karl Marx (1818–1883) argued that the human capacity for labor is our distinguishing trait. Through productive activity, we not only survive, we also develop our humanity. Under capitalism, however, people become alienated from this potential. Under capitalism, the process of labor is controlled by others and the products of labor are owned by capitalists. Capitalism reduces workers to commodities who must sell themselves in a labor market. Capitalism alienates workers and deforms human potential. Rather than living to work (as the expression of creative activity), people must work (under alienated conditions) to live. Because labor makes us human, its alienation is a fundamental assault on our human nature.

Marx was also a materialist who believed that the most important feature of any society is how it meets people's material needs. The material base of society is the foundation for everything else. It contains forces of production, such as technology, resources, and labor. It also contains relations of production, consisting of a small, powerful group of owners who benefit from the labor of a much larger group of producers. This material base is an engine of change as new technologies and skills are developed. It is also a source of conflict as producers resist exploitation by owners. Arising from the material base, there is a superstructure consisting of politics, kinship, and culture as well as ideas, beliefs, and worldviews. This superstructure is largely controlled by the same powerful class that controls material production. They shape politics, culture, and ideas to reinforce their power over the masses. Marx was highly critical of how these relations allowed the few to benefit at the expense of the many.

Under capitalism, the relations of production involve capitalists who own the means of production and live off profits and workers who sell their labor-power and live off wages. Marx endorsed the labor theory of value: that workers create all economic value. Capitalists create no value, although they organize the productive process. Because capitalists have economic control, political power, and legal rights, they own the products created by labor. When they sell them, they divide the proceeds between their profits and worker's wages. This arrangement is exploitative because workers create all value but only get a portion back as wages. Moreover, competition between capitalists drives each to maximize exploitation of their workers. Marx recognized that capitalism revolutionizes technology and creates unprecedented wealth. The problem is that this wealth is created by one class but owned by another. Once again, the human capacity for productive labor is turned against the vast majority who actually do the labor. This exploitation was the main target of Marx's critique.

As capitalism developed, Marx expected that workers would resist exploitation and become class-conscious agents of social change. He thought that as workers were brought together in large factories, they would realize their shared exploitation, identify with each other, recognize their common enemy, and challenge capitalist power. Over time, Marx thus expected increasing solidarity within classes and polarization between them. As the battle lines became clearer, he expected workers to overthrow capitalism and create a more equitable society.

Worker resistance creates instability, but capitalism experiences increasingly severe economic crises for several reasons. Overproduction occurs because the value of the goods workers produce is greater than the value of the wages they receive; hence there is a shortage of purchasing power that can become an overproduction crisis. There is also a tendency for the rate of profit to fall because capitalism replaces human labor with technology. If labor is the source of all value, and if labor shrinks while technology expands, then profits become harder to realize. Many capitalist practices are responses to these crisis tendencies. By seeking new markets, cutting labor costs, destroying surplus goods, and offering consumer credit, capitalism has sought to maintain profitable production. But the structural tendency toward crisis remains. When combined with worker resistance, the potential exists for a revolutionary transformation to a more equal society.

Marx's sociology took both scientific and humanistic forms. What places it in the critical sociology camp is its commitment to promoting progressive social change on the basis of sociological knowledge.

Critical Theory

By the early twentieth century, it was evident that history was not following Marx's script for socialist revolution. In this context, a group of German, Jewish intellectuals founded the Frankfurt School for Social Research in 1923 (Jay 1973). Along with other neo-Marxists, their collective work came to be known as critical theory. This school is a major contribution to critical sociology. These thinkers were sympathetic to Marx's analysis, but they had serious doubts that the working class would become the revolutionary agent of history. The challenge before the Frankfurt School was to critically build on Marx's work. The central question was how a society based on class exploitation could nonetheless remain stable over time.

The Frankfurt School argued that Marx focused too narrowly on labor and the material base of society. Although economic exploitation is important, modern capitalism controls people in many different ways. Whereas Marx focused on one dimension, the Frankfurters focused on multiple dimensions of domination. They accepted his analysis of economic exploitation, but were most interested in other methods of social control. This led the Frankfurters to focus on the superstructure of society. In many respects, they saw this superstructure of politics, culture, symbols, and ideas as just as important as the material base in sustaining an unjust and unequal society.

Antonio Gramsci (1971) was not a member of the Frankfurt School, but his work exemplifies critical theory. He was interested in hegemony, or cultural domination. Hegemony is like a subtle kind of thought control. When this occurs, people embrace beliefs that contradict their own interests. With hegemony, domination becomes almost invisible, because people don't realize how they are being manipulated by their beliefs. Marx expected workers to develop class consciousness around their real interests. Hegemony is a kind of false consciousness that obscures real interests. Such distorted beliefs often rest on a false unity; people identify with their rulers, their nation, their culture, their race, or their religion—but not with their real interests or allies. The concept of hegemony allowed critical theory to explain the persistence of capitalism because material control over resources was reinforced by symbolic control over ideas; both benefited elites at the expense of ordinary people.

Nazi Germany confirmed the worst fears of the Frankfurt School, as Hitler rose to power in a nightmarish example of hegemonic control. However, although the Nazi movement was specific to Germany, the broader phenomenon of Fascism occurred in Italy, Spain, and elsewhere. The most chilling message of the Frankfurt School was that an authoritarian, militaristic fascism could emerge in any modern, capitalist nation.

The contributions of the Frankfurt School continued throughout the twentieth century and will receive more extensive treatment in the next chapter. Their work continued Marx's critical spirit even while subjecting his ideas to critical scrutiny.

World System Theory

Whereas critical theorists expanded Marx's analysis "up" into the superstructure, world system theorists expanded it "out" across national boundaries. Marx recognized the expansionary tendency of capitalism, but world system theorists make it the centerpiece of their analysis. Thus, Immanuel Wallerstein (1974, 1980, 1989) details how capitalism has been a global, world system for several centuries. This world system is politically divided but economically integrated.

This integration is not harmonious. It is rooted in the same exploitation that Marx identified. The extraction of profits from the labor of workers is simply a global rather than a national phenomenon. This means that capitalism's relations of production have become international. The working class includes everyone on the globe who sells their labor for a wage. The capitalist class includes everyone who owns means of production and purchases labor to derive a profit. This poses new challenges to class formation, because cheaper labor in poorer nations is used to undermine living standards for workers everywhere else. Before workers can defend their interests in a world system, there must be communication, consciousness, and solidarity *across* national boundaries. It is only by improving the position of the worst off that the position of all workers can be defended.

The current composition of the world system reflects the imperialism and colonialism that helped create it. The core of the world system consists of former colonial and neocolonial powers. They retain the economic power, political clout, and military might to ensure that the world system provides substantial profits to them. The periphery of the world system consists of former colonies. Their natural resources and cheap labor continue to generate profits that flow from the periphery to the core. Standing between these two extremes is the semi-periphery. It is a diverse group that includes former socialist nations and more advantaged former colonies. Core nations exploit both peripheral and semi-peripheral nations. Semi-peripheral nations exploit peripheral nations while being exploited by core nations. And peripheral nations experience a double exploitation by both core and semi-peripheral nations.

Inequalities between nation-states make the class relations of the world system very complex. Nation-states are good examples of "status groups" (Weber 1968) that provide their members with cultural identity and group affiliation. In the world system, national status identity can undermine global class identity. When workers follow nationalistic, patriotic, or militaristic appeals, it weakens class solidarity across national boundaries and strengthens global capitalist interests. But this is not simply "false consciousness." In core countries, workers derive real material benefits from their national identity; they might be exploited as workers but benefit as consumers with comfortable standards of living. The world system creates real contradictions among classes and nations. These political divisions within an economically integrated world system help maintain the power of the dominant class.

The world system has a dynamic history. Different nations have changed positions over time, and the leadership of the core and the system as a whole has changed hands. As we shall see in a later exploration of globalization, these dynamics have important global and domestic ramifications.

World system theory is a prime example of critical sociology. It explains why the demise of formal colonialism has not ended global inequality. It illuminates how ongoing postcolonial struggles continue to challenge the core's domination over the labor, resources, and cultures of the worlds' peoples. It studies global capitalism to identify the changes that could create a more equitable system for producing and distributing the world's resources.

Feminist Sociology

Another example of critical sociology and its commitment to progressive social change is feminist sociology. It analyzes gender in much the same way that Marxism analyzes class. Most importantly, feminist sociology focuses on how gender is socially constructed to create inequality.

The emergence of feminist sociology is itself revealing. Sociology prides itself on seeing beyond appearances, but sociology historically ignored gender. In part, this was because sociology was a male-dominated discipline. Because gender rarely works to the disadvantage of men, this helps explain why it remained off sociology's radar screen. There have always been women who provided incisive understandings of how gender shapes the world (Freedman 2002), but their work was rarely accepted as "real" sociology. It was the feminist movement that provided leverage for feminist sociology. As feminism challenged male domination in the late 1960s, a feminist perspective gradually entered sociology.

This perspective took multiple forms. Liberal or equal rights feminism criticized segregation and discrimination that limited opportunity for women and advocated for their integration into mainstream institutions. Social or cultural feminism emphasized distinctively female temperaments and aptitudes and argued for their preservation as core social values in place of male competition, aggression, and violence. Socialist feminists and feminists of color analyzed how multiple inequalities rooted in class and race as well as gender intersected and reinforced each other. Through such feminist insights, gender eventually took its place on sociology's agenda.

Feminism entered sociology relatively recently, but its insights have always been profoundly sociological. The slogan "the personal is political" means that seemingly individual issues are shaped by gender power differences. The "personal" is "political" when female self-esteem is tied to male-defined body images reinforced by relentless advertising and marketing. This recalls Mills's (1959) distinction between personal troubles and public issues. If the sociological perspective involves seeing political issues in place of psychological troubles, then feminists have always been solid sociologists. This also suggests that good sociology is as likely to be done by people challenging domination as by credentialed professionals.

Another link between feminism and sociology concerns levels of analysis. Whereas sociologists have struggled to integrate their understandings of macro and micro levels of social order, feminists have always understood gender as a multi-level phenomenon. In so doing, they have enriched sociology's understanding of both levels of analysis.

On the macro level of social structure, including gender has meant broadening conventional notions of material production. Although such activities are often male-dominated, they are sustained by equally basic forms of *social* production and reproduction. The latter are often female-dominated, and sexist biases have frequently ignored or trivialized the social significance of domestic labor, household production, and child rearing in sustaining social life.

Through the gender division of labor, gendered assumptions are embedded in major social institutions. Whether the focus be economics, politics, media, culture, education, medicine, religion, or sports, each institution incorporates and perpetuates basic assumptions about gender differences and inequality. The daily operation of these institutions makes these appearances seem utterly natural. As critical sociology, feminism looks beyond these seemingly natural appearances to examine the social mechanisms that sustain them.

Macro-level gendered patterns are intertwined with micro-level gendered practices. Gender is part of social structure; it is also a fundamental social identity. Sociologists have long studied socialization, but feminism reinvigorated the topic by revealing how socialization is always gendered. As such, it constructs differences between women and men that in turn foster gender inequality.

Gender-laden notions about women and men circulate in the culture but also get embedded in individual minds. As people come to see themselves through a gendered lens, they learn common sense understandings about the world and their place in it that differ sharply by gender. When they act on those understandings, they perpetuate a world so familiar that it seems like the only possible social order. When micro-level common sense dovetails with macro-level social reproduction, gender becomes a pervasive type of inequality and domination.

Feminist sociology grew out of political struggles for social change. Sociology has been greatly enriched by its understanding of gender, and feminist sociology has retained a commitment to both analyzing and changing gender dynamics.

Postmodern Insights

Postmodern analysis provides a final example of critical sociology. This work spans many disciplines, and some of it challenges critical sociology's project of emancipation. Nonetheless, there are important strands of postmodernist thinking that exemplify critical sociology.

Postmodernism claims we are in a transition from the modern era that has always been sociology's subject matter to something else. Although economics and politics retain many modern features, culture best illustrates postmodernist claims. Here's an example. Modernism assumes we can distinguish between reality and representations of reality. In a postmodern era, such distinctions break down.

Consider how much of our daily experience is mediated through television and other symbolic media. We often take these images as faithful representations of an underlying reality. Yet, if you have ever been at a televised event and later seen it rebroadcast, you know that media representations are partial and selective at best. Given how many such images we see, how selective they inevitably are, and how we nonetheless take them as "real," it could be said that the images are more "real" to us than the "reality" they supposedly represent. It could even be said that media create our reality rather than reflecting a preexisting reality. A postmodern world is like a house of mirrors in which we mistake images for the "real" thing when they are all merely reflections of other reflections.

Consider another example. Every spring I attend a "Festival of Nations," where people from dozens of cultural groups prepare ethnic food, dress in native costumes, and perform traditional music and dances. This event seems to authentically represent existing cultures around the world. In actual fact, many of these cultures exist mainly in the memories of the people staging the festival. For better and for worse, many of these traditional practices have been superseded by social change, cultural diffusion, colonial domination, and globalizing forces. Hence, we have the peculiar situation of witnessing a copy of something for which there is no longer an original. In such a "hyperreal" world of endless "simulations" (Baudrillard 1983), modernist distinctions between reality and representations no longer hold up.

Some postmodern thinking thus recalls sociology's debunking tendency. It questions not only the surface appearance, but also whether there even is an underlying reality. Some other postmodernist thinking resembles the critique of domination that is central to critical sociology. And still other postmodernist thinking challenges critical sociology itself.

Good examples of the "critique of domination" version of postmodernism can be found in Foucault's (1965, 1975, 1979) historical case studies of the rise of modern psychiatry, medicine, and corrections. Although each discipline claimed to be more humane than its predecessors, Foucault detects new forms of domination in each case. This domination derived from new discourses about madness, disease, or deviance. While couched in the language of scientific objectivity, these discourses created new power relations between privileged experts with specialized knowledge and dependent clients, patients, or prisoners at their mercy. The rise of expertise through scientific discourses created a new elite with the power to define reason and madness, health and sickness, and conformity and deviance. Behind the benevolent facade, new forms of power are embedded in many contemporary social institutions.

The most radical, postmodern challenge is to the Enlightenment premise that reason and knowledge can lead to freedom and equality. Foucault (1980) speaks of "power/knowledge" to suggest that every quest for knowledge is really a grab for power, and that knowledge inevitably leads to domination rather than freedom. For other postmodernists, the Enlightenment dream of reason leading to emancipation is merely another "grand narrative" (Lyotard 1979) that cannot possibly be true because "Truth" itself is no longer possible in a postmodern era. Such arguments challenge the foundations of critical sociology (and every other modern system of knowledge). Although I do not find them ultimately persuasive, they provide critical sociologists with a critical lens on their own work even as they seek to analyze and change a problematic world.

This dual commitment to analyzing and changing domination is the hallmark of critical sociology. It is the common thread running through Marx's work, critical theory, world system theory, feminist sociology, and some versions of postmodernist thought. It is also the thread that sets critical sociology apart from scientific and humanistic sociology.

CONCLUSION

Sociological theories are complex, and any attempt to categorize them is somewhat arbitrary. My purpose here has been to highlight critical sociology as one of several orientations within the discipline.

Chapter one discussed sociology's double critique. We can now see how all sociological approaches are *critical* in the first sense of the term. They all have a debunking quality that does not take the world at face value. They look beyond surface appearances. They assume the world is something other than what it claims to be. They look for unintended consequences and latent functions.

Both scientific and humanistic sociology are critical in this sense. The functional analysis that typifies scientific sociology specializes in finding latent consequences of social action. It recognizes that while people are doing one thing, their actions create other outcomes as well. It reveals precisely how the world is not always (or only) what it appears to be. Humanistic sociology is also critical in this sense. It gave rise to the idea of debunking in the first place (Berger 1963). Humanistic sociology is especially good at seeing how society consists of multiple, symbolic meaning systems. Any system that claims to be the central one is ripe for a debunking analysis.

Among my categories, only critical sociology is also critical in the second sense. Scientific and humanistic approaches embrace value neutrality and scientific detachment that limit their critique. Critical sociology is rooted in particular values that motivate sociological work from the start. It advocates freedom, equality, and emancipation. It is the only approach that fully embodies sociology's double critique. This approach is the main focus in this book, and it receives more detailed discussion in the next chapter.

Critical sociology is also best qualified to address the flawed legacy of Enlightenment thought more generally. The critique of domination has traditionally focused on inequalities of class and injustices of capitalism, and those topics loom large in what follows. But this critique has also been extended to inequalities of race, ethnicity, and gender as well as injustices of colonialism and globalization. These issues also receive more detailed analysis in subsequent chapters.

Chapter 3

Toward a Critical Sociology

This chapter sketches some major themes of critical sociology. The remainder of the book applies this perspective to a wide range of topics.

THE FRANKFURT SCHOOL REVISITED

The first generation of the Frankfurt School developed critical theory from the 1920s through the 1960s. A second generation has carried this work forward into the twenty-first century. This tradition is central to critical sociology.

Marx once encouraged workers to revolt because they had nothing to lose but the chain of economic exploitation. The Frankfurt School suggests a different image: Rather than a single chain, domination involves a complex web of social controls (How 2003, ch. 2). The web traps people in the existing society and discourages the pursuit of alternatives. By revealing how the web creates unjust inequality and limits human potential, the Frankfurt School hoped to encourage progressive social change.

Traditional Theory
One strand in the web of domination is traditional theory, or what I have called scientific sociology, with its emphasis on value neutrality. This approach emerged in natural science to study a natural world that exists apart from human activity. Society, by contrast, is a social construction that is precisely the product of human activity. When we study society through the method of the natural sciences, we create the illusion that it exists apart from our actions and that it can only be organized in one way. Although we cannot change the laws of physics or chemistry, we *can* change the "laws" of society. Studying society as if it were a natural phenomenon denies this possibility.

Traditional theory also excludes values from science. It claims that we can scientifically study "what is" but not "what ought to be." This also tends to "naturalize"

35

the social world by denying the possibility of alternatives. The role of values in social science is complex, but the Frankfurt School argued that it is neither possible nor desirable to exclude them. Rather than claiming a false objectivity, they recognized that values inevitably inform social inquiry. Indeed, critical theory is founded on the Enlightenment values of reason, freedom, and equality as well as on the belief that knowledge can lead to emancipation.

Given these premises, the Frankfurt School's position is clear. Traditional theory naturalizes the social world, endorses the status quo, denies the validity of alternatives, embraces a false objectivity, and presents itself as the only valid form of knowledge. This amounts to the scientific domination of knowledge, and it thereby composes one strand in the web of domination in modern society.

Instrumental Rationality

Another strand is the prevailing form of rationality in modern society. Here the Frankfurt School built on Max Weber's insight that rationalization is the master trend of modern society. Weber saw a dark side here, fearing it would lead to an "iron cage" of bureaucratic control and cold efficiency. The Frankfurt School built on these ideas to identify another type of domination.

Instrumental rationality is a partial and limited use of the human capacity for reason. It reduces reason to a mere instrument or technique that can be applied to any goal whatsoever. As such, highly rational means can be used to pursue highly unreasonable goals. If reason is limited to the choice of means and not extended to goals themselves, then a society can simultaneously become more instrumentally rational and less socially reasonable.

This is perhaps what Einstein had in mind when he characterized the modern age as involving the perfection of means and the confusion of ends. In limiting the application of reason to means, instrumental rationality resembles traditional theory. Just as traditional theory excluded values from science, instrumental rationality denies rational decisions about ends. In both cases, the possibility of rational value choices is ruled out. This turns value neutrality and instrumental rationality against human interests in using reason to create a more autonomous social world.

Instrumental rationality becomes domination in several ways. By focusing debate on *how* do to things, it stifles debate about *whether* it is reasonable to do them in the first place. Whether the issue is nuclear weapons, economic growth, military superiority, or free markets, instrumental rationality asks how to achieve such outcomes efficiently. It deflects attention from broader questions about whether these outcomes make sense to begin with. It simply accepts these priorities as unquestioned necessities. Standing behind these priorities are powerful institutions and interests who benefit when their priorities are seen in this way. Instrumental rationality becomes domination when it prevents critical examination of goals by confining rationality to a discussion of the means to achieve those goals.

Instrumental rationality also becomes domination by enhancing social control over ordinary people. In economics, the unquestioned goal of profitability brought the assembly line, which achieved greater efficiency while also granting managers much greater control over work and workers. In politics, the unquestioned goal of power has promoted bureaucratic control and executive privilege that consolidates power for elite decision makers. In military circles, the unquestioned goal of superiority has spawned more expensive and lethal weapons that have made people around the world increasingly vulnerable to devastating military force.

All these dimensions came together in one of the most appalling examples of instrumental rationality: the Holocaust. In their systematic efforts to exterminate the Jews, the Nazis developed a rationalized, industrialized form of genocide in which millions of people were identified, transported, incarcerated, annihilated, and disposed of. The system had all the classic hallmarks of instrumental rationality: efficiency, calculability, predictability, and control. Yet there is no better example of how instrumental rationality can serve domination, and how instrumentally rational means can serve horrifically unreasonable goals.

Instrumental rationality thereby limits the scope of reason, portrays special interests as unquestioned necessities, develops new forms of social control, enhances the power of elites, and cloaks these processes in claims of rationality. This is an ideological distortion of rationality and yet another strand of domination.

State Capitalism

The Frankfurt School agreed with Marx that capitalism exploited workers to the benefit of capitalists. They were, however, more skeptical about the ability of workers to challenge this system. Rather than oppositional class consciousness, the Frankfurt School feared that "false" consciousness would prevail.

These thinkers focused on new forms of capitalism. Marx had analyzed a competitive, entrepreneurial capitalism. It was an economy of many small producers competing for small market shares. Such an economy at least approximated the virtues of competition in free markets. The relatively small size of capitalist enterprises was matched by the relatively small size and role of government. The philosophy of laissez-faire was at least partially realized as government kept its "hands off" economic activity and minimized its impact on the operation of the marketplace.

By the early twentieth century, the economic concentration and centralization that Marx himself had predicted was producing dramatic effects. Increases in the size and scale of both business and government gave rise to a qualitatively different capitalism, as many small businesses were displaced by fewer large corporations. Frankfurters variously described this new economy as state, monopoly, corporate, or advanced capitalism.

As corporations grew in size, they changed in form. They became complex, bureaucratic hierarchies, concentrating economic power in the hands of the few who owned and controlled them. This changed the basic relation between businesses and the market. Rather than small producers being subordinate to the market, the market became subordinate to the large corporations. As firms became larger, they could monopolize production, set prices, eliminate competition, manipulate demand, create needs, and control government. Corporations dominated workers directly and the entire society indirectly. They began to shape not just economic but political, military, social, and cultural priorities.

Government underwent a parallel transformation. States grew in size, functions, and responsibilities. Even more than corporations, they perfected the complex, hierarchical, bureaucratic organization that typified Weber's "iron cage." State bureaucracies concentrated political power in the hands of the administrators of various state agencies.

As corporations and states grew in size and function, their relationship also changed. Laissez-faire policies were abandoned as states put their "hands on" the marketplace. The corporate economy and state bureaucracy forged an alliance that cemented their interdependence and pursued their joint interests. State capitalism evolved into a system in which states intervened in the market to sustain profitability for corporations, and corporations returned the favor by providing state managers with resources to extend their bureaucratic control.

The rise of state capitalism resting on private corporations and state bureaucracies posed the danger of a "totally administered society." This new capitalism concentrated power in the hands of corporations and states, forged a closer alliance between them, and created more extensive control over workers and citizens. This is a more elaborate form of economic domination, and yet another strand in the web of multiple dominations.

Political Authority

The state grew in response to economic pressures, but also because bureaucratic power follows its own expansionary logic. Once established, bureaucracies centralize their control, expand their reach, and justify their power in the language of instrumental rationality. The Frankfurt School again built on Weber's insight to suggest that bureaucracy was expanding as a form of political domination at the expense of democracy.

The bureaucratic state increasingly intervenes into every aspect of modern life. The bureaus, agencies, departments, and divisions that typify the modern state *might* be required to meet citizen needs. But it is undeniable that they centralize state power over citizens. Even when the motives for creating bureaucracies are laudable, goal displacement and organizational self-perpetuation place bureaucratic interests before anyone or anything else. As a result, bureaucracies reduce citizens to powerless clients and passive consumers of government services. The proliferation of bureaucracy thereby expands political domination.

The rise of authoritarian political bureaucracies and authoritarian economic corporations created an alliance of common interests in profitability and power. A third partner in this alliance was authoritarian military organizations that also followed the bureaucratic model of top-down control. Wars are not new. But modern states foster a culture of militarism that becomes a new form of social control. Militarism can be justified as patriotism, but it often means unquestioned allegiance to a particular government that deflects criticism of political leaders. Marx recognized nationalism was a form of false consciousness. But the consequences only became fully apparent with World War I, as the working classes of rival capitalist countries slaughtered one another, while their capitalist countrymen engaged in war profiteering.

Political domination also rests on propaganda. The Nazi party under Hitler was extremely effective at linking the genuine frustrations of the German people with the expansionary goals of the authoritarian state. The success of Nazi propaganda was partly owing to Hitler's charismatic leadership, but it also relied on generic methods of mass manipulation. The techniques that sold fascism to the German people strongly resemble the marketing, advertising, and public relations methods that sell all sorts of products to consumers in capitalist economies everywhere. The kinship between advertising and propaganda is another expression of instrumental rationality, in which efficient techniques serve destructive ends and produce irrational consequences.

When state capitalism, bureaucratic control, widespread militarism, and official propaganda combine in these ways, democracy yields to authoritarianism. This was not merely an aberration of Nazi Germany. It is a potential outcome anywhere these forces are present. Political domination thereby makes its own contribution to the overall web of domination in modern society.

Personality Dynamics

While domination grew "outside" people, it was also planted "inside" them. The Frankfurt School was troubled by new personality types that were eager to conform to external authority and unable to resist social pressures. They were concerned with psychological forms of social control because they were a more subtle type of domination in which people policed themselves. In C. Wright Mills's (1959) memorable phrase, they could produce a society of "cheerful robots."

The family helped instill such overconformity. The traditional German family was patriarchal and authoritarian, with rigid power differences between adults and children and men and women. Such families raised children excessively attuned to authority, comfortable in hierarchical relations, and predisposed to reproduce authoritarian relations (How 2003, ch. 6).

The Frankfurters thus identified the "authoritarian personality" in modern society. This personality favors rigid thinking that sees the world in simplistic categories of black/white, good/bad, or right/wrong. Such thinking embraces prejudice and scapegoating and readily blames outsiders for problems. This helps explain pro-Nazi and anti-Semitic beliefs. But the same process can emerge whenever psychological insecurities encounter strong authority. When Stanley Milgram (1974) found that a high percentage of Americans would inflict severe pain on others before they would disobey an authority figure, it revealed the same dynamic in a very different cultural setting.

Psychological domination involves trade-offs between individual freedom and social order. Freud (1955) famously argued that social order requires individual repression. Antisocial impulses must be sublimated into socially acceptable behaviors, if society is to be possible. Although this argument seems plausible, some Frankfurters argued that modern society had created *surplus* repression that went far beyond what might be necessary for social order (Marcuse 1964). Surplus repression, or overconformity, maintains elite power through mass manipulation. Authoritarian societies maximize surplus repression, whereas a rational society would maximize freedom.

Contemporary U.S. society seems far removed from Nazi Germany. We pride ourselves on free expression. In Freud's language, we seem to have desublimated repressed drives concerning pleasure, sexuality, and the like. But it is possible for such desublimation to be repressive itself (Marcuse 1964). This happens when people's desires are manipulated and their energy is dissipated with no lasting social benefits. The potential of desublimated desires to create a more liberated society is turned against people. Consider how each generation embraces its own variation of a rebellious pose that has become a staple and harmless feature of popular culture. People think they are rebelling when they are simply recreating the dominant society.

When personal needs, self-worth, and emotional insecurities are manipulated by larger social forces, psychological domination exists. Consider how millions of jobs and billions of dollars are devoted to manipulating people into buying whatever advertisers are selling to fulfill desires that have been created by those very same forces. This amounts to a type of "internalized oppression" that is an especially potent form of control because it exists without overt conflict. It thereby composes a significant strand in the web of domination.

Mass Culture

The Frankfurt School is perhaps best known for their critical analysis of the *culture industry*. The term summarizes their argument. Culture is how people create meanings, maintain traditions, sustain identities, and integrate groups. Culture is potentially the most creative sphere of human activity where hopes for a better society are expressed. Linking the word *industry* to *culture* implies that the creative possibilities of cultural expression have given way to the standardized methods of instrumental rationality. Culture becomes another commodity produced with efficiency, calculability, predictability, and control; it becomes another form of domination (How 2003, ch. 5).

The target of this criticism is mass culture, or the intersection of mass media, public relations, and consumer marketing. Mass culture turns meanings into commodities that follow the logic of the marketplace. Profitability means standardization to reach the largest market and alienate the fewest consumers. Creativity and artistry are pushed to the margins as the culture industry packages products into familiar genres and styles. We think our role is to consume products, but don't realize that we have become the product because the goal of mass media is to sell audiences to advertisers. Content is irrelevant as long as it creates audiences for sale.

The media are not "just entertainment." They are also a form of domination. The culture industry reduces people to passive spectators and consumers of culture rather than active participants in its creation. Consider how mass media turn political issues—and elections in particular—into spectacles to be consumed as entertainment. This is a far cry from democratic ideals of active citizenship, as mass culture reinforces the authoritarian tendencies of the political system.

A second way the culture industry becomes domination is consumerism. The culture industry taps into people's needs and desires in a highly unequal society. Through the psychological domination discussed earlier, mass media links needs to consumerism as the universal solution to human problems. In the logic of the culture industry, there is no human dilemma for which a product cannot be created, marketed, and profitably sold. And if the desire or need is not already there, it can be created by the advertising industry. By tapping real needs, creating false needs, and linking both to consumption, the culture industry creates the demand required for a profitable economy.

A third way in which the culture industry becomes domination is that its products are "weapons of mass distraction." The culture industry colonizes the "free time" left to us after the physiological need for rest and the economic compulsion to work. Our leisure is less a time of relaxation and reflection than another form of work in which buying, watching, listening, and otherwise consuming cultural products becomes a compulsive lifestyle. The more people participate in this world, the more they are likely to take it for granted and the harder it is to envision any alternatives. When people cannot envision alternatives, domination has been accomplished.

When meanings, symbols, and identities become commodities, people become passive consumers rather than active creators of their social world. Cultural domination thereby takes its place alongside other forms of social control that compose a dense web of domination in modern society.

The Frankfurt School: An Assessment

The Frankfurt School thinkers were like hunters seeking new forms of domination. Their prey, however, was not especially elusive. It turned out that domination was everywhere in modern society (How 2003, ch. 3). Whether one focused on science, rationality, economics, politics, psychology, or culture, there was an almost perverse tendency for each to become another means of controlling masses to the benefit of elites.

This was a major irony they called the dialectic of Enlightenment. The phrase summarized the inability of the Enlightenment to deliver on its promises. On the positive side, it had moved Europe out of an intellectual dark age that subordinated knowledge to religious authority. It was progressive in this context by suggesting that reason and science could emancipate people from unjust authority and arbitrary domination. In their place, the Enlightenment promised autonomous people building a rational society.

On the negative side, the Enlightenment created more powerful techniques of social control. Reason and science did not automatically lead to freedom and autonomy. It turned out they could be used for other purposes altogether. When rationality becomes an instrument in the service of power, then the dark side of the Enlightenment appears. Nuclear power is a poignant example. Unlocking the secrets of the atom was an astounding scientific accomplishment that epitomized an Enlightenment dream. The use of such knowledge to develop nuclear weapons that could destroy life on earth illustrates an Enlightenment nightmare. In darker moments, the Frankfurt School foreshadowed postmodern themes by detecting power everywhere and becoming deeply suspicious of reason (How 2003, ch. 3).

The Frankfurt School is crucial to understanding the modern world through the lens of critical sociology. Its work, however, is also open to criticism. Many people are frustrated by the seeming lack of solutions. They say that the critique of domination is fine but they want to know how to fix things. Easy answers are not forthcoming from the Frankfurt School. Of all people, they would insist that solutions cannot be handed down by elites (including intellectuals) but rather must be created democratically. Only then might it be possible to formulate solutions that don't recreate the dynamics of hierarchy and authority.

Their reluctance about solutions is also a reaction to Marx, who combined sociological reasoning and political hope to conclude that the working class would become the grave diggers of capitalism. Many of Marx's followers emphasized the hope over the reasoning and turned working-class revolution into an article of faith. This faith has proven unfounded, and it has been used to justify revolutions that have not advanced human emancipation. The Frankfurt School rejected this faith from the beginning, and it was unwilling to identify any group that had an inside track on overthrowing domination.

There is a related problem that runs deeper. The Frankfurt School has no theory of agency. In a way, these thinkers did too good a job in detecting domination. By finding it everywhere, they portrayed a social system so powerful that no one could ever escape its grasp. When theories grant this much power to abstract systems of control, they inevitably depict people as passive victims of overpowering forces. To deny agency means people are not seen as capable of ever deviating from what the system wants them to do.

Such a view is not plausible. Even in the face of domination, people resist. Such resistance might not fit traditional images of revolution, but neither can it be dismissed. Thus, critical sociology must reject the cultural pessimism of the Frankfurt School concerning agency. A better premise is that wherever there is domination, there is also resistance. However powerful, domination is always contested. Society is not a product of one-way domination but of multidirectional struggles. This insight is crucial to a viable critical sociology.

HABERMAS'S CONTRIBUTIONS

The most well-known member of the "second generation" of the Frankfurt School is Jürgen Habermas. His work began appearing in the early 1960s and continues to this day. His writings span the social sciences and philosophy. Although sometimes dense and difficult to understand, his ideas are central to critical sociology and offer intriguing solutions to the problem of agency.

The Public Sphere

Habermas's work has always endorsed democracy as a system in which all citizens have real input into political decisions. By this standard, what we call democracy is a highly diluted version in which voters select between elite candidates already beholden to powerful interests. Habermas's concern is how to enrich democracy and maximize participation for all.

In the early days of European capitalism, Habermas (1989) finds one model of democracy in the public sphere. Publics emerged in newly urbanizing areas, as literacy became more widespread. These publics had important democratic features. In social settings like pubs and coffeehouses, people debated ideas with few restrictions on the basis of status. As they did so, it was the power of the better argument that was most highly prized. In this, Habermas sees the germs of an important form of *substantive* rationality.

In these discussions, reason was not a mere instrument in pursuit of other goals. Reason was central in deciding the goals themselves by debating what kind of society was most desirable. Here Enlightenment values of reason, democracy, equality, and freedom were fused in a positive way. With the spread of the printing press, such democratic debate reached larger audiences. From the very beginning, Habermas's work thus examines occasions of democratic decision making in which people are agents seeking a better world.

Habermas is also careful not to romanticize the public sphere. In a capitalist society, the public sphere is both an idea and an ideology. As idea, it links substantive reason, citizen agency, and democratic decision making. As ideology, the public sphere sustains the illusion that capitalist society is more democratic than it really is or ever could be. Think of the coffeehouse again as a metaphor for the public sphere. Within its doors, people participate as equals, and the best argument wins. When people step outside, they resume their roles in the private sphere with sharp differences among wealthy business owners, small farmers, and wage laborers. The public sphere thus contains a contradiction. The kernel of an egalitarian, democratic society is within the shell of an unequal, capitalist economy. Such a society is a long way from the democratic potential implied by its public sphere.

Indeed, contemporary capitalism is even farther from the positive model of the public sphere under the influence of large corporations and massive bureaucracies. The rational-critical debate that used to define the public sphere has largely evaporated. Modern "debates" rarely involve ordinary citizens; they are fabricated by pollsters, advisers, and experts, who work for elite political interests. With this transformation, the public sphere is less a place where democratic decisions are made and more a place where private priorities gain a veneer of public legitimacy.

When the public sphere is reduced to mass culture, it becomes another tool of domination. Habermas shares Frankfurt School pessimism about mass culture, but retains optimism about the potential of a public sphere. It is crucial that elite decisions still need the legitimation that the public sphere provides. As long as such legitimation is required, the potential of the public sphere for fostering genuine democracy persists.

Labor and Interaction

The public sphere is really about communication, which is another of Habermas's central concerns. He developed his ideas through a type of dialogue with Marx on what defines the human species.

Marx equates being human with the ability to labor. It is through labor that we survive, but it is also through labor that we develop as individuals and evolve as a species. When we work, we create and recreate ourselves through the knowledge, skills, and capacities we develop in order to work effectively. This includes reflexivity. We think, plan, and design before we act, work, or build. Human labor is an interactive cycle between reflection and activity. Marx argued that this is what distinguishes the worst of architects from the best of bees: Both build elaborate structures, but bees use instinct, whereas humans use imagination. Unlike instinct, imagination improves through practice. Labor thus makes us human. This is why alienation is such a serious problem. A society that alienates people from their labor alienates people from themselves; it is an inhumane society.

Habermas agreed that we develop as a species through our own activity, but he felt that Marx defined it too narrowly. Labor is one dimension, but communication or interaction is another. Where Marx has a one-dimensional view of human activity as labor, Habermas has a two-dimensional view as involving both labor and interaction (How 2003, ch. 4).

Habermas (1969) sees labor as purposive-rational action. What matters here is the achievement of an external goal. Success requires rational decisions about the most efficient way to achieve the goal. Marx's "labor" thus becomes Habermas's "purposive-rational action," but both agree that this activity has been crucial to our development as a species.

For Marx, the story ends there; for Habermas, there is a part two. Alongside purposive-rational action, communicative action is also crucial in the development of the species. The goal of purposive-rational action is external success, and it is motivated by self-interest. The goal of communicative action is establishing understanding, and it is motivated by reciprocity. Each action seeks a different outcome. Purposive-rational action seeks technical control over an external environment. Communicative action seeks intersubjective agreement among interacting people. Successful purposive-rational action results in greater control, while successful communicative action results in communication that is *free from domination*.

Consider the difference between two scenarios. Sitting down at a poker table implies the *instrumental* goal of winning other people's money. Doing so requires calculating the strength of your hand and the size of your bet relative to your opponents'. Success means leaving with more money than you started with.

Sitting down in a therapist's office implies the *communicative* goal of achieving understanding. Doing so requires open dialogue to identify symptoms, causes, and solutions to psychological problems. Success means gaining a mutual understanding and insight that helps the client overcome a problem. The deception that is integral to good poker strategy would undermine successful therapy, just as the honesty required in therapy could lose you a lot of money at the poker table. The contrast suggests how instrumental and communicative actions are qualitatively different.

Both Marx and Habermas use their theories as a baseline for critical analysis. Marx's baseline is unalienated labor, where people develop and express their human nature through work. Marx uses this baseline to criticize alienation and as a goal for progressive change. Habermas's baseline is undistorted communication, where people use language to reach understanding. Habermas uses this baseline to criticize distorted communication and as a goal for progressive change. This explains Habermas's interest in the public sphere. It was a situation of relatively undistorted communication geared to reaching democratic understanding. This is an important standard for criticizing any situation in which communication becomes distorted by purposes other than seeking understanding.

Discourse and Truth

Habermas's interest in communication led him to analyze language. What he found met a big challenge for critical theory by revealing a basis for the values at its foundation. This basis is language itself.

"Habermas's argument is, simply, that the goal of critical theory—a form of life free from unnecessary domination in all its forms—is inherent in the notion of truth; it is anticipated in every act of communication" (McCarthy 1981, 273). The very structure of language endorses the values of truth and freedom, because every speech act implies four things. First, that what we are saying is grammatically correct or understandable. Second, that what we are saying is true. Third, that we are truthful, sincere, and reliable. Fourth, that it is appropriate for us to say these things. Every speech act anticipates achieving consensus and establishing truth. Language itself is the foundation for the values at the basis of critical theory.

These implicit claims are not always fulfilled when people talk. People often say things that are grammatically incorrect, false, insincere, or things they are not qualified to say. But we still judge their speech by these standards built into language itself. The claims help us judge the correctness, truthfulness, sincerity, and rightness of speech. When speech does fulfill these claims, we have communication that establishes a consensus and points toward truth. When it deviates from them, we have *distorted* communication. Speech used to deceive others violates the underlying nature of language itself. If believed, such distortions can be a powerful tool of control. One goal of critical theory is to reveal such distortions by measuring them against the standards of language itself.

Another goal of critical theory is to promote undistorted communication. A model of such communication is the "ideal speech situation." This is an imaginary scenario in which discourse leads to a genuine consensus. To do so, several conditions must be met. People's motivation must be to seek the truth. Power cannot intrude on the discourse. Everyone must have equal opportunity to participate. People must provide convincing reasons for their positions. The only "power" permitted is that of the better argument. In this hypothetical situation, undistorted communication would flourish and lead to consensus and to truth.

The ideal speech situation can never be fully achieved. It nonetheless serves two purposes. First, it is a standard for identifying distorted communication. The more the conditions of ideal speech are violated, the more distorted communication becomes and the more it serves domination rather than consensus. Second, it provides a goal for real world discourse. The more we can approximate the ideal speech situation, the more likely we can arrive at a genuine consensus. In a rational society, every effort would be made to minimize distorted communication and to approximate the ideal speech situation.

Consider political speech in the United States, where wealthy interests literally buy broadcast time and figuratively buy the allegiance of politicians whose campaigns they fund. Money is power that distorts the issues, motives, and stances of those who accept it. Even though politicians want to convince us they speak the truth, we are right to be suspicious. Now consider a system of publicly financed campaigns in which each viable candidate receives funds out of general revenues with no strings attached. Although hardly a complete solution, this would move political speech from more to less distorted, by neutralizing the corrosive influence of private money. The ideal speech situation thus provides both a positive goal of undistorted speech and a critical standard for judging distorted speech.

Two Forms of Rationality

The early Frankfurt School used the term *instrumental rationality* to criticize the use of reason as a mere instrument. They endorsed a substantive rationality that would extend to goals and values as well, but did little to develop the idea. Habermas's analysis of language provided a new basis for substantive or communicative rationality.

Instrumental and communicative rationality are both products of social evolution (Habermas 1987). Early societies made little distinction between natural and social worlds. People "socialized" nature; they thought it was alive with forces, spirits, and gods who intervened in human affairs. They also "naturalized" society; they thought it was part of nature, over which they had no control. A big step in social evolution was the distinction between nature and society. Nature was "desocialized," as people came to see it as an inanimate world, and society was "denaturalized," as people came to see it as a social construction.

Society can also be seen as both system and lifeworld (How 2003, ch. 7). Society as a system must meet survival needs through material production. Over time, such abilities have developed enormously. This development is a type of rationalization or increase in instrumental rationality.

This is evident whenever we do things with greater efficiency, precision, calculability, and control. Instrumental rationality has thus been crucial to the survival and development of the species. It is not a problem in itself. It becomes a problem when it is seen as the only kind of rationality that exists.

This is why Habermas is so keen to describe an alternative: the communicative rationality of the lifeworld. This lifeworld involves practical, everyday interactions, where people use language to establish meanings, express identities, clarify norms, and reach understanding. Such communicative action seeks agreement among participants. It is rational because people give reasons for their positions and defend them against criticism. Communicative action becomes rationalized as it becomes free from domination or external authority.

Like instrumental rationality, communicative rationality evolves. In earlier societies, mythical, magical, or religious ideas provided answers to life's uncertainties. Questions about birth and death, the existence of suffering, or the meaning of life found answers in these belief systems. In these societies, communicative action provided mutual understanding but left little room for debate.

With social evolution, mythical, magical, and religious beliefs lost some of their power. Automatic acceptance through belief gave way to reasoned judgment through dialogue. Questions about norms and values were not automatically settled by authorities; they became subject to discourse.

In such discourse, people present positions, defend them with reasons, and move toward consensus based on the best argument. As this process emerged, normatively ascribed agreement was replaced by communicatively achieved understanding. Put more simply, there was a shift from being told what to do and think by an external authority to deciding what to do and think on the basis of discussion and consensus. Traditional knowledge was replaced by communicative action as a guide to everyday action.

There is a sense in which each person's life replays this story of social evolution. As infants and small children, we obey adult authority without question. As we mature, we become capable of understanding the reasons behind adult decisions, and eventually we can discuss, challenge, and perhaps even change such decisions. The individual progression from unthinking obedience to deliberative reasoning about how to act replays the broader evolution of communicative rationality in society itself.

Rationalization thus follows two paths. Instrumental rationality evolved as the system became more efficient in meeting survival needs. Communicative rationality evolved as the lifeworld became more democratic in reaching mutual understanding.

The Colonization Thesis

With social evolution, the system also becomes "detached" from the lifeworld. This detachment means that economic and political decisions in the system are no longer justified through communicative action. There is no rational explanation for why certain actions are undertaken.

In place of communication, the principles of money and power drive system decisions and priorities. The economic and political systems are hardwired to do whatever will enhance profitability and power. These goals are taken for granted; they are rarely if ever discussed or justified through reasoned deliberation.

This is an ironic development. Just when communicative rationality has emerged as a more democratic basis for lifeworld decisions, system decisions are absolved from any such justification. Instead of discourse, money and power are "automatic pilots" for decision making. The instrumental rationality of the system goes unquestioned. This is a new version of an old argument about how instrumental rationality becomes social domination.

There is a larger problem: the colonization of the lifeworld (Habermas 1987). Consider the metaphor. Colonizers exploit indigenous peoples, take their resources, and dominate their culture. In the metaphor, the instrumental rationality of the system becomes a colonial power that dominates the lifeworld and its communicative rationality. This creates a major power struggle between two forms of rationality.

Colonization means that rather than using communicative rationality to arrive at meanings, identities, norms, and understanding, these processes are overtaken by instrumental rationality. Social activities ideally based on communicative action and justifiable reasons are reshaped by the priorities of money and power.

Consider mass culture again. Cultural creativity could be the ideal medium for communicative action, but mass culture colonizes this potential. Culture becomes a commodity and profitability becomes the measure of value. When the "best" books, movies, and music are defined as those that make the most money, culture has been colonized by the system.

Or consider health care. There are major contradictions between health-care needs and for-profit medicine. Offering health care as a commodity creates massive inequalities among recipients, drives up costs and restricts availability, underwrites a profitable if dangerous pharmaceutical industry, and creates complex layers of inhumane, bureaucratic decision making. Although markets can be an effective way to provide some goods and services, profit-based health care is a striking example of how system priorities colonize and distort human needs.

Such colonization reinforces passivity. As consumers, we are encouraged to define and meet our needs by buying commodities. As clients, we are encouraged to define and meet still other needs through bureaucratic services. Colonization "monetarizes" and "bureaucratizes" human needs, so that meeting them makes us dependent on the system and enhances its power. Recent trends toward privatization offer further examples of colonization. Whether the issue is education, prisons, or Social Security, privatization means meeting human needs through commodities that place corporate profitability before human welfare.

Colonization means instrumental rationality intrudes into social life. Although these forces are powerful, they are not uncontested. Wherever instrumental rationality intrudes, it clashes with the communicative rationality of the lifeworld. The colonization of the lifeworld is less an accomplished fact than one side in an ongoing struggle between two different kinds of rationality.

New Social Movements
Colonial relations provoke resistance. The colonization of the lifeworld expresses domination but also provokes resistance. This is a big step beyond the traditional Frankfurt School's inability to identify any countervailing forces against the web of domination.

The potential for such resistance is new social movements. In place of the "old" working-class response to capitalism, new social movements challenge the instrumental rationality of the system as a whole (Habermas 1987). Such movements are often diverse. They include people from different social classes. They often organize on the basis of gender, race, ethnicity, nationality, culture, sexuality, age, or disability. Sometimes they attract people more on the basis of a pressing issue than a common identity. Such issues include human rights, peace and justice, environmental causes, consumer health and safety, or globalization dynamics.

New social movements often are "post-materialist"; they are not primarily about gaining material resources. Their goals have more to do with defending the quality of life, the identity of a group, or the autonomy of a community. One consequence of such goals is that it might be harder to co-opt these movements. Materialist movements can sometimes be "bought off" with partial concessions. Post-materialist movements pose bigger challenges because their demands cannot be reduced to material rewards. This post-materialist aspect is itself a challenge to instrumental rationality by rejecting the idea that everything has a price and can be reduced to money.

New social movements resist lifeworld colonization. Consider the environmental movement. The logic of corporate capitalism defines the natural world as private property to be owned and marketable commodities to be sold. In either case, the goal is short-term profitability. Such logic colonizes the natural world and the ecosystem that sustains human life. In myriad ways, the environmental movement challenges this colonization. Whether the issue is resource depletion, industrial pollution, global warming, or species extinction, the environmental movement challenges the logic of instrumental rationality and profitability with the deliberate discourse of communicative rationality.

Peace, justice, and antiwar movements are also responses to colonization. The logic of nation-states is to seek, maintain, and enhance power in the form of national superiority through military force if necessary. Such logic colonizes the cultures and peoples of the world by subordinating their needs to the dictates of national security and military superiority. Peace, justice, and antiwar movements challenge this colonization. Whether the issue is defense spending, supporting dictators, clandestine operations, or overt warfare, each challenges the unspoken premises of national security and military superiority. Once again, the minimal goal of such movements is to undermine the unquestioned logic of instrumental rationality and power with the deliberate discourse of communicative rationality.

Identity-oriented new social movements challenge the system in other ways. Systems of domination are not tolerant of diversity. They tend to deny it or use it against people in the form of discrimination. Identity-oriented movements challenge such denial and domination by seeking autonomy and self-determination for those who are "different." Whether the constituency is women, "minorities," or gays and lesbians, self-determination is a central challenge to instrumental rationality, because it can only be achieved through communicative rationality attuned to meanings, values, norms, and identities. The more "space" created for communicative rationality, the bigger the challenge to instrumental rationality.

New social movements also nurture discourse. Because they exist outside the colonized spaces of the corporate economy and mainstream politics, they have unusual opportunities to engage in communicative rationality. In order to define their own priorities and purposes, these movements must engage in dialogue. As a result, they can become laboratories of communicative action that approximate the ideal speech situation in which discourse revolves around how we should live. This is why the metaphor of colonization must be interpreted carefully. It involves not one-way domination but two-way struggle between domination and autonomy.

Habermas: A Brief Assessment

The early Frankfurt School lacked a foundation for the values driving their critique and a theory of agency that might offer some hope about overcoming domination.

Against this backdrop, Habermas makes two real advances. First, he finds a basis for critical theory. His work shows that the very structure of language points toward truth and provides standards to judge truthfulness. The ideal speech situation describes a hypothetical model in which discourse would lead to consensual truths, but there are real examples of communicative rationality in the lifeworld, the public sphere, and new social movements. This rationality points toward a society free from domination.

Like his predecessors, Habermas does not identify any group who will necessarily challenge domination. But unlike his predecessors, he offers insights about the potential for change. It is built into the lifeworld and its characteristic form of communicative rationality. Unless lifeworld concerns about meaning, purpose, identity, and belonging are completely colonized, it will always be a basis of resistance to domination. This potential takes a more concrete form in every new social movement that arises to defend the lifeworld and challenge the system. Whereas the Frankfurt School ultimately saw people as passive victims of domination, Habermas sees ongoing potentials for resistance.

Habermas did not solve all the problems of critical theory, and his own work has received criticism. He has been faulted for an overly dualistic view of a system free of norms and a lifeworld free of power. Feminist critics have been astute in identifying how power operates in the lifeworld and in challenging the dualism of these spheres (Fraser 1989). Nevertheless, this work is a considerable advance on the early Frankfurt School, and it provides an important foundation for critical sociology.

CONCLUSION

The Frankfurt School analyzed a web of domination that seemed all-powerful. They were ingenious in exposing it, but pessimistic about transcending it. Habermas recast the web of domination as the colonization of the lifeworld. This metaphor illuminates domination while recognizing potentials for transformation.

In many respects, the clash is between capitalism and democracy. The logic of capitalism is based on private interest and profitability. The logic of democracy is based on public interest and consensus. "Between capitalism and democracy there is an indissoluble tension; in them two opposed principles of societal integration compete for primacy" (Habermas 1987, 345). The modern world has been shaped by this competition, so a critical sociology based on these ideas is essential to making sense of that world.

The Frankfurt School also exposed the contradictions of the Enlightenment by demonstrating how reason and science do not necessarily promote autonomy and equality. Indeed, they can become new forms of domination, as evidenced by instrumental rationality and lifeworld colonization. In subsequent chapters, the colonization thesis guides discussions of economics, politics, and culture.

There are other Enlightenment contradictions the Frankfurt School ignored. They said little about how seemingly universalistic assertions about "mankind" concealed the deeply rooted biases of white, male, Eurocentric thinkers. Later chapters on inequality and difference will introduce other critical voices addressing class, race, and gender. Still other voices will address issues of self and society. The concluding section of the book draws on all these themes to analyze globalization, social movements, and democratization.

PART TWO
POWER AND DOMINATION

Chapter 4

A Late Capitalist World

For critical sociology, capitalism is the dominant force in the modern world. Its corporations dwarf the social landscape. Its pursuit of profit shapes all social priorities. Its logic saturates our culture. Without understanding capitalism, we can't know where we came from, what we are doing, or where we are going.

We begin with Marx, followed by an analysis of the advanced capitalism that matured in the twentieth century and is expanding globally in the twenty-first century. We then explore potential crises that might emerge in advanced capitalism and conclude with some economic trends shaping our world as the new century unfolds.

MARX'S ANALYSIS OF CAPITALISM

Marx saw capitalism as a historically specific economic system. It is not eternal. It was preceded by other economic systems and will be followed by still others. It is distinguished by three elements. First, it is devoted to the realization of profit. Second, this occurs through the production and sale of commodities. Third, these commodities are produced by wage-labor. This combination of private profit, commodity production, and wage-labor sets capitalism apart from all other economic systems.

Labor Theory of Value
Marx begins with a seemingly simple question: Where do profits come from? How is it possible for a capitalist to invest in resources, labor, and technology to create products whose sale results in more money than was there at the beginning? Not every business succeeds, but there is a systematic quality to the accumulation of capital as a whole. How does this happen?

Any commodity has two types of economic value. It has use-value because it meets some human need. This use-value is realized when someone consumes the commodity. Commodities also have exchange-value. One commodity can be exchanged for another commodity. The exchange-value of a commodity is realized when someone trades it for another. This raises another question: How is the exchange-value of a commodity determined? Why are some more valuable than others?

Mainstream economics points to supply and demand, but this is merely a theory of price fluctuation. Low supply and high demand increase prices, whereas high supply and low demand decrease prices. But what is the "real" value of a commodity when supply and demand are in balance? The question is difficult because the use-values of commodities are qualitatively different. You can't wear a cheeseburger to stay warm or eat a stocking cap to relieve hunger. So why do cheeseburgers, stocking caps, and every other commodity in the world have a specific exchange-value?

There is only one common feature of all commodities: They are products of human labor. From this, Marx advocated the labor theory of value: Commodities have economic value because they are the products of human labor. Moreover, the amount of exchange-value that any commodity has is based on the amount of labor that goes into its production. The more labor that goes into the production of a commodity, the greater its exchange-value. Some commodities are more valuable than others because more labor went into their production.

Another defining feature of capitalism is wage-labor. Workers sell labor-power (their ability to work) to capitalists for a wage. In other words, capitalism turns labor-power into a commodity that is bought and sold. As with any commodity, the price of labor fluctuates with changes in supply and demand. But what is the "real" value of labor-power when supply and demand are in balance?

Marx's logic is consistent. If labor-power is a commodity, then its value is determined by the amount of labor that goes into its production. Because labor-power is embodied in a person, the production of labor-power really means the survival of the person. People must consume a variety of commodities to sustain themselves and their ability to labor. So the value of labor-power is equal to the value of all the commodities people need to survive at a culturally acceptable level. If capitalists buy labor-power at its real value, they pay workers wages that allow them to survive and reproduce their labor-power.

The labor theory of value explains the exchange-value of all commodities in terms of the single baseline of human labor. It is the only common element in the production of every commodity, including labor-power itself.

Surplus Value and Exploitation

If we assume that all commodities exchange at their true values, we still have the question: How is profit possible? Where does the "extra" value come from? It turns out that labor-power is the only commodity that can create new value greater than its own value. The more productively it is organized, the greater the surplus that will result.

Consider a simple example. A small capitalist spends $1,000 each on raw materials, means of production, and labor-power to make pencils. Her total investment is $3,000. She then sells her pencils for $6,000 and makes $3,000 in the process. Where does the extra three grand come from? If labor-power is the only commodity that can create a surplus, then it must come from labor. The raw materials and means of production do not create new value. Their value is simply transferred to the pencils in the production process. The new value comes from labor and its unique capacity to produce a surplus. The question can now be answered. Profits come from labor.

Starting from a symmetrical situation where all commodities exchange at their value, we arrive at an asymmetrical outcome. Our capitalist created no new value but received a $6,000 return on a $3,000 investment. This new value is created by workers, but they only receive a portion of it back to reproduce their labor-power. The remaining value created by labor goes to capital. When workers create all the new value and capitalists take a portion of it, that is exploitation. Capitalists exploit workers by taking advantage of labor-power's unique capacity to produce a surplus.

This exploitation is obscured by how workers are paid. Consider economic production on a large scale. Every day some commodities are completely consumed and others are partially consumed. Survival requires that a certain amount of production occur every day simply to replace what is used up. Call this necessary labor. A society could hypothetically do only this much labor and survive. However, there would be no surplus and no growth. In reality, all societies produce some surplus. Put differently, they engage in surplus labor above and beyond the necessary labor needed to ensure survival.

We can thus hypothetically divide a workday into two components. The first is necessary labor required for survival. The second is surplus labor beyond that minimum. The value created during necessary labor comes back to workers as wages. It must, if they are to survive by buying commodities to reproduce their labor-power. The value created during surplus labor goes to the capitalists as surplus value, or profits.

It's as if workers work part of the day for themselves and part of the day for capitalists. If the day were really divided this way, logical workers would go home after necessary labor with all their wages and leave capitalists without any income. The wage form prevents this. It takes the money workers need and spreads it out over the entire workday, so they must work a full shift to receive their wages.

Imagine that workers produce eight hours of new value and get four hours back as wages, and capitalists take the other four hours as surplus value. This ratio is the rate of surplus value; it expresses what capitalists get relative to workers. It is also the rate of exploitation; it reveals what workers get relative to their contributions. Such exploitation is inherent in capitalism; it makes profits possible.

It gets worse. Capitalism systematically increases exploitation in two ways. One is by lengthening the working day. If workers can be forced to work twelve hours rather than eight, the rate of surplus value increases dramatically: Four hours for workers and eight for capitalists. The other method is to increase the productivity of labor. If workers double their output, necessary labor (and workers' wages) shrinks from four to two hours and surplus labor (and capitalists' profits) expands from four to six hours. In both cases, workers still create all new value, but their share shrinks to an ever-smaller proportion of the total, and capitalists' share expands.

Capitalism increases exploitation because capitalists compete amongst themselves. As powerful as they are, even capitalists are subject to the laws of competition. The primary strategy in the competitive struggle between capitalists is to maximize surplus value by exploiting workers more extensively than rival capitalists. Over the long run, capitalism becomes more competitive between capitalists and more exploitative of workers.

Marx recognized the revolutionary power of capitalism to develop the forces of production. But he was highly critical of the price workers paid for such advances. Capitalism inevitably creates increasingly exploitative and antagonistic relations between a wealthy minority and the vast majority of the population. Marx's ultimate target was not capital*ists* but rather capital*ism,* because it deforms human relations.

This deformation includes alienating workers from their product, their work, their potential, and other people. It includes commodity fetishism where commodities become more important than people. Even though people are required to create them, commodities often acquire a life of their own, and we "forget" their origins. Marx punctured these illusions by referring to commodities as "dead labor," reminding us that they would not exist without the past efforts of workers. In a similar fashion, the socialist slogan that "property is theft" reminds us that what exists now as private property was once the creation of laborers who could not own what they produced. And most generally, Marx insisted that capital is not a thing but a social relationship. It comes into existence through the productive efforts of workers. Its ownership by others should not blind us to how it was created or to whom was exploited in the process.

Contradictions and Crises

Capitalism is a dynamic, unstable system because of capitalist competition and worker resistance. Its instability goes even deeper because capitalism rests on contradictions. Some contradictions develop into major economic crises that threaten capitalism's survival.

One contradiction is between social production and private appropriation. Capitalist production is socially organized; it requires the coordinated activity of many people. Appropriation, however, is private and individual. Resources that are socially produced are privately owned. As a result, capitalism is good at producing private commodities but bad at producing public goods. Capitalism produces lots of cars but not efficient mass transit. It produces lots of drugs but not affordable health care. It produces countless products to clean your house but can't sustain clean air and water. The contradiction between social production and private appropriation contributes to capitalist instability.

Another contradiction is between internal organization and market anarchy. Internal organization occurs within the corporation, which becomes a highly rational and bureaucratic firm seeking to control and predict its environment in pursuit of profits. In sharp contrast, there is economic anarchy in the larger society. There is little economic coordination, no overall plan for using scarce resources wisely, and little regulation of rapid fluctuations in commodity and labor markets. The revenues for essential services like health, education, and welfare thus become highly unpredictable. Although the wealthy can survive such instability, it threatens the livelihood of many ordinary citizens.

A third contradiction is the polarization of wealth and poverty. Because capital is concentrated in fewer hands, the rich become richer. Even when workers' living standards improve, capitalist standards often improve more rapidly, creating a relative polarization of wealth and poverty. When measured on a global scale, the polarization between rich and poor nations is staggering. Such extreme inequality creates further instability.

A fourth contradiction is that capitalism produces for profit and not for use. Imagine two circles that partially overlap. One circle represents products people need. The other represents products that are profitable. Capitalism responds to the second circle. It produces some things that are needed—but it does so because they are profitable and not because they are needed. It also produces some things that are profitable but not really needed (visit any shopping mall for examples). Finally, it does not produce things that are needed but not profitable; affordable housing is one of many examples. Production for profit and not use creates further instability by allowing the extreme affluence of some to coexist with the unmet needs of others.

Some contradictions become major economic crises. Consider how overproduction or under-consumption occurs because capitalism produces more than can be sold at an acceptable profit. Recall that workers produce more value than they receive back as wages, so they don't have the purchasing power to buy all the commodities they produce. Even when capitalist consumption is added to the equation, there is a tendency toward overproduction or under-consumption that becomes an economic crisis. On the production side, profits shrink, investment slows, production declines, inventories accumulate, and productive capacity goes unused. Stagnation, recession, or even depression can result. On the consumption side, firms seek new markets, destroy surplus products, tap government as a consumer of last resort, advertise more heavily, and extend consumer credit, so that even people without money can buy.

Another crisis tendency involves a falling rate of profit as capitalists invest in new technology to stay competitive. This means their investment in labor becomes a smaller portion of their total investment. Because labor is the only source of new value, it becomes increasingly difficult to sustain profits. Again, various strategies come into play. Capitalists can increase exploitation or depress wages to counter a falling rate of profit. In the long term, they must cheapen the cost of new technology to sustain acceptable profits. Unless they can do so fast enough, profits remain low and the entire economy experiences stagnation.

These contradictions and crisis tendencies cannot be eliminated. What capitalists and their political allies try to do is minimize and redirect their most harmful effects. The value of this crisis theory is not that it predicts an inevitable downfall of capitalism; it is rather that it identifies powerful economic tendencies that trigger certain responses. The dance of crisis tendencies and counterstrategies offers important insights into capitalist economies.

Capitalism is a system in which labor's ability to produce a surplus is turned against a majority of the population. Rather than shared abundance, surplus becomes profit for a tiny minority. Moreover, capitalists must maximize exploitation to survive in a system increasingly subject to inherent contradictions and crisis tendencies. Marx is a vocal critic of capitalism, but capitalism is really its own critic. Every unmet need in a context of affluence reveals how far capitalism remains from a rational society in which production would be organized to meet the needs of all before the wealth of a few.

FROM LIBERAL TO ADVANCED CAPITALISM

Capitalism has obviously changed over the past 150 years. A critical sociology for our time retains Marx's core insights while updating his crisis theory of capitalism. This is precisely the strategy of Habermas's *Legitimation Crisis* (1975): to analyze new crisis tendencies deriving from the dominant institution of our time.

Consider the notion of crisis. In medicine, a crisis occurs when a patient faces a grave threat to survival with the possibility of recovery. A social crisis poses an equally grave threat while also allowing for recovery and transformation. A genuine social crisis occurs on two levels. It threatens *system* integration by undermining the production and distribution of material goods needed for physical survival. It simultaneously threatens *social* integration by weakening the social norms, cultural values, and personal identities that hold society together. It is when *both* system and social integration are imperiled that societies face a real crisis.

This logic fits Marx's crisis theory. In the liberal capitalism of the nineteenth century, the market provided system integration by coordinating the production and distribution of material goods. It also provided social integration by providing norms, values, and identities that reinforced people's economic motivation. These included beliefs about upward mobility, equal opportunity, the work ethic, and the belief that hard work would be economically rewarded.

Because the market provided both types of integration, liberal capitalism was very fragile. It was predisposed to crisis. The instant the market faltered, system integration was imperiled by its inability to produce and deliver material goods. At the same time, social integration was imperiled because the market's failure demonstrated that mobility, opportunity, and rewards for hard work could be illusions. Problems on either level quickly translated into problems on both levels. Liberal capitalism was thus highly prone to crisis.

Marx was right: Liberal capitalism experienced a major crisis. But unlike medical patients, societies have possibilities other than death or recovery. Capitalist societies underwent a transformation from a market-based, liberal capitalism to a corporate-dominated, advanced capitalism. This advanced capitalism has two distinguishing features. First, it is dominated by large corporations and multinationals that can monopolize production, set prices, and manipulate demand. As a result, the free market benefits of competition, price reduction, and the rest have evaporated in many sectors of advanced capitalism.

The second distinguishing feature of advanced capitalism is the high degree of state intervention into the economy. This intervention was, in part, a response to the crisis of liberal capitalism. That system failed when the market became overburdened and could no longer provide system and social integration. State intervention was like a lifeguard coming to the rescue by supplementing a faltering market. It provided needed but unprofitable goods and services, maintained the infrastructure, subsidized education and training for workers, provided social insurance for the unemployed, disabled, or retired, met the social costs of capitalist production by repairing environmental damage, and much more. The crisis of liberal capitalism triggered massive state intervention which, in turn, acted like a midwife in the birth of advanced capitalism.

Consider a historical example. The 1929 stock market crash in the United States led to the Great Depression, which threatened the survival of capitalism in the United States. The only way to save the capitalist "patient" in crisis was a massive transfusion of state intervention into the economy. The New Deal promoted recovery. It put many people back to work through federally subsidized employment. It provided a system of social security for those unable to work. It increased government's role as a regulator of economic activity through monetary, fiscal, and tax policies. The New Deal helped the patient survive. The economic stimulus of World War II helped the patient thrive. By mid-century, the patient seemed cured. But from this point forward, a steady dose of state intervention remained necessary for ongoing economic health.

In advanced capitalism, markets are subordinated to large corporations and partially replaced or supplemented by state intervention. This raises a basic question: Has advanced capitalism achieved real stability, or is it still subject to crisis?

CRISIS TENDENCIES IN ADVANCED CAPITALISM

To answer this question, we must examine four institutions in advanced capitalism: its economic system, its administrative system, its legitimation system, and its class structure.

The economic system has three sectors. The private, monopoly sector consists of capital-intensive enterprises like corporate businesses. The private, competitive sector consists of labor-intensive enterprises like small businesses. The public, monopoly sector involves state-controlled production through government contracts. The rise of this sector is yet another expression of state intervention into the economy.

The administrative system is the federal government that intervenes in the economy in several ways. It does limited planning to regulate economic cycles. It channels capital by offering tax incentives to bring investment to socially needed areas. It supplements or replaces the market as described previously. This intervention has an important consequence. By intervening, the state acknowledges that markets no longer organize economic production efficiently on their own. However, whereas markets were seen as natural forces beyond human control, states are supposed to represent citizens and act on their behalf. When states fail, they can be blamed in ways that markets rarely are.

The legitimation system emerges because the market no longer provides legitimation by itself. The purpose of this system is to gather diffuse support for elite decisions while deflecting any real input that might interfere with elite priorities. This is done in several ways. Formal democracy reduces politics to elections and limits citizens to voting for elite candidates. Technocratic decision making favors specialized experts over ordinary citizens. Finally, a lifestyle of civic privatism encourages people to focus on careers, families, consumption, and leisure while avoiding any larger role in the public sphere. The legitimation system thereby provides diffuse support for elite priorities with little meaningful role for citizens.

The class structure of advanced capitalism involves a partial class compromise. The working class has become a highly differentiated group in terms of skills, security, wages, and benefits. This has promoted a partial breakdown of class identity and a fragmentation of class consciousness. It has allowed better-off workers to negotiate good contracts through collective bargaining in exchange for not challenging capitalist priorities. It has also allowed the state to shift negative economic consequences to the least powerful groups in society. Although class conflict still occurs, it is episodic and limited rather than persistent and broad.

Advanced capitalism is prone to new crisis tendencies. In liberal capitalism, crises were clearly economic. In advanced capitalism, there are multiple crisis tendencies and a logic of crisis displacement from one sector of society to another.

Economic Crisis Tendencies

There were numerous sources of economic crisis in liberal capitalism. The question is whether they continue to provoke crises in advanced capitalism.

The answer hinges on the effect of state intervention into the economy. Consider some examples. Because the state supplements the market, small problems might not be allowed to develop into a full-blown crisis. Fluctuations in interest rates or inflation that might spin out of control are now moderated by monetary and fiscal policy. Large corporations whose bankruptcy might destabilize entire industries are now rescued by government bailouts because they are "too big to fail." Unused capacity is now activated as government becomes a consumer, creates economic demand, and mitigates under-consumption problems. Think of a nautical metaphor. Unregulated markets are like huge ships at sea that can tip over when seas are rough. State intervention is like adding stabilizers that minimize tipping and keep the ship on an even keel.

State intervention goes deeper. It is heavily invested in educating and training the workforce and in underwriting research and development. This means that capitalists don't pay for the full value of labor-power or means of production. These savings can counteract the tendency of profits to fall. The state is also involved in regulating the contracts of workers who engage in collective bargaining. This means that the cost of labor power is no longer set in a purely economic fashion but rather is influenced by political processes.

Advanced capitalism remains exploitative and prone to crisis. Because of state intervention, however, the likelihood of a purely economic crisis is remote. In real-world terms, economies like the United States are less likely to experience a Great Depression again, because government is committed to doing everything in its considerable power to prevent it.

Although a purely economic crisis might have been averted, this is just the beginning of the story. The same intervention that prevents an economic crisis displaces the crisis from the economy to the state. Hence, we must follow the trail of potential crises from the economic world of financial markets to the political realm of government institutions.

Rationality Crisis Tendencies

State intervention creates new obligations for government. It pushes state resources beyond their limits. The outcome might be a rationality crisis. This means that the state is unable to generate and rationally distribute enough revenue to fully offset economic crises. A rationality crisis is evident when chronic problems in monetary inflation, interest rates, federal deficits, public debts, and budgetary shortfalls cannot be managed effectively. Hence, the price paid for averting an economic crisis is to transfer the crisis to the polity.

Rationality crises are likely in advanced capitalism because the state must respond to the two contradictory needs of accumulation and legitimation. Accumulation means that the state must do everything in its power to make capitalism as profitable as possible to avoid an economic crisis. This means maintaining infrastructure, subsidizing corporations, training workers, reducing regulations, cutting taxes, and much more. The state pays high costs to foster accumulation.

At the same time, state power is severely limited by property rights in capitalism. The state can never dictate how or where capitalist investments are made. It can merely seek to create a climate in which capitalists will invest capital. Moreover, when the state does this, it is really siding with capitalist interests in profits. But the state is supposed to represent all citizens and not just a particular class. When the state acts to enhance capitalist accumulation, it risks legitimation problems with the rest of the population who might resent the class bias of this state intervention.

The state must therefore be concerned with legitimation as well as accumulation. This entails costs that undermine accumulation. To gain legitimation, the state provides needed but unprofitable goods and services as well as social welfare programs for various recipients. It monitors consumer rights, worker safety, and environmental protection. It underwrites the cost of education and health care. As the state fulfills at least some of the genuine needs of its citizens, it earns legitimacy by creating the appearance that government works for everyone.

The legitimation role of government creates its own tensions. The mere fact of state intervention creates a potential trap for the state. People can accept a market crisis like a natural disaster that is unfortunate but no one's fault. But when state intervention is the norm, people are more likely to hold political leaders accountable when things go bad. In addition, every time the state creates a new program, it creates new constituencies and expectations about continued governmental support.

The net effect leaves the state in a very difficult position. It must promote accumulation, but this is costly and state power is limited. It must sustain legitimation, but this is also costly, and doing so raises expectations. Fostering accumulation and maintaining legitimacy are thus contradictory and yet both are necessary. Caught in this cross fire, the state is often reduced to crisis management, responding to the most urgent problems with little capacity for long-term solutions. Hence, the result of avoiding an economic crisis through state intervention is to transfer the crisis from the economy to the state.

When a rationality crisis becomes severe, it disrupts the production and distribution of material resources, threatening system integration. The interesting question is whether such problems also undermine social integration, leading to a full-blown crisis. To explore this possibility, we must turn from the economic and political dynamics of the system to the legitimation and motivational processes of the lifeworld.

Legitimation Crisis Tendencies

Legitimation is especially important in advanced capitalism. Unlike liberal capitalism, the market no longer sustains beliefs about mobility, opportunity, and fairness. The state assumes new responsibilities to many groups who might hold officeholders accountable if they fail. Whereas the economic system was the most vulnerable part of liberal capitalism, it is the legitimation system that is the most vulnerable part of advanced capitalism. When advanced capitalism loses legitimation alongside rationality problems, it faces a genuine crisis. What kind of society might replace advanced capitalism, and which groups would shape such a society would then become crucial political questions.

Crisis tendencies provoke various responses that become an ongoing political struggle. For instance, one might think that political elites want strong legitimation where the vast majority of people actively support their decisions and policies. But this might not be the case. If ordinary people become active in politics, there is always the danger that such activism could turn against the current leadership. For this reason, leaders might prefer a weaker form of legitimation in which people provide shallow and diffuse support for leaders without becoming too involved in the political process. Following this logic, political elites benefit whenever people support the system as a whole while minimizing their actual involvement in political decision making. Elites thus prefer a passive population providing vague support to one that is actively engaged in politics and could turn against them. A politically passive population reduces legitimation pressures on elites and minimizes the chance that chronic rationality problems will translate into legitimation difficulties.

Several aspects of advanced capitalism produce exactly this result. In each case, they reinforce political passivity and reduce legitimation pressures. Collectively, they become a blank check allowing political leaders great latitude to act with very little accountability. This makes it easier for elites to promote accumulation for capitalists without suffering legitimation deficits vis-à-vis citizens.

Consider technocratic decision making. Its premise is that some issues are too complicated for ordinary people to understand, because those people lack specialized knowledge. Hence, they should leave the issues to experts and trust their supposedly better judgment. There is thus a tension between technocratic and democratic decision making.

If people accept the premise of technocratic decision making, they effectively disenfranchise themselves from meaningful input into political decisions. By forfeiting their right to decide, they also reduce legitimation pressures on the state. Technocratic decision making thus contributes to a politically passive populace. Such a situation is dangerous in several ways. Technical experts are narrowly trained and might not be in the best position to assess wider risks concerning nuclear energy, genetic engineering, tax policy, or drug safety. Technical experts might be biased or corrupted by power holders. And when experts are wrong, it is ordinary citizens who live with the harmful consequences. Nevertheless, a politically pacified population offers little resistance to technocratic decision making, and it thereby lessens the likelihood of a legitimation crisis.

Another aspect of legitimation is material goods. In principle, state action must be justifiable to citizens based on legitimate reasons. In reality, citizens might be willing to "trade" legitimate reasons for material goods. Put bluntly, as long as the system delivers the goods, citizens might accept government action that is unjustifiable or even corrupt. Put even more bluntly, people might accept any foreign policy or environmental damage that keeps gasoline prices within acceptable limits. Such a trade-off reduces legitimation pressures, because people no longer hold government accountable to any principle other than maintaining their lifestyle.

Although this can be a viable short-term strategy for elites, there are reasons to doubt its long-term effectiveness. First, it is questionable whether people would permanently set aside moral, ethical, and religious principles for material gain. Although capitalist cultures are materialistic, they also experience waves of reaction that reintroduce other principles into public discussion that could raise legitimation pressures. Second, the ability of the system to deliver material goods might itself be limited. Living standards are increasingly dependent on public goods like health care, quality education, and sustainable environments. Even if people are willing to trade legitimation for material rewards, the system's ability to provide them is limited by capitalism's historic difficulty in providing public goods. Nevertheless, if the public makes this bargain, it reinforces political passivity and reduces legitimation pressures.

A third aspect of the legitimation system is electoral politics and the idea that voting is the ultimate political act for citizens. This amounts to a very impoverished notion of what democracy is. A "rich" notion of democracy would emphasize much broader citizen participation, including ongoing political education, robust voluntary associations, and active social movements. This would approximate participatory democracy in which everyone affected by a decision has meaningful input into that decision. Measured against these possibilities, the idea that democracy is about voting once every four years is an impoverished notion indeed.

Another term for this impoverished version is *elite democracy*. It implies that otherwise passive citizens choose every four years between preselected candidates. This model of elite democracy is constantly reinforced by media coverage of politics. While speaking in reverential tones about the power of voters, media rarely recognize any other form of political action or explore how candidates are preselected on the basis of money long before they are elected on the basis of votes. Elite democracy reduces politics to elections that are easily controlled by powerful interests. To the extent that citizens accept this reduction and see voting as their only political act, their political passivity again reduces legitimation problems.

A final aspect of the legitimation system involves "civic privatism." In simpler language, this means that people seek their greatest satisfactions in private life rather than public engagement. Civic privatism emphasizes family life, interpersonal relations, and personal gratifications. It encourages people to focus on what they can get as consumers or clients as opposed to what they can do as producers and citizens. This mind-set reflects another trade-off. Civic privatism basically says that because public activities are unfulfilling and alienating, then personal life is where we should focus our psychic energies.

The problem is not that these are false pleasures. Intimate relations can be deeply satisfying, and consumption can be enjoyable. The problem is that civic privatism implies that these are the only possible pleasures. It also implies that we should see them as compensation for the alienation of the larger social world. When people embrace civic privatism, they lower their expectations of what is possible in social life and the public sphere. Lowered expectations reinforce passivity and reduce the likelihood of legitimation pressures that might otherwise occur.

To sum up, advanced capitalism is unstable because when the state intervenes to prevent an economic crisis, the crisis shifts to the state. It is very difficult for the state to simultaneously foster accumulation for capitalists and retain legitimation by citizens. Advanced capitalism thus relies on a legitimation system to manage this problem. To whatever extent people leave decisions to experts, accept material goods in exchange for legitimation, limit political activity to voting, and embrace civic privatism, they become a passive population. This reduces legitimation pressures, offsets crisis tendencies, and allows an unequal, unjust, and exploitative society to persist.

Legitimation pressures increase when the above scenarios are reversed. Whenever citizens question the right of experts to make decisions for them, they challenge technocratic decision making. Whenever citizens demand political accountability in addition to material rewards, they are refusing to be bought off. Whenever citizens engage in political activity above and beyond the simple act of voting, they are challenging elite democracy. And whenever citizens step outside the cocoon of civic privatism into the public sphere, they seek collective fulfillment above private pleasures. Legitimation difficulties can thus be either contained or heightened, depending on how these scenarios play out.

This analysis illuminates many political issues. Recall that the legitimation increasingly found in advanced capitalism is not detailed support for specific policies but rather broad and diffuse approval of political leaders. Now consider how often leaders create or capitalize on fears about crime, drugs, immigration, or terrorism to gain such legitimation. By "standing up to the threat," the symbolism of their stance often means more than the logic of their policies in gaining legitimation. When leaders commit troops to war, "supporting the troops" displaces questions about the logic or even the truth of the war's rationale. When leaders appeal to religious values, the validation felt by true believers overrides consideration of whether government policies embody or contradict those values.

Sometimes leaders retain significant support even though a majority of the population disagrees with most of their policies. When this occurs, it means that diffuse, symbolic, and uncritical support has become the primary form of legitimation. This turns political leadership into a spectacle that rewards those who can effectively manipulate the symbols required to elicit this legitimation. This diffuse support, in turn, gives politicians great latitude to implement even unpopular policies.

Consider another example. In the mid-1970s, much concern was expressed about a "crisis of democracy" in the United States. From the perspective of state managers, the "crisis" was that too many people had too much influence over political decisions, making it difficult for elites to pursue their objectives. This prompted attacks on "big government" that persist to this day. The strategy is to lower people's expectations about what government will, can, and should do for its citizens. Whether expressed through fearful portrayals of big government running amok or through uplifting pleas for personal responsibility, the message is the same: People must lower their expectations about what government can do.

This strategy makes perfect sense as a legitimation struggle. Rationality and legitimation crises emerge in part because people develop high expectations about government. Elites can reduce the likelihood and severity of such crises if they alter what people expect from government. Lowered expectations take the heat off the state and allow it to do less for ordinary people while continuing to serve elite interests. They lessen the tension between fostering accumulation and earning legitimation by reducing the need for the latter. When elites can reduce the need for legitimation and frame it as broad symbolic support, they maintain power while ignoring genuine needs. This is the kind of political domination that has long interested the Frankfurt School.

If lowering expectations is the strategy, cutting taxes is the tactic. Economic elites have been the major beneficiaries of the tax cuts undertaken by conservative governments of the past three decades. The long-term goal is reducing and eventually eliminating all taxes on wealth and investment, so that taxes on the wages of ordinary people become the main source of government revenue. Reduced government revenue forces the state to reduce expenditures as well. These reductions undermine state funding for education, health care, housing, and social welfare. Finally, it will be difficult to maintain or restore these programs as the tax burden shifts to the middle and working classes, who thus have reason to oppose them. The combined reduction and shift in the tax burden means that the state will do less for ordinary people at the same time that its strategy of lowered expectations gets people to accept less without withdrawing their legitimation.

This is an argument about tendencies. The strategy of lowering expectation has not provoked serious legitimation problems yet, but the possibility remains. If tax cuts outrun spending cuts, deficits will rise, triggering other economic problems requiring additional state intervention. Hence, the tension between fostering accumulation and securing legitimation never disappears.

Motivation Crisis Tendencies

Social integration involves values, beliefs, norms, and identities. When these break down, social integration is jeopardized. When political beliefs break down, legitimation crises can emerge. When cultural values break down, motivational crises might emerge, as people no longer find compelling reasons to conform to social expectations. Motivational problems can also lead to a questioning of political authority that heightens legitimation difficulties.

The big issue is how people find meaning, purpose, and motivation in life. Throughout most of human history, people found these things through religious beliefs that made sense of their world and their place within it. When modernity emerged, secular beliefs challenged religious beliefs, and traditional sources of meaning and motivation lost some of their power.

Even so, the early days of liberal capitalism still relied on religious motivations. Weber's (1904) analysis of the Protestant Ethic showed that early entrepreneurs were driven more by religious than economic motives, because the accumulation of wealth was believed to signify moral worthiness in God's eyes. Even today, there is no shortage of religious belief. But in many respects, late modern societies have moved in secular, scientific directions. As secular views displace religious ones, the question becomes acute: What meanings and motivations replace religious ones in a secularizing world?

This question returns us to the lifeworld where the rise of communicative rationality has displaced blind obedience to authority with the idea that actions must be justified by reasons. Modern, child-centered socialization practices incorporate communicative rationality by promoting autonomy and self-direction as children mature into adults. The same goals are increasingly evident in the educational system with its emphasis on "critical thinking." As this occurs, younger generations become carriers of communicative rationality for which actions and decisions need clear and compelling justifications. If actions and decisions fail this test, people socialized to these standards might reject them.

In the late modern world, the lifeworld and system are on a collision course. On one hand, young people are socialized to value autonomy and rational justifications. On the other hand, the occupational roles of the economic system and the bureaucratic organizations of the political system operate through instrumental rationality, money, and power. The economy and polity still expect compliance and obedience even from recent generations schooled in autonomy and self-direction. Put differently, although the cultural lifeworld has encouraged people to question authority, the system requires people to conform. The mismatch between socialized expectations and institutional realities sows the seeds of a motivation crisis.

A motivation crisis is expressed in alienation and anomie in modern society. A common thread is the inability to coherently link meanings, purposes, values, and identities. This condition might be particularly acute for younger generations, because identity formation is crucial in this stage of the life cycle. Possible responses to motivation crises are withdrawal, social isolation, destructive behavior, or compulsive attachments. Whatever the response, these signify the fraying of social integration.

The sociologically intriguing question is when motivational problems will lead people to question the legitimacy of social arrangements. Such transitions depend on political and historical context. Imagine a similarly alienated youth generation in two different historical periods. In one case, there is a potent, political issue that quickly translates motivational issues into legitimation challenges. In another case, there is no equally potent issue, and the anomie does not translate into legitimation problems.

An example is the contrast between responses to the Vietnam War and more recent wars in Afghanistan and Iraq. In the earlier case, the draft symbolized the power of the system over people in the lifeworld; it thus became a catalyst for resistance to war. In the latter cases, the "volunteer" army has eliminated that catalyst. But no one can anticipate which issues will provide such catalysts, so motivational crises retain the potential to spill over into legitimation crises.

To sum up, capitalist societies are prone to crisis because of inherent contradictions and conflicts built into them. Advanced capitalist societies respond to this threat with massive state intervention. This has displaced the crisis from economy to state. Chronic rationality problems in the state are the price of avoiding economic crisis. Under certain conditions, problems of state intervention trigger legitimation difficulties. Meanwhile, motivational problems have also become chronic features of modern societies, which also have the potential to translate into legitimation difficulties.

Legitimation is the most vulnerable aspect of advanced capitalism because it operates under the double pressure of a state that cannot rationally make decisions and a culture that cannot convincingly provide meaning. When rationality problems of system integration combine with legitimation problems of social integration, a genuine crisis occurs. Although such a crisis could be resolved in many ways, the optimal response would be transformation toward a rational society less dominated by instrumental rationality and more grounded in communicative rationality.

CAPITALISM UNBOUND

Advanced capitalism remains a dynamic, complex, and contradictory system. Since the 1970s, several trends are especially prominent. They can be summarized as "capitalism unbound," because each involves an expansion of capitalism or the removal of limits on how it operates. Each is a response to prior economic difficulties as capitalism sought to maintain or enhance profits. At the same time, each can provide only temporary respite while fostering more serious problems down the road.

One trend is globalization. Capitalism has always been a global system, but the globalization of national economies has accelerated since the 1970s. This was a response to an unusual combination of economic problems including energy costs, rampant inflation, chronic stagnation, and declining profits. In the advanced capitalist countries, capitalism was "unbound" in geographical terms as capital flight, runaway shops, and deindustrialization shifted a great deal of economic activity outside core countries. Better-paying manufacturing jobs declined, and lesser-paying service jobs increased. The net effect was to undermine the living standards of working people and leave many communities with permanent economic stagnation and high unemployment. Such aggressive, cost-cutting strategies harmed many workers while restoring profits for corporate capital. Although ordinary people paid the price, the globalization strategy at least temporarily revived many national economies.

Another trend is commodification. Whereas capitalism was unbound externally through globalization, it was unbound internally through commodification. Capitalism has always promoted commodification, but the strategy has intensified recently. It is yet another response to stalled profits that seeks new ones. Commodification turns social resources into private products for profitable sale. The fast-food industry is one example; it replaces use-values for direct consumption (home-cooked meals) with exchange-values for corporate profit (burgers and fries). Commodification also substitutes private products for declining public goods. Think of bottled water. Or think of highly polluted cities where clean air is scarce but you can buy ten-minute doses of pure oxygen as a private commodity from street-side vendors. Whether the issue is housing, policing, health, welfare, education, prisons, or the military, commodification puts profitability before quality, utility, or service. Accelerated commodification of social resources is yet another response to problems of profit realization. Although it has boosted profits, it is doubtful that these problems have been permanently averted.

A third trend is privatization. Capitalism has also become unbound from forms of state intervention that impede profit making. In some ways, privatization is another expression of commodification. But the term *privatization* accentuates the reversal of long-standing governmental regulation of economic processes. With the philosophy of neoliberalism, the strategy of reducing government, and the tactic of deregulation, governments have abandoned much of their role as defenders of the public interest. Whether the issue is worker safety, environmental protection, or unemployment compensation, privatization displaces government safety nets with the logic of the marketplace. Debates over Social Security in the United States illustrate the trend. For more than half a century, the system was so popular and successful that no politician dared to challenge it. Under the banner of privatization, conservatives now seek to convert a cost-efficient, publicly administered, social insurance program into millions of highly profitable, privately owned investment accounts. Like globalization and commodification, privatization is yet another capitalist strategy to sustain profitability.

A final factor crucial to the future of global society is ecological sustainability. Globalization, commodification, and privatization are all designed to enhance short-term profitability rather than long-term sustainability. These capitalist strategies mean we will reach many ecological limits sooner rather than later. Two limits are especially significant. Not only are fossil fuels being depleted, but their costs will continue to increase as they become more difficult to locate and extract. Global warming is also creating long-term consequences that might be devastating for capitalist profitability if not human survival itself. As new capitalist strategies are implemented, their environmental consequences loom large as a source of future crises.

An "unbound" capitalism has intriguing implications for social stability. Globalization, commodification, and privatization each shift power from the public sphere of citizens to the private economy of corporations. They heighten the tension between capitalism and democracy. In political terms, they are designed to repeal the New Deal. That is, they seek to reduce or eliminate the very kinds of state intervention that were necessary to rescue liberal capitalism from a catastrophic economic crisis. These moves might be necessary to sustain short-term profitability, but they might simultaneously increase legitimation pressures for the system as a whole. As advanced capitalism follows this trajectory, the question of whether it can retain legitimacy will be essential to the prospects for progressive social change.

Chapter 5

The State of the State

Imagine the following scene. A stranger walking down a country road encounters a farmer on his property. The stranger compliments the farmer on his land and asks how he got it. The farmer replies that he inherited it from his father, who inherited it from his grandfather, who inherited it from his great-grandfather. The stranger asks how the farmer's great-grandfather got the land. The farmer says that his great-grandfather fought for the land. The stranger says, "OK, I'll fight you for the land" (adopted from Luhman and Gilman 1980, 3).

Even though the land belongs to the farmer because an ancestor fought for it, the stranger's proposal to fight for it now seems ludicrous. The scenario says a lot about power. It suggests that political systems we take for granted were often created through overt conflict. It further suggests that when coercive force is converted into legitimate authority, it becomes more stable and harder to challenge. It finally suggests that the stranger has an uphill battle because the farmer's property claims are backed by governmental authority. Don't bet on the stranger in this contest.

Similar dynamics apply to relatively recent historical inventions known as nation-states. Our global map only emerged within the past few centuries, as the nation-state became the prevailing form of political organization. But the national boundaries we take for granted are highly arbitrary. As European states emerged through conflicts, they expanded and colonized other regions. These regions subsequently gained independence by overthrowing colonialism and creating their own nation-states. Although we applaud the constitutional principles and representative governments that emerged in many cases, getting there often involved conflict and bloodshed until the victors established laws that normalized the privileges of the winners. Like the farmer's ancestors, people fought to establish the nation-states and political boundaries of our world. In many places, the fights continue to this day. The connection between states and coercive power runs very deep.

In this chapter, we begin with some general sociological observations about states that are primarily derived from Max Weber. The heart of the chapter presents a long-standing debate about the power structure in the United States and one recent attempt at a synthesis. The chapter closes with a brief consideration of the future of the state in the face of globalization pressures.

DIMENSIONS OF THE STATE

Since the origins of the modern state, people have feared its centralized power. Thomas Hobbes described the state as a Leviathan that threatened to crush the individual and civil society. A good deal of political theory is preoccupied with limiting state power and protecting individual rights. The framers of the U.S. Constitution explicitly created checks and balances to limit state power and defend individual rights. Although their concerns did not extend to class, race, and gender inequalities they took for granted, they recognized that concentrated state power was a dangerous thing.

Classical sociologists were also interested in state power. For Marx, the main conflict was not between a centralized state and individual citizens; it was rather between the two major classes of capitalism. Moreover, the most basic power resided not in the state but in ownership of capital and control of property. Material conditions and class conflict were primary, and political resources and conflicts were secondary.

Marx thereby understands the state and political power through the lens of capitalism and economic power. Seen this way, the state can never be a neutral umpire for resolving conflicts. In contrast to this liberal view, Marx claims the state will inevitably be an ally of the most powerful class in capitalism. The people who need to fear state power are not all citizens, but rather workers whose interests are not likely to be represented in a state inevitably dominated by capitalist interests.

Whereas Marx understood the state through the lens of class, Max Weber saw it as a more independent institution with considerable power (Weber 1921). Indeed, Weber emphasized the links among states, power, coercion, and violence. His definition of the state sees it as a social organization that successfully claims a monopoly on the legitimate use of physical force within a given territory. States are preoccupied with establishing, defending, and expanding their boundaries, because boundaries determine the scope of state power. Within them, the state is sovereign.

Notice the heart of the definition. The state is defined by physical force; this is what makes a state a state. But unlike other coercive organizations, the state's use of force is seen as legitimate. This doesn't mean that other groups don't resort to force. Rebels, criminals, terrorists, gangsters, or revolutionaries might all resort to force in pursuit of their goals. As long as state power is intact, however, such force will be defined as illegitimate and criminal, and state coercion to control it will be seen as legitimate. Legitimation leads people to accept and even support state violence while rejecting violence done by others.

A crucial question is how states convert power into authority. Power is the ability to achieve goals despite the resistance of others. In the case of the state, this power is considerable, but it has an Achilles' heel. Power expressed as coercive force creates simmering resentment and overt resistance. Power can be very effective in the short run, but it is unstable in the long run.

For this reason, power holders seek to convert power into authority. Authority is power that has acquired legitimacy in the eyes of the people subject to that power. It doesn't mean that people agree with every decision; it means they recognize the right of those in power to make decisions. Legitimacy is not a quality of power holders as much as it is a relationship. It is people without power who ultimately determine whether power is legitimate by granting or withholding legitimation. When granted, legitimacy converts power into authority and creates a much more stable state.

This led to Weber's well-known typology of authority. Traditional authority makes power legitimate by appealing to long-standing customs. Throughout most of human history, people granted legitimacy to tribal chieftains, clan leaders, shamans, or patriarchs, because they were entitled to their positions on the basis of cultural traditions. People owed allegiance to a particular person designated by tradition, and there were usually clear rules about succession that spelled out how authority was passed from one generation to another.

Charismatic authority makes power legitimate on the basis of unique qualities attributed to a charismatic leader. Such leaders are rare in history, but when they appear as prophets or revolutionaries, they can inspire fanatical devotion among their followers. True believers attribute superhuman abilities to charismatic leaders and are often willing to sacrifice their lives for them. Weber thought charismatic leadership was the most revolutionary force in history, capable of overthrowing established authority and instigating radical change. For all its volcanic force, charisma tends to be short lived. When charismatic leaders die, their charisma dies with them. This creates problems of succession. Eventually, the routinization of charisma leads back to more conventional forms of authority.

Rational-legal authority makes power legitimate on the basis of a rationalized system of legal requirements and bureaucratic procedures spelled out in constitutions and other legally binding documents. This is a system of rule by law and not persons. People owe their allegiance not to a person but to an office that endures while individuals cycle through it. This type of authority was part of a broader process of rationalization in all spheres of society. As societies modernize, this becomes the most common form of authority, often accompanied by the spread of bureaucracy.

There are thus several ways in which power can be converted into authority. Legitimation is also a matter of degree; states can have more or less legitimacy. Moreover, legitimation is often contested. In the previous chapter, legitimation defined the central crisis tendency of advanced capitalism. Weber's analysis suggests that this is true for many political regimes because states are ultimately rooted in coercion but cannot survive on this basis alone. The quest for legitimacy is crucial to state survival, just as legitimation difficulties create opportunities for transforming states.

Three other issues are central to understanding the modern state. First, nation-states exist in a larger, interstate system, so they are shaped as much by external relationships as internal dynamics. Indeed, many states were born out of conflict with a preexisting state. Although states often arise through conflict, they also develop alliances with other states. Within the nation-state system, we thus find blocs of states united against other blocs. In stable times, a balance of power limits the actions of each bloc. In less stable times, power imbalances may tempt states to extend their reach to the detriment of their rivals.

As noted earlier, nation-states are recent historical inventions. Some argue that they are now losing power in a globalizing economy. The future of the nation-state is a complex question, and we will return to it at the end of this chapter. What is clear is that the nation-state system has been a major cause and consequence of modernity over the past few centuries. It created the political worlds we now take for granted.

Second, nation-states have always been intertwined with nationalism. It is particularly strong in states with a single ethnic group; here nationalism translates ethnic identity directly into state power. More typically, states contain more than one nationality or ethnicity. In these cases, nationalism promotes a new identity that transcends diverse ethnicities and unites people on the basis of common citizenship. Nationalist identities can combine or compete with other identities in complex ways.

For instance, the same nationalism that unites people within a nation-state might impede the development of broader identities like global citizenship. When nation-states engage in conflict, nationalism can become prejudice, scapegoating, and racism, and it can promote discrimination, ethnic cleansing, and genocide. Nationalism can also be used by elites to manipulate citizens. In a climate of fear, nationalism can be used to boost legitimation, recruit armies, and justify wars. When faced with legitimation challenges, it is common for state managers to appeal to nationalist sentiments.

Third, states are militaristic. Domestic state power is embodied in police forces, law enforcement agencies, militias, national guards, and the criminal justice system. Although states prefer voluntary compliance from citizens, they will invest unlimited resources to enforce "law and order" if necessary. Even when rarely used, such power is significant in ensuring "domestic tranquility."

The more obvious expressions of militarism are standing armies and lethal weaponry. States without military forces are rare, and they survive only by adhering to strict neutrality in all conflicts. More often, militarism is a symbolic indicator of state power and that its leaders are to be taken seriously. There have always been conflicts between groups using whatever weapons were available. Modern states, however, have raised the bar by maintaining substantial armed forces during peacetime and by equipping them with weapons of unprecedented lethality. In the twentieth century, states deployed militaries to conduct the most destructive conflicts in human history.

States are thus repositories of tremendous power. At their best, they enshrine noble ideals, promote democratic participation, and meet social needs. At their worst, they repress citizens, provoke wars, and conduct genocide. At all times, the issue of legitimacy is crucial. We therefore turn to some crucial questions about who exercises state power.

THE POWER STRUCTURE DEBATE

The power structure of the United States has been much debated since the middle of the twentieth century. The debate began with the pluralist perspective advocated by political scientists, which was challenged by sociological advocates of the power elite model. The debate was then joined by neo-Marxist theories of the state. The issues persist to the present day, so the debate provides a lens into who exercises state power and how they do so.

The Pluralist Perspective

Pluralists maintain that political power is dispersed across a plurality of groups (Truman 1951). The strongest case for pluralism came from Robert Dahl (1961), who focused on overt, observable, political decision making. Dahl reasoned such observations would reveal how power is distributed. If the same groups repeatedly dominate decision making, it would support power elite theorists. If different groups succeed on different issues, it would support the pluralist position.

Dahl's findings suggested that power is dispersed across many interest groups. The pluralist perspective that emerged through this research rested on several concepts (Ricci 1971). The first concerns the difference between *potential* and *actual* *influence.* People's potential influence is not necessarily the same as their actual influence. No matter how potentially powerful someone might be or how big that person's reputation for power might be, we should confine our analysis to actual influence.

A second pluralist concept is *scopes of power.* If a political actor (individual or group) has a wide scope of power, it means that they can influence decision making on many issues. If they have a narrow scope of power, it means they are influential only on a few issues. The pluralist contention is that although some political actors are undeniably powerful, they have narrow scopes of power. This means different groups prevail on different issues and no one group prevails on most issues. Pluralists thereby acknowledge the undeniable power of some groups while retaining a pluralist conclusion.

A third concept is *noncumulative resources.* Political resources take different forms: money, position, information, influence, networks, alliances, and the like. Although such resources are unequally distributed, the inequalities are not cumulative. If people have a lot (or a little) of one resource, it does not necessarily mean that they will have a lot (or a little) of others. This allowed pluralists to acknowledge political inequities but deny that they lead to elite control.

A fourth concept is *slack power.* In any political system, there will always be slack power, but this is especially true in democracies. Slack power is always available to ordinary citizens if they feel their interests are not being served by those in power. Moreover, power holders factor slack power into their political calculations. They try not to provoke this slack power, which thus limits their exercise of power. This concept acknowledges that most citizens are not politically active most of the time. Even so, they have (slack) power, and its mere existence limits elite power.

A fifth concept involves a philosophical distinction between *homo civicus* and *homo politicus*. Dahl reasoned that most people follow the homo civicus model, where being nonpolitical expresses a natural inclination to seek life's satisfactions from something other than politics. It is only a minority—homo politicus—who are "wired" for intense political involvement. This distinction frames the political apathy of most citizens not as a problem but rather as an expression of deeply rooted human predispositions.

A sixth concept divides society into *political* and *apolitical strata*. Homo politicus translates into an active, political minority, while homo civicus becomes a passive, apolitical majority. Dahl thus acknowledges elites but retains pluralist conclusions by stressing that members of the apolitical strata can become involved in political activity if they wish. Access to the system is available to all. The passivity of the apolitical strata reflects a conscious choice. Most importantly, members of the political strata compete with one another, and the support of the apolitical strata is crucial to their success. Rather than a top-down, elite dominance model, Dahl offers a bottom-up, pluralist model, because even elites must recruit support from nonelites to maintain their positions and attain their objectives.

The final concept is the *democratic creed*. This includes beliefs about democracy as the best form of government, the importance of majority rule and minority rights, the legitimacy of governmental institutions, and the like. Here, Dahl makes an intriguing claim. The issue is not whether the democratic creed is factually accurate. The issue is rather whether the creed is widely believed. If so, it provides legitimation for the system as a whole. Thus, the believability (if not the accuracy) of the democratic creed reinforces a pluralist political system.

Dahl provides a sophisticated statement of "elite pluralism" that acknowledges the existence of elites, while stressing the competition between them that can only be won by recruiting nonelite support. In the last analysis, the system is therefore a pluralist one.

Pluralism has nonetheless come in for much criticism. The claims that scopes of power are narrow and political resources are noncumulative are unconvincing. The argument seems contradictory when it minimizes the potential influence of elites while stressing the slack power of nonelites. The distinctions between homo civicus/homo politicus and apolitical/political strata seem more like justifications than explanations of political passivity.

The latter was a crucial issue in the debate. Pluralists interpret passivity as a conscious choice, because people always have the option to become politically active in a formally open system. Even further, they see passivity as an endorsement of the status quo and an expression of people's political satisfaction; otherwise they would get involved. Elite theorists interpret passivity in a dramatically different way. For them, it signifies political resignation, withdrawal, and alienation. Expressed in the form of low voter turnout, political passivity reflects a futile sense that there are no meaningful ways for ordinary citizens to influence politics. For elite theorists, such passivity is a criticism and not an endorsement of the political system.

The pluralist focus on observable, community decision making has also drawn criticism. One concerns generalizability. Even if there is support for pluralism on the local level (and the picture is mixed at best), the conclusion might not apply to national politics. A second problem is the equation of power with governmental decision making. This ignores how economic power can trump formal political power. A third problem is observable decision making. Winning an overt conflict does indicate power. But there are more important forms of power. If a group controls the political agenda, it can decide which issues come up for decisions and which don't. The ability to set agendas is an extremely effective form of power that would never be detected by the pluralist focus on observable decision making. On the basis of these problems, many critics were willing to consider alternative approaches.

The Power Elite Perspective

Elite theories have a long history, but C. Wright Mills (1956) provided a compelling version in the power structure debate. Mills began with the pluralist focus on decision making but pointed out that not all decisions are equally important. They differ in impact, depth, and scope. Moreover, some decisions set agendas and determine whether other issues will even be considered. Mills emphasized such key decisions as the best indicator of power. Treating all decisions equally might support a pluralist conclusion, but looking at key decisions reveals that power is concentrated in the hands of a "power elite."

Mills uses an institutional analysis of power to identify this elite. Top positions in major institutions provide their occupants with great power. To locate the power elite, we must look to the most powerful positions in the most influential institutions of our society. It is here that we will find a small group of people who make key decisions that have a profound effect on the rest of the society.

Mills focused first on the corporate economy. Like a pyramid, the corporate economy has many levels, but at the top there is highly concentrated power to make decisions of enormous consequence. These decisions about corporate behavior affect employment rates, pay levels, environmental conditions, health care, workplace safety, retirement security, community vitality, and foreign policy. Despite their impact, corporations are not remotely democratic. Power is monopolized by the top officers, the board of directors, and the largest shareholders. This very small group makes key decisions with profound impacts on society.

Mills turned next to the political hierarchy. It also has many levels, from local to federal. At the top of the national state, there is concentrated power to make key decisions whose impact matches that of corporate decision making. Mills emphasized the increased power of the executive branch. It is the president, vice president, cabinet, their staffs and advisers, and the appointed directors of major agencies that compose the political wing of the power elite. Once again, this small group makes key decisions of enormous consequence.

Mills then identified the military as the third pyramid in the power elite. Power is concentrated at the top of the military hierarchy, which is the most authoritarian structure of all. Here one finds the Joint Chiefs of Staff and top positions in the

Pentagon, intelligence agencies, and the Department of Defense. Mills acknowledged that the military is formally subordinate to civilian power. But he argued that a military mind-set had permeated the civilian sector, so that military options had become a routine part of political and corporate decision making. Mills wrote during the Cold War, but the persistence of huge military budgets and pervasive military mind-sets long after the Cold War exemplifies the ongoing role of the military in the power elite.

It is hard to deny that these groups are exceptionally powerful. But a pluralist might respond that these elites compete with one another, and they must get the support of nonelites to maintain power. If so, an "elite pluralist" argument might still be tenable. For this reason, Mills further argues that the power elite is a relatively unified group. On most issues, in most circumstances, most of the time, members of the elite agree on priorities, goals, strategies, and even tactics. To whatever extent they are unified, the "power elite" argument becomes more persuasive.

Mills identifies four sources of elite unity. The first is the rotation of personnel through different sectors of the power elite. Corporate lawyers get political appointments. Military brass sit on the board of directors of arms manufacturers. Politicians move in and out of the corporate sector. This "revolving door" means that members become familiar with the concerns of elites in different institutional positions, because they have been there themselves. This circulation of elites breaks down divisions among economic, political, and military leaders and contributes to greater unity for the power elite as a whole.

A second basis of unity is long-term structural interests. Corporations obviously seek profits, but a profitable economy also supports strong state revenues and big military budgets. Politicians seek a stable political system, but this also helps corporate and military interests strategize effectively around their goals. The military seeks increased budgets, but this also serves corporate interests abroad and political ones at home. These shared interests are another basis of unity. Moreover, the interests that unite elites often distance them from nonelites. Profitable economies don't benefit ordinary people if the profits come from outsourcing and downsizing; stable political systems don't benefit ordinary people if some groups are regularly denied a political voice; big military budgets don't benefit ordinary people if they are funded at the expense of domestic programs. The interests that unite elites often separate them from the rest of the society.

A third basis of unity is social class. Elites disproportionately come from upper-class backgrounds. They are accustomed to privilege and power, moving from wealthy families and neighborhoods to exclusive prep schools, Ivy League colleges, and prestigious social clubs. Even before they enter the power elite, they develop a worldview and class consciousness that links them to other elites and distances them from ordinary people.

A final basis of elite unity involves recruitment and cooptation. Members of the power elite carefully recruit people for elite positions. The more someone reflects their interests, the better their prospects. When recruitment fails and a maverick gets in, cooptation takes over. Nonconformists are offered a combination of rewards and punishments to get them to realign their views in keeping with elite interests. In the final analysis, elite members who refuse to conform can be marginalized, isolated, or convinced to "offer" their resignations.

For pluralism, divided elites compete against one another. This limits their power and empowers nonelites. For elite theory, elites are unified and coordinated. This augments their power and disempowers nonelites.

Mills then analyzes the overall power structure in society. Envision one large pyramid. The power elite sits at the top. Below them are middle levels of power. Many lesser decisions are not directly made by elites but rather made at this level. Congress, the courts, labor unions, religious groups, citizen lobbies, and many other players exercise some influence in these lesser decisions. But don't overestimate the importance of middle levels of power. If there are key decisions to be made, they will be made by elites. If they do not have a vital interest in the outcome of a decision, or if taking a position might hurt more than it helps them, then they are happy to leave the decision to middle levels of power. Even then, previous elite decisions often limit subsequent decisions.

The middle levels are not a check on elite power. They rather play a largely ideological role. That is, they make the overall power structure *appear* more open to the influence of ordinary citizens than it really is. Mills doesn't deny the pluralist image of power as much as he puts it in its place. Pluralist processes can indeed be found on the relatively inconsequential middle levels of power. This should not obscure the fact that much more fundamental decisions are made by elites. Without middle levels of power, it would be more obvious who is running the show, which might provoke more opposition. Middle levels of power provide legitimation by making the power structure appear more democratic than it really is.

Below the middle levels of power is mass society, composed of ordinary people, whom Mills depicts as socially isolated and politically alienated. They feel (correctly, as it turns out) that they have no real influence on political decision making. They seek satisfactions elsewhere while withdrawing from political life. This recalls Habermas's civic privatism and Dahl's apolitical strata. However, whereas Dahl presents this as a conscious choice of people with other options, Mills presents it as a structural reality of how power is distributed. Where pluralists see political withdrawal as a choice and even an endorsement of the status quo, elite theorists see it as the ultimate expression of political alienation in a society that allows ordinary people few meaningful options.

Mills's elite theory is a powerful challenge to pluralism. From the perspective of critical sociology, it provides the stronger argument while acknowledging a sliver of truth in the pluralist vision regarding middle levels of power. Mills's theory has nonetheless come in for criticism.

First, critics challenged the equivalence of the three sectors of the elite. Critics from both the left and the right claimed he attributed too much power to the military, which might better be seen as a "junior partner" implementing decisions made by other elites. Critics from the left also suggested that Mills understated the impact of corporate power. Control of economic decision making and the overall economic climate can allow corporate elites to shape the environment in which other elites operate. These critiques would redraw the power elite so that the corporate hierarchy looms larger than the political one, which in turn looms over the military.

Second, critics challenged the top-down image of elites monopolizing power with no counteracting, bottom-up power. During the 1960s, elites came under serious challenge from various social movements. The movement against the Vietnam War is particularly interesting. Elites *were* largely unified in the early 1960s when the United States invaded Southeast Asia—just as Mills's theory would predict. But opposition to the war helped create a division among elites. This division, in turn, helped change U.S. policy in Southeast Asia. Such examples of bottom-up challenges to elite power suggest that Mills's image is too monolithic. Like the Frankfurt School, Mills's efforts to document political domination overstated the case and obscured the potential for resistance by nonelites.

Neo-Marxist Perspectives

The debate between pluralism and elite theory was subsequently joined by neo-Marxist theories of the state. Compared with pluralism, these theories broadened the conception of power beyond the state to examine the relationship between economic and political power. Compared with elite theory, these theories downplayed politicians and the military and underscored economic power rooted in social classes rather than a power elite.

Neo-Marxist theories of state power subdivide into instrumentalist and structuralist approaches. Both assume that economic power conditions political power and that capitalists typically prevail over workers in exercising both types of power. Where they differ is how economic power is converted into political power.

The instrumentalist approach derives from Marx's claim that the state is an executive committee for managing the affairs of the capitalist class. The state is thus an instrument or a tool capitalists use to pursue their class interests. If successful, the political power of the state complements the already considerable economic power of the capitalist class. The instrumentalist approach predicts that capitalists or their close allies will directly occupy positions of state power to align it with capitalist interests.

This does not mean that capitalists always control the state. There might be rare circumstances—warfare, social upheaval, elite divisions—that undermine capitalist power and allow the working class to temporarily redirect state policy to its interests. Marx's support of British legislation limiting the length of the working day implied that in at least some circumstances, the state could be an instrument on behalf of worker's interests. The instrumentalist state is thus an object of class conflict that determines which class will control state power.

To say it is a fight is not to say it is a fair fight. The resources of the capitalist class—their wealth, their cohesiveness, their consciousness—favor them from the beginning. Because state agencies are bureaucratically organized, capitalists don't need to occupy many positions; they merely need the most powerful offices that set priorities and policies. In addition, capitalists can often rely on managers and professionals to serve their interests. Such officeholders aren't technically capitalists, but their livelihood is so closely tied to capitalist interests that they can be counted on to represent them faithfully.

Regulatory agencies provide more explicit examples of how capitalists control the state. Such agencies are established to monitor and regulate activities in particular industries and defend the public interest. Over time, however, capitalists and pro-capitalist managers gain access, influence, and ultimately control of such agencies. Their purpose is then redirected, and they become avenues for capitalists to tap federal resources and shape policies and regulations that favor their interests. In these cases, an instrument meant to counteract capitalist interests and priorities is turned into one for achieving them.

In the broader society, many forces legitimize capitalist control of state power. Political parties, churches, mass media, education, advertising, and mass culture implicitly support capitalist values. Further reinforcement comes from prevailing ideologies about equality, mobility, freedom, and nationalism that can render class control of the state harder to see.

The instrumentalist approach does not see capitalist control as inevitable. The state in capitalist society is rather an object of class struggle. Capitalists, nevertheless, have the upper hand in that struggle, except in the most unusual circumstances (Miliband 1969).

The structuralist approach makes the intriguing claim that the capitalist state serves capitalism even when it is not directly controlled by capitalists. Indeed, such a state might be more useful to capitalists than one under their direct control.

The structuralist logic is as follows. In capitalist societies, the state has a "relative autonomy" from direct economic control compared with past societies. This relative autonomy is very useful to capitalism, because the capitalist class consists of different factions with somewhat differing interests. Think of differences between large corporations and small businesses over health care policy or of differences between domestic and export businesses over tariffs and trade policy. This means that the class as a whole could never control the state; it could only be one faction or another that might do so.

If this were to happen, it could be harmful to the capitalist class as a whole, because the dominant faction could use state power against other factions of the capitalist class and perhaps destabilize capitalism as a whole. The relative autonomy of the state is a blessing in disguise for capitalists, because it reduces the likelihood that any one faction of capitalists will use state power against rivals.

In this view, the state is where the general, long-term interests of capitalism are identified and pursued. The relative autonomy of the state helps organize the capitalist class as a whole by providing an institution that maintains the general conditions of capitalist production that benefit all capitalists. Indeed, this arrangement makes it possible for the state to act against the narrow interests of one capitalist faction when they jeopardize the overall conditions of capitalist production. Structuralists thus interpret inter-capitalist disputes over tariffs, taxes, or antitrust initiatives as short-term losses for some capitalists that produce long-term stability for capitalism as a whole.

Although the capitalist state helps organize the capitalist class, it disorganizes the working class through electoral politics. Elections reflect individual preferences rather than class interests. This is particularly important in winner-take-all voting systems like in the United States, where up to 49 percent of voters may be utterly ignored rather than proportionally represented. The relatively autonomous state thus helps capitalists formulate their class interests while obscuring those of workers.

The "relative autonomy of the state" thus requires careful interpretation. "Autonomy" means that the capitalist state is free from the *direct* control of capitalists. "Relative" means that there are important *indirect* limits on how far the state could ever depart from general capitalist conditions. This indirect power over state policy derives from capitalists' control of economic resources. Governments depend on tax revenue from productive economies. When capitalists are unhappy with government policies, they can redirect their investments or even stage a "capital strike." Mere threats of such action can destabilize financial markets, heighten inflationary pressures, and exert substantial influence on government policies. Given these capacities, the "autonomy" of the state is very "relative" indeed (Poulantzas 1975).

The neo-Marxist perspective on the state addresses other issues as well. One is the tension between accumulation and legitimation. Capitalist states promote capital accumulation for all the reasons just discussed. States must also maintain legitimation. These quickly become contradictory requirements for the state. Fostering accumulation in too obvious a way will raise legitimation problems, and gaining legitimation through social spending might undercut capitalist accumulation. Capitalist states constantly renegotiate the contradictions between fostering accumulation and maintaining legitimation (Habermas 1975; O'Connor 1973).

A related tension confronting the capitalist state is between commodification and decommodification. Commodified practices mean buying and selling goods and services in a marketplace for profit. Decommodified practices mean government-sponsored social services. Capitalists typically want to commodify as many practices as possible to maximize their opportunities for profit making. However, this leaves poor people unable to meet basic needs around housing, education, transportation, and health care. In these situations, states might have to decommodify some goods and services to prevent suffering, blunt opposition, and maintain legitimation. The rise of the "welfare state" in the twentieth century thus involved the decommodification of basic needs that were met as part of the state's obligations to its citizens. The more recent push toward "privatization" seeks to recommodify those relationships by shifting them from government services to marketplace commodities (Offe 1985).

The power structure debate among pluralism, elite theory, and neo-Marxism continues, because the issues defy easy resolution. Thus, pluralism endorses a passive citizenry choosing among competing elites. Elite theory claims that this amounts to elite dominance rather than pluralist participation. Neo-Marxist theory claims that elite theory ignores class conflict and bottom-up power. Pluralists take this as evidence that power is dispersed across different groups. And so it goes. Such debates are rarely solved. Their value is to provide analytical tools for a basic sociological task: to see beyond the surface appearances of political activity to the underlying dynamics and interests that drive it. A number of these tools have been conveniently summarized in a more recent statement on the power structure debate.

Domhoff's Synthesis

G. William Domhoff entered the power structure debate as a critic of pluralism, blending insights from elite theory and neo-Marxism (Domhoff 1967). His most recent statement (Domhoff 2002) offers a "class-dominance" perspective and a good example of critical sociology. In this synthesis, the power elite is the vehicle that translates class dominance into political power. This elite emerges from the intersection of three groups: the corporate community, the upper class, and policy organizations.

The corporate community consists of large corporations that dominate the economy through capital investment. Its members have always been upper class. Moreover, they form a surprisingly cohesive community that is revealed through network analysis. The overlapping memberships and interlocking directorates of this small group of people link their interests, strategies, and tactics. Like the structuralist neo-Marxists, Domhoff concludes that the corporate community has substantial power over government simply through its investment decisions. Yet, this does not guarantee pro-capitalist outcomes. There is more to the story.

The upper social class is another key component. Although it is based on enormous wealth, Domhoff emphasizes its social and cultural role. People born into this class experience privileged lives from cradle to grave. They attend exclusive prep schools and Ivy League colleges. They join upper-class social clubs and travel to exclusive resorts. This class is an incubator nurturing a "class awareness that includes feelings of superiority, pride, and justified privilege" (Domhoff 2002, 68). Such awareness helps unite the class while also distancing its members from anyone outside the group. However, not all members of this class are politically active. Some simply enjoy luxurious lifestyles far from the political arena. It is not the upper class as a whole that joins the power elite; it is a subset of politically active members who link up with other groups in the power elite.

Policy organizations round out the power elite. They include charitable foundations, think tanks, and other organizations that formulate elite policies. They are typically underwritten by corporate wealth and perform several functions. They allow members of the upper class and the power elite to study issues and formulate proposals that represent their interests. They provide a training ground for people to hone skills required for powerful political offices. They explore how to promote pro-capitalist policies in language that will appeal to a broader spectrum of people. They provide "experts" to media outlets who advocate elite views on the issues of the day. Although Domhoff acknowledges a handful of left-liberal groups, the great majority of these policy organizations reflect conservative viewpoints.

The power elite derives from the intersection of the corporate community, the upper class, and the policy organizations. The structural power of the corporate community combines with the class consciousness of the upper class and the specialized expertise of the policy networks to create a formidable political force.

Although the power elite doesn't win on every issue, and although it has periodic internal friction, it remains a powerful mechanism for converting class dominance into political power.

Four processes achieve this dominance. First, in the special interest process, businesses compete with one another on the basis of their particular, short-term interests. This often reveals divisions over taxes, subsidies, tariffs, regulations, and the like. These battles among different interest groups approximate the pluralists' multiple centers of power, Mills's middle levels of power, and the neo-Marxists' factions of the capitalist class. But there is more to the story.

Second, in the policy formation process, elites come together in the policy network to identify common, long-term, dominant class interests and translate them into government policy. Whereas the special interest process (which makes politics appear more pluralistic than it really is) attracts news coverage, the policy formation process is a quieter, behind-the-scenes affair. Policy formation is less about winning overt conflicts than setting the agenda in the first place. It precedes overt decision making and makes a big contribution to elite unity—a key aspect of Mills's original argument about the power elite. It also echoes the neo-Marxist idea that the state is an institution where the capitalist class formulates its long-term, class interests.

Third, in the candidate-selection process, the upper class and the power elite shape who becomes viable candidates for national office. This is made easier by a system of winner-take-all elections that favor only two major parties. Elite economic resources are vital in financing campaigns, so that viable candidates enter races already indebted to their financial backers (in more ways than one). In twentieth-century U.S. politics, this has typically narrowed the presidential field to lawyers from wealthy backgrounds, who are "very ambitious people who are eager to 'go along to get along'" (Domhoff 2002, 143). Most importantly, a majority of national, elected officials have been pro-business conservatives. The consistency of these outcomes argues against pluralist notions of "competing elites" and in favor of a largely unified elite.

Fourth, in the opinion-shaping process, the power elite uses public relations firms, advertising agencies, polling organizations, and mass media to influence public opinion in its interests. This could mean support for specific policies, but it more often means reinforcing cultural values (freedom, nationalism, free markets) and linking them to elite preferences. Opinion shaping is most successful on foreign policy, with more mixed success on economic policy. On social issues, it often promotes conflict that is helpful to elites by diverting attention from more substantial issues. For example, if people are distracted by debates about intelligent design or gay marriage, they are less likely to notice tax cuts that benefit the wealthy and defund social services. These attempts to shape public opinion suggest that it is a potential source of opposition that elites would prefer to convert or neutralize if possible.

In sum, the power elite is a mechanism for translating class dominance into political power. It is derived from the corporate community, upper class, and policy organizations. Although differing over special interests, the general interests of the power elite emerge in the policy-formation process and are implemented through the candidate-selection and opinion-shaping processes. The power elite is clearly the most powerful political force in the society.

Even so, there have been at least two significant exceptions to this class dominance. Both involved labor struggles, and both were defeats for elites and victories for workers. The first was the National Labor Relations Act of 1935, which affirmed the right of workers to form unions. The second was the establishment of the Occupational Safety and Health Administration in 1970. In both cases, government policy became at least a temporary instrument of working-class power that extended protections to workers and limited the power of employers (Domhoff 2002, 169–180). Elites subsequently sought to ignore or undermine both these working-class gains, but they nonetheless signify the possibilities of two-way power.

Although no one perspective can resolve all the questions, the class-dominance approach is a powerful synthesis of many issues in the power structure debate that has been under way for half a century. It is also a good example of critical sociology.

STATES IN DECLINE?

This chapter began by noting that nation-states are recent historical inventions. They emerged alongside capitalism, urbanization, and industrialization. States have since become major global actors, sponsoring exploration, establishing colonialism, underwriting imperialism, creating alliances, incubating democracy, and conducting wars. Rebellions against states still promote the nation-state form, as national liberation movements have decolonized the globe and created a world of some two hundred nation-states. Just as nation-states have become a worldwide form of political organization, some sociologists are predicting a steady decline in their power.

The reason involves another recent historical invention: the corporation. From their inception, corporations have affirmed Marx's predictions about the concentration and centralization of capital, as the most successful corporations became oligopolies or monopolies at the expense of their competitors. By the end of the twentieth century, many corporations have become global, transnational entities. Indeed, the largest transnational corporations dwarf the economies of many nations.

As corporations become transnational, the power balance between states and corporations shifts. When they were essentially national entities, corporations were subject to the legislation, taxation, regulation, and general influence of the nation-states in which they were located. As they become transnational, they escape this influence. The strategy of playing one government against another has now been institutionalized in the World Trade Organization. Under recent treaties, transnational corporations can use weak labor and environmental or regulatory standards in some countries to overturn stronger standards in other countries as barriers to "free trade." With some exaggeration, it could be said that we are moving from a world in which corporations were subordinate to states to one in which states are becoming subordinate to corporations.

Another expression of this power shift is the rise of neoliberal economic policies. Neoliberalism advocates "free trade" or "free markets" along with the commodification and privatization of goods and services. Under this banner, governments are shedding social welfare obligations in favor of policies more acceptable to corporate interests. The effect has been to limit and subordinate government policy to the priorities of financial markets in a globalizing economy.

Although all states are subject to these pressures, they differ in their power and ability to resist them. In the periphery and semi-periphery of the world system, many states are too weak to offer meaningful resistance to neoliberalism and its subordination of such states to transnational capital. Others have cultivated populist defiance that seeks to limit transnational power within their boundaries. In the core of the system, states are much stronger and more likely to engage in real negotiations, with corporate forces driven by common interests as well as tensions between transnational goals and state policies.

Core states have also found new ways of strengthening military power. Dwight Eisenhower's famous warning about a military-industrial complex ranks among the best sociological predictions of the mid-twentieth century. "Military Keynesianism" solved economic problems of surplus capital and lagging demand through increased federal spending for military purposes. Massive military budgets were sold to the public as vital to national defense during the Cold War, but that "war" is over. The fact that military budgets continue to increase suggests the importance of the military-industrial complex to an advanced capitalist economy.

Militarism serves other purposes as well. A venerable sociological principle is that conflict with an out-group increases in-group cohesion and decreases in-group conflict. This is why nations at war are more likely to pull together and less likely to tolerate dissent. This principle can even foster a search for enemies (Coser 1956), whereby leaders seek or exaggerate external threats to reap the benefits of internal cohesion and control. This is why the Cold War was so useful to elites; external threats justified internal control. The demise of the Cold War removed the threat and some of its benefits to elites. The "need" for such threats perhaps explains why even domestic policy is often couched in militaristic language as a "war" against poverty, or drugs, or crime. It is certainly relevant to understanding foreign policy and the tendency to provoke or exaggerate external threats to justify militaristic policies.

In an interesting analysis of the 1991 Gulf War, David Brown (2004, 163–171) argues that war has a theatrical dimension. War *is* violent conflict, but it is also a symbolic ritual that can reinforce legitimacy, increase cohesion, promote nationalism, and suppress dissent. Brown cites the 1997 film *Wag the Dog* about leaders who completely fabricate a war to reap the domestic benefits of nationalist sentiments. Although the complete fabrication of war for these purposes is best left to Hollywood and conspiracy buffs, the notion that state managers use external conflicts to promote internal control is beyond dispute.

Consider recent U.S. wars. The terrorist attacks of September 11, 2001, were immediately framed not as an international crime but as an act of war requiring a "war on terror." This rhetoric glossed over the fact that wars are conducted between states and that terror is a tactic and not a state. Such subtleties were lost in the ideological battle to frame this conflict in ways that would promote internal cohesion and renewed nationalism. The metaphorical war on terror was quickly followed by real wars in Afghanistan and Iraq, even though no Iraqi threat was ever convincingly identified.

The wars abroad allowed the "war at home" to proceed with little opposition (Piven 2004). The "war at home" involves aggressive pursuit of neoliberal policies that benefit elites at the expense of ordinary citizens, including tax cuts for the wealthy, increasing federal debt, attacks on civil liberties, and the undermining of social programs. Fighting wars while cutting taxes is historically unprecedented; making those cuts permanent would be a major victory for neoliberal efforts to shrink government. The successes of the war at home resulted in part from the diversion afforded by the "war on terror." The twin towers of U.S. state policy have become neoliberalism and neonationalism. The latter is sustained by both real and exaggerated external threats, and it has provided effective cover for the former.

This example suggests a broader lesson. The idea that nation-states are losing power in the face of corporate expansion and globalization is at odds with sociological conceptions of states as rooted in the control of force and violence. The image of states in decline—especially core states—is too simplistic. The future of states involves a more complex dialectic among corporate agendas, military power, the need for legitimation, and the collaborative *and* contradictory ways in which state managers and transnational capitalists pursue their respective interests.

Chapter 6

A Mass-Mediated World

"Image is everything," according to a famous advertising campaign. Such claims are designed to sell products by associating them with desirable images. But the slogan acknowledges that more than just the product is being sold.

Our world is saturated with such claims. Because they are so widespread, we take them for granted. Such taken-for-granted claims should set off sociological alarm bells. The more familiar some aspect of our social world becomes, the more critical it becomes to use the sociological imagination to look beyond surface appearances.

This chapter examines several aspects of our mass-mediated world. We begin with a broad look at culture and proceed to some core concepts of critical sociology that emerge at the intersection of culture and power. We then examine the political economy of mass media, a propaganda model for understanding media output, and the pervasiveness of consumer culture.

CULTURE 101

The concept of culture is basic to the sociological tool kit. Culture refers to the products of organized social life. Material culture involves physical products. They range from pottery and agricultural implements in traditional societies to computers and cell phones in contemporary societies. Ideational culture refers to equally real but less tangible products like ideas, beliefs, values, symbols, and worldviews.

Culture is often juxtaposed with instinct, in claims that other animals are determined by instinct and humans are guided by culture. In extreme circumstances, we might fall back on something like instincts, but the vast majority of human action is guided by cultural learning rather than natural instinct.

It is culture that makes the world understandable by assigning meanings to it. Some meanings interpret the natural world through magical, mythical, religious, or scientific beliefs. Other meanings make sense out of the social world through a similarly broad range of belief systems. Still others attempt to answer existential questions about the purpose of life, the significance of death, or the existence of God. Our ability to make sense of the natural environment, the social world, and existential questions requires a culture of symbolic meanings.

One of the most important social acts is the transmission of culture from one generation to another. Because culture is not natural or instinctive, it must be learned. The process of socialization means cultural learning or enculturation. Through socialization, we learn and internalize the values, norms, and beliefs of our culture and integrate them into our identity. In this sense, culture is a profoundly conservative institution: It preserves and transmits the accumulated products of past generations and embodies their meanings in the identities of successive generations.

A classic statement of the importance of culture is the Sapir-Whorf hypothesis. According to this idea, language does not merely reflect the world "out there" like a mirror. It rather creates our sense of the world by providing linguistic categories through which we understand the world. Thus, some cultures and languages have distinctions and understandings that others do not. As a result, people raised in different cultures have distinct worldviews. They experience the world in different ways, depending on the tools their language provides.

The world consists of many cultures, so that culture helps distinguish one society from another. Culture is intertwined with ethnicity, language, religion, territory, and nationality. The world is clearly a multicultural place, and many nations are increasingly multicultural within their own boundaries.

Cultural diversity among and within societies poses classic sociological issues. Through socialization, our culture becomes deeply embedded in our identity and daily life. Our way of seeing and doing things feels normal and even natural. This embedded culture becomes a habitual, taken-for-granted way of making sense of the world. This is why encounters with other cultures often create culture shock.

When confronted with other cultures, we often respond in an ethnocentric fashion. That is, we tend to assume that our culture provides the correct guidelines to the world and that others do not. The taken-for-granted quality of culture can easily become a bias about the superiority of our way and the inferiority of any alternative. Prejudice, discrimination, and racism often flow from ethnocentrism. The antidote to ethnocentrism is cultural relativism. This means a respectful recognition that cultures are relative to time and place, that everyone feels an ethnocentric link to their own culture, but that no cultures are inherently superior or inferior to any other.

Culture provides a snapshot of what is distinctive about a society. For example, every introductory sociology text identifies values that typify U.S. society and culture. Although not unique, it is the centrality and interconnections between them that make U.S. culture distinct. The standard list includes achievement, success, individualism, efficiency, practicality, science, technology, progress, material comfort, democracy, equality, and racism (Henslin 2005, 49–53).

There are still other aspects of cultural diversity. We speak of subcultures when people adapt mainstream values and modify them into a unique social world or lifestyle. We speak of countercultures when people explicitly challenge and reject some mainstream cultural values and deliberately create alternative values and even build counterinstitutions as well.

The concept of culture is basic to sociological analysis. It fits especially well with humanistic sociology, with its emphasis on how people construct meanings and act on them. The concept of culture has also proven useful for critical sociology.

CULTURE MEETS CRITICAL SOCIOLOGY

Sociology typically sees culture as unifying society. In the functionalist tradition in both sociology and anthropology, culture is a repository of common values and beliefs that provide social cohesion. In this view, culture is the glue that holds social elements together.

Critical sociology sees it differently. It is interested in culture when it intersects with power and domination. Whenever culture expresses or embodies power, it becomes relevant for critical sociology. Put differently, although mainstream sociology is interested in all aspects of culture, critical sociology is interested in cultural domination and resistance. Several examples illustrate this intersection of culture and power.

First, consider mass society. On one hand, such societies contain massive, bureaucratic organizations. On the other hand, they promote extreme individualism. The result is a mass society of isolated, atomized people who experience anomie and alienation from these massive bureaucracies and from other alienated individuals. Intermediate social groups that might provide a buffer between dominant organizations and isolated individuals are lacking in mass society. Mass society theory anticipated recent trends of declining social involvement in neighborhoods, churches, voluntary organizations, and other social activities that could connect people to each other.

The decline of intermediate social organizations was paralleled by the rise of mass culture. Their differences are crucial. Intermediate social organizations provide face-to-face interaction that allows people to be active participants in cultural activities. They foster a sense of agency that reduces alienation and powerlessness. They also provide reference groups and a knowledge base to judge claims made by authorities. Such groups sustain a public sphere of engaged citizens.

In sharp contrast, mass culture involves mediated, one-way transmissions in which people become passive consumers of cultural messages and products. Such media undermine agency and often heighten alienation and powerlessness. They replace the reference group and knowledge base provided by intermediate social organizations with more media outlets. These media become an echo chamber of "talking points," and it becomes increasingly difficult to evaluate their validity in the absence of face-to-face contact in small groups. As a result, the prospects for a public sphere in which ideas come under critical scrutiny are correspondingly diminished.

Culture *can* provide the symbolic glue holding society together. But when it becomes mass culture, it also becomes a means of domination that disintegrates social life, increases social isolation, creates passive consumers, and enhances elite power. Mass society is one intersection of culture and power of interest to critical sociologists.

A second such intersection is ideology, defined as meaning in the service of power (Thompson 1990, 7). It is very common for symbols and meanings to assume ideological functions and serve powerful interests. The impact of such ideology is heightened when transmitted through mass media, because the receiver of the message often has no independent context for judging its validity.

There are several ways meanings serve power and become ideological. Some ideologies provide legitimation. They acknowledge domination exists but portray it as legitimate and therefore acceptable. Other ideologies involve dissimulation. They conceal domination and seek to render it invisible. Other ideologies involve unification. They portray people as part of a false unity that obscures control of some by others. Other ideologies involve fragmentation. They divide potential challengers by identifying false enemies and directing attention away from common foes. Still other ideologies involve reification. Here, ideology interprets a temporary, historical condition as if it were permanent, natural, or timeless. These ideologies might acknowledge domination but deny the possibility of ever overturning it (Thompson 1990, 52–67). These processes each maintain domination by enlisting cultural meanings in the service of power.

A third example of the intersection of culture and power is cultural capital. Economic capital involves wealth; such wealth is obviously unequally distributed. Cultural capital involves specialized knowledge, technical skills, and professional credentials; these are also unequally distributed. Groups high (or low) in economic capital are likely to be high (or low) in cultural capital, but other variations are possible. Some groups inherit or acquire wealth without a corresponding amount of cultural capital (think *Beverly Hillbillies*). Others lacking economic capital might nonetheless have substantial cultural capital, which in turn could allow them to achieve economic capital (think computer geeks who create successful companies).

Cultural capital has a direct relation to power and domination. Pierre Bourdieu has examined how social hierarchies are reproduced over time without provoking resistance—or even being recognized. Part of the answer involves culture as symbolic power. Just as people pursue material interests and profits through economic behavior, they also pursue symbolic interests and "profits" through cultural behavior. Symbolic power is the ability to shape people's understandings of the world in ways that reinforce current arrangements and deny the viability—or even the possibility—of alternatives (Swartz 1997).

Symbolic violence is the imposition of beliefs that sustain and reproduce hierarchies. Symbolic violence is strongest when people accept their subordination as just, legitimate, or correct. Those who control cultural capital have an obvious advantage in using symbolic violence, because of their skill at using knowledge, language, and meanings. Effective symbolic violence can prevent people from recognizing that a cultural struggle is occurring in the first place—not to mention that it is working to their disadvantage.

The most intriguing part of this argument involves habitus, or unconscious predispositions to act in certain ways. Such habitual predispositions often guide our action. Here's the important part: Habitus is class specific. People in privileged classes acquire one set of habitual predispositions about how to act in the world, and people in subordinate classes acquire different predispositions. Both derive from socialization; mainstream sociology is correct that socialization transmits culture from one generation to the next. What critical sociology adds is that socialization transmits different amounts and types of culture to different social classes.

Here's the even more important part: Habitus reproduces hierarchy precisely through the different predispositions that become "second nature" in different classes. Habitus creates self-fulfilling prophecies. Privileged classes learn habits that lead them to act in ways that perpetuate their privilege. Conversely, subordinate classes acquire habits that lead them to act in ways that perpetuate their subordination. The predispositions of such groups have a self-defeating quality; it's as if they are predestined to screw things up. Culturally embedded habits lead to actions that reinforce the habits. And so it goes. Bourdieu thus tackles one of the most basic sociological puzzles: How is inequality maintained without resistance and sometimes even without recognition? His answer sees culture as power: Cultural capital and habitus maintain inequality (Swartz 1997).

A final example of the intersection of culture and domination is the concept of power/knowledge (Foucault 1980). It challenges the cultural fable of modernism. According to this fable, people since the Enlightenment have used reason in a scientifically disinterested way to develop knowledge leading to a single, universal, and uncontested Truth. In the process, they created discourses or systems of knowledge that reveal this Truth.

For Foucault, each premise is dubious. First, the goal of a single, universal Truth is outdated in a postmodernist world of partial, relative truths. Second, the image of reason and science as a disinterested, objective pursuit of "pure" knowledge is dubious. If there are no universal truths and if reason and science are not disinterested, then we must reevaluate the pursuit of knowledge itself. This leads Foucault to power/knowledge. It means that although people were claiming to pursue objective truth through disinterested science, they were actually acquiring power through specialized knowledge. The discourses that supposedly express scientific rationality are really exercises in creating expert power.

The concept of power/knowledge summarizes how every quest for knowledge is also an exercise in power, because specialized discourses are a scarce resource monopolized by a minority of experts who thereby gain power over nonexperts. This power is masked because these discourses are still perceived through a modernist lens. We think we are getting "Truth" from these discourses, when we are really getting "truth effects" or "regimes of truth." The discourses create the appearance of "Truth" while establishing the reality of power.

This conclusion was reached after historical studies of modern knowledge systems, including medicine, psychiatry, and the social sciences (Foucault 1965, 1966, 1969, 1975, 1979). In each case, Foucault detects a "will to power" lurking underneath the "will to knowledge." To whatever extent we have become a knowledge society, Foucault's arguments are crucial to understanding how the cultural artifact of knowledge can become the political resource of power.

The concepts of mass society, ideology, cultural capital, and power/knowledge illustrate intersections of culture and power. As such, they are crucial tools for understanding culture through the lens of critical sociology.

THE POLITICAL ECONOMY OF MASS MEDIA

We increasingly experience culture through mass media. This mass culture has created a world where we have less *direct* experience of life, earth, dirt, blood, nature, and death, while having massively more *indirect* experience of these things through mass media.

To a time traveler from a traditional world, the images and products of mass culture would seem fantastic. To us, they are taken for granted. In fact, we are likely to think they reflect the "real" world. It requires the sociological imagination to recall that this world is a social construction. This basic sociological insight is especially useful when analyzing how mass culture constructs reality for us. Understanding mass media requires a sociological lens attentive to context, history, and the logic of how social institutions operate in society.

In other words, we need a political economy of mass media to understand how they emerged and how they function in the context of capitalist markets and state power. The first lesson of such an approach is that "the media" are large, bureaucratic, corporate enterprises. They follow a basic capitalist logic of maximizing profits. In the pursuit of such profits, they create worlds that we take to be real, because it serves their economic purposes to do so.

The economics of the relationship is more evident in some cases than others. When we buy music, books, or movie tickets, the financial exchange is obvious. When we consume "free" media, like television or radio, the economics are less clear, but no less real. Mass media sell audiences to advertisers. The media are an intermediary whose goal is to gather the largest possible audience, so they can derive the largest possible revenue from advertisers who buy access to that audience. With mass media, people are turned into audiences and sold as commodities to advertisers who pay media to reach them.

The commercial basis of this seemingly "free" transaction has important consequences. For one thing, it means that media content is secondary to commercial purposes. Although media occasionally offer content that is artistic or educational, these goals take a backseat to profitability. Artistry and education are quickly ignored if they conflict with the bottom line.

Another consequence is programming that follows familiar formulas so as to recruit large audiences. These formulas include sexual titillation, "realistic" violence, moral uplift, and sitcom humor. More recent formulas involve "reality" programming and talent contests that are very cheap to produce. They generate large ratings that increase advertising revenue and allow programmers to defend their unimaginative fare as "giving people what they want."

Yet another consequence is that the commercial logic of the marketplace displaces any other rationale for mass media and its products. If the ultimate goal of mass media is financial gain, then it should be no surprise that even news and editorial policy come under pressure to maximize the bottom line.

There is nothing natural or inevitable about a market-oriented, profit-driven mass media. It emerged through a series of critical junctures where corporate motives intersected with government policy making (McChesney 2004, 1–56). For example, in the early twentieth century, the National Association of Broadcasters established commercial broadcasting as the norm for organizing the media. "With the passage of the Communications Act and the formation of the FCC in 1934, the NAB accomplished its mission. Congress no longer debated the propriety of commercial broadcasting" (McChesney 2004, 41). While endorsing commercial broadcasting, this legislation contained provisions to ensure competition and require broadcasters to serve the "public interest."

Subsequent media policy followed a predictable story line, as "the FCC has become the classic 'captured' regulatory agency" (McChesney 2004, 45). Captured agencies reverse their original purpose. Agencies created by government to regulate industry and protect the public instead become vehicles for industries to shape government policies that benefit them. As a result, the norm of serving the public interest in exchange for commercial broadcasting licenses has all but disappeared. For most media, this commitment begins and ends with a few public service announcements aired in the middle of the night. The remainder of the broadcast schedule is exclusively devoted to commercial interests.

The other regulatory goal of ensuring competition has been under constant industry attack. The Telecommunications Act of 1996 eliminated some of the few remaining restrictions on media consolidation. Amid much talk of new technologies, the underlying rationale of the act was promoting neoliberal, market-based "solutions." Judging from the solutions, the "problem" was that media giants couldn't merge fast enough, because the "deregulation" advanced by this act fostered rapid concentration of media assets. The same neoliberal, privatizing approach that has promoted a capitalism "unbound" also drives media policy and practice.

These changes accelerated horizontal integration of media firms, leading to oligopolies in which a few firms dominate the market for a given product. Ironically enough, such oligopolies produce the opposite of free market benefits. Rather than many small suppliers driving up quality and driving down prices, oligopolies can manipulate prices with little concern for quality. Instead of the market driving business to produce collective benefits, corporations dominate the market and maximize private gain. Horizontal integration and oligopolistic control underscore how mass media are no different from other corporations.

This logic also pushes media firms toward vertical integration, where the same firms own both the content and the means of distribution. It is economically rational for firms to seek such control and predictability over their environment.

But what is good for them is not necessarily good for consumers or the public. Vertical and horizontal integration lead to fewer and larger economic interests owning and controlling formerly unrelated businesses. Such conglomeration becomes self-perpetuating as competitors follow the same strategy to survive. The result is that the vast majority of cable stations are owned by a handful of firms, which in turn own broadcast stations, movie studios, daily newspapers, radio stations, and music companies. Behind the seeming diversity of media outlets is a shrinking number of massive corporate interests in control of the "real world out there" (McChesney 2004, 175–210).

These dynamics undermine quality. Artistic cultures of writing, journalism, acting, and musicianship have long coexisted with commercial goals. The rise of conglomerates has elevated commerce over craft and managerial priorities over artistic creation. It is not just that artistic products are turned into commodities. It is that the people making decisions are less likely than ever before to understand the culture of creativity. When decisions are increasingly made only with respect to the bottom line and shareholder interests, a vital tension between creative potential and financial incentives has been lost. Despite lip service about artistry, the logic of profitability is unforgiving.

This is evident in book publishing. Consider two books about books. The first was *Books: The Culture and Commerce of Publishing* (Coser, Kadushin, and Powell 1982), which documented the healthy tension and occasional synergy between the creative and commercial sides of book publishing. Fewer than twenty years later, Andre Schiffrin (2000) published *The Business of Books: How International Conglomerates Took Over Publishing and Changed the Way We Read,* which is an insider's report of how the commercial side of publishing overwhelmed its cultural side.

The traditional balance between commerce and culture worked as follows. A press could stay in business even if most of its books lost money—as long as a few books made healthy profits and thereby supported the press as a whole. This logic allowed publishers to take chances on books whose profitability was uncertain, or to simply publish good books they knew would be unprofitable. This trade-off preserved a culture of book publishing that saw many high-quality, low-profit volumes reach the marketplace, because they were subsidized by better-selling books, and because presses were not subject to rigid economic priorities. Moreover, the decisions were made by editors who sought to balance artistry and commerce.

This changed drastically when conglomeration turned independent publishers into small divisions within media giants. In some cases, entire categories of books that had made presses famous were simply eliminated. In other cases, rigid rules requiring that every book generate a profit were established. In one transaction, Random House was sold to the German conglomerate Bertelsmann, which immediately imposed a 15 percent profit target on its operations. At the time of the takeover, Bertelsmann employed four thousand accountants at its headquarters, a figure far exceeding the number of editors in all its holdings around the world (Arnove 2000). The subordination of artistic creation to financial pressures is increasingly common, as small media businesses become divisions of larger conglomerates.

In advanced capitalism, culture becomes mass culture under the control of powerful corporate interests. The economic dynamics are familiar. We have seen them in the production of automobiles, computers, water heaters, and lightbulbs. But to see them in the "production" of stories, novels, movies, and songs should give us pause. Processes that *might* have led to better automobiles and water heaters do not necessarily lead to better novels or songs. If culture makes us human, then the profit-driven production of mass culture is ominous. It is not only bad for culture; it is also dangerous for democracy.

NEWS, PROPAGANDA, AND JOURNALISM

Here's an interesting correlation: The number of media outlets has increased, while ownership of those outlets has become more concentrated. Here's another: People's use of media has increased, while political involvement has decreased (McChesney 2000, 1). As we have "invested" in media, we have "disinvested" in citizenship. Although a correlation is not necessarily a causal relationship, it suggests a connection worth exploring.

To understand the depoliticizing effects of media, remember that their product is a social construction. Did you ever notice that every day, there is exactly enough "news" to fill a half-hour broadcast (minus commercials)? Unless you watch cable, where there's enough "news" to fill a twenty-four-hour "news cycle" (minus commercials). Or perhaps you are one of the declining number of people who read newspapers. Same question: Why is there exactly enough news to fill the newspaper (minus advertising)? There are never empty moments in the broadcast or blank pages in the paper. The observation underscores that choices are made about what becomes "news." This brings up the questions of who decides, and on what basis?

To answer this question, think of media as a giant funnel. Above the funnel are countless events and issues—more than could ever be coherently presented in existing media formats. Most events and issues fall outside the media funnel and receive little or no attention. A small minority fall inside the funnel and pour into media outlets where they become "news." According to the media's own proclamations, they only report what is newsworthy, but this is circular logic. The question remains: How do media interests decide what is "newsworthy"?

The process involves a series of filters within the funnel, from its broad entry to its narrow exit. "Potential news"—the broad world of events and issues—must pass through these filters to become real news. The filters sift what becomes news and what does not. By identifying the filters, we can learn how media constructs the news—and maybe how it stifles political involvement.

This suggests a propaganda model of how elites manufacture consent in democratic societies (Herman and Chomsky 1988). In this model, the main function of media is to mobilize popular support for the special interests of political and corporate elites. The argument is not a conspiracy theory. It is rather an institutional analysis of how bureaucratic organizations pursue their interests. It suggests that the subtle self-censorship of the market might create a more effective system of propaganda than the heavy censorship of an authoritarian state.

This propaganda model "traces the routes by which money and power are able to filter out the news fit to print, marginalize dissent, and allow the government and dominant private interests to get their message across to the public." The filters "fix the premises of discourse and interpretation, and the definition of what is newsworthy in the first place, and they explain the basis and operations of what amount to propaganda campaigns" (Herman and Chomsky 1988, 2).

The first filter at the top of the funnel derives from the size, ownership, and profit orientation of mass media themselves. As we have seen, media are large, corporate entities. They are often tied to other corporations and government agencies. This creates institutional interests in promoting some views and marginalizing others.

Sometimes the connections are obvious, as when General Electric's ownership of NBC prevents any critical examination of GE's business practices by that network (McChesney 2000, 52). More often the connections are indirect but still effective in shaping what becomes "news." These interests don't guarantee exclusively pro-corporate news, but they begin defining what is "newsworthy" in keeping with elite interests. Some stories don't survive the obstacles posed by this first filter. Some do, only to encounter still other filters (Herman and Chomsky 1988, 3–14).

The second filter involves advertisers. When revenue comes from direct sales like magazine subscriptions, buyers have some potential power. When advertising revenue displaces direct sales, advertisers exercise control. Put differently, advertisers become the real buyers, and the market responds more to them than to consumers. As we have seen, advertising pressures mean media become vehicles for assembling audiences.

Although there are cases of virtual censorship by advertisers, this filter generally works in more subtle ways. Advertisers become reference groups guiding decisions about what is newsworthy. Most generally, the pressure is to avoid complex or controversial topics that might conflict with promoting consumption (Herman and Chomsky 1988, 14–18). Once again, this filter does not provide direct control of all media content, but it helps set the parameters of what is "newsworthy."

The third media filter involves sources who define what is "news." In a romanticized image of journalism, reporters hit the streets, identify clandestine sources, find the story, and reveal the truth. In reality, official sources have all but displaced reporters, so that journalists become mouthpieces of officially sourced news. Government sources are always happy to provide facts and interpretations that suit their interests (and conceal those that don't). Official sources have automatic prestige and status, and they are easier and cheaper to access than unofficial ones. Good journalism used to begin by investigating what sources said; it now too often ends with an uncritical regurgitation of a source's claims.

As media become more dependent on official sources, the latter grant stories to cooperative reporters and withhold them from others. The result is a pacified press that has traded independent analysis for access to power holders. A tamed press corps might gain additional access by featuring "experts" who endorse official views

(Herman and Chomsky 1988, 18–25). Like the other filters, this one does not result in seamless control of the news. But along with other filters, it further defines what is newsworthy in ways that reflect elite interests.

The fourth filter is flak, which is like an insurance policy on the other filters. If issues detrimental to elite interests survive the first three filters to become news, elites generate flak that can be very costly to media organizations and detract attention from the initial story. Some flak is promoted by government, and some comes from think tanks and policy organizations on behalf of elite interests. Even when it is false, well-financed flak can divert attention and deflect challenges to elite interests (Herman and Chomsky 1988, 26–28). Indeed, there is a veritable industry devoted to generating right-wing flak about the supposedly liberal bias of the media. Aside from accuracy, sheer repetition of the charge has shaped what becomes "newsworthy" (McChesney 2004, 98–137).

Writing in the 1980s, Edward Herman and Noam Chomsky identified a final filter of anticommunism. Though crucial during the Cold War, this filter lost much of its power with the demise of the Soviet Union. But the logic remains. This filter emphasized an external enemy, but its vagueness made it very flexible. When anticommunist fervor is aroused, "the demand for serious evidence in support of claims ... is suspended, and charlatans can thrive as evidential sources" (Herman and Chomsky 1988, 30). In the early twenty-first century, terrorism has replaced communism as the vague and amorphous external threat. Replacing communism, terrorism has become the final filter in socially constructing both what is newsworthy and how we interpret this news.

These filters are not foolproof, but they have an emergent power. The funnel is greater than the sum of its parts, because even when one filter fails, others might succeed. The result is that when stories serve elite interests, they receive a tremendous amount of attention and repetition; when they do not, they are likely to disappear quickly if they surface at all. Even very imperfect control undermines informed, democratic decision making.

The "debate" leading up to the U.S. invasion of Iraq in 2003 is a telling example. Political elites selectively interpreted and distributed ambiguous intelligence about an Iraqi threat, suppressed conflicting information, and endlessly repeated ominous threats about weapons of mass destruction. A compliant press faithfully transmitted and amplified these concerns. The rare dissenting voice attracted heavy flak and intimations of treason for challenging the government's line. It should not be surprising when governments act this way, but it is disappointing when journalists—supposedly the "fourth estate"—uncritically echo elite views in the name of neutrality.

It was not always so. For much of our history, we had a partisan press whose members took sides and advocated positions. Such partisanship promoted democratic debate as long as there were numerous independent media outlets representing diverse views. The first wave of media consolidation in the early twentieth century undermined this model of journalism. As ownership was consolidated, a partisan press would increasingly be perceived as speaking for the narrow interests of its owners. The traditional model of partisan journalism thus faced a crisis (McChesney 2004, 57–64).

"Professional" journalism emerged in response. With professionalization, standards of neutrality and balance replaced partisanship and advocacy. If journalism became neutral and balanced, then concentrated ownership was not a problem because the standards of professional journalism would ensure unbiased news coverage. In this way, the professionalization of journalism legitimized the concentration of media ownership (McChesney 2004, 64–66).

There were several flaws here. In other fields, professionalism meant partnerships or independent ownership of medical, legal, or psychiatric practices. Journalists, however, remained employees who worked at the discretion of their bosses. Moreover, professional journalism contains its own biases. It rejects criticism and alternative perspectives from outsiders who are—by definition—unprofessional.

Professional journalism also tends to equate neutrality with acceptance of official sources as a basis for legitimate news. This is often coupled with a lack of context for stories, because this might be construed as introducing partisanship. By attempting to avoid partisanship and mimic professionalism, "journalism smuggles in values conducive to the commercial aims of owners and advertisers and to the political aims of big business" (McChesney 2004, 72–73). This is most often expressed in the kinds of stories that are covered and how such choices reflect elite interests (McChesney 2004, 67–77).

The model of professional journalism was always deeply flawed. With recent media consolidation, it has succumbed to further commercialization. Broadcast news has historically been unprofitable, but this was a source of professional pride, because it "proved" that the news wasn't driven by commercial concerns. Unprofitable news divisions were subsidized by more profitable operations (like the publishing industry). With further commercialization, news divisions are now expected to become profit centers in their own right.

As a result, news divisions have seen budget and staffing cuts. Investigative reporting has become a rarity. Expensive factual reporting has given way to endless commentary and spin. Content has moved toward entertainment and celebrities to generate ratings. Traditional distinctions between business and journalism have eroded, leading to a steady diet of "infotainment" and "advertorials" (McChesney 2004, 77–97). The pace of change has surprised even professionals. "Whereas only ten or fifteen years ago prominent journalists were among the staunchest defenders of the commercial media system, today, in what amounts to almost a sea change, journalists have emerged as among its foremost critics" (McChesney 2000, 52).

These developments culminate in the production of "news" by corporate firms or government agencies for distribution to the media for direct broadcast. Such public relations gimmicks are a standard corporate strategy, but the federal government is quickly catching up. "In all, at least 20 federal agencies, including the Defense Department and the Census Bureau, have made and distributed hundreds of television news segments in the past four years.... Many were subsequently broadcast on local stations across the country without any acknowledgement of the government's role in their production" (Barstow and Stein 2005).

Propaganda is a loaded term, but it is difficult to know what else to call such corporate and government production of "news." It is not surprising that underfunded news departments broadcast such "news," but it is a sad comment on a field that once aspired to professional standards. Indeed, it is the lingering veneer of professionalism that provides added legitimation to corporate-produced or government-sponsored propaganda masquerading as news.

These developments help explain why increasing media exposure coexists with declining political participation. Consider a final example of how televised news decontextualizes its stories. "The result is a litany of events with no beginning and no real end, thrown together only because they occurred at the same time. So an earthquake in Turkey turns up next to proposed budget cuts, and a championship sports team is featured alongside a big murder trial. These events are reduced to the level of the absurd because we see only those elements that can be shown on television at a given moment, cut off from their antecedents and consequences" (Bourdieu 1998, 6–7).

As mass culture specializes in such fragmentary images, it is no mystery why those most attuned to it are least able to make sense of it—much less to fashion a political response to their world.

AN ALL-CONSUMING CULTURE

At the beginning of the twentieth century, Max Weber (1904) published a classic analysis of the rise of capitalism. He argued that Protestantism created a unique impetus to entrepreneurial activity. One the one hand, it endorsed hard work and acquisitive activity as a religious duty and a sign of moral worth. This made the acquisition of wealth an ethical imperative rather than an expression of greed. On the other hand, Protestantism required a simple lifestyle that renounced material pleasures. The combined prescription to create wealth but not consume it had a logical if unexpected result: the accumulation of wealth needed to launch capitalism. Weber noted that although something like the Protestant Ethic might have been necessary to launch capitalism, it was not required to sustain it.

At the beginning of the twenty-first century, we can update the analysis. A sparse, ascetic lifestyle might have been necessary to launch capitalism, but it poses a major threat to its long-term health. Capitalism has only survived by encouraging ever-increasing levels of consumption. As Marx expected, capitalism is prone to a crisis of under-consumption, because the value of commodities created by workers exceeds their purchasing power. Hence, capitalism must systematically promote consumption to offset this crisis.

Critical sociologists identify several problems with consumer culture. The emphasis on individual consumption promotes class inequality and undermines public goods. Consumerism requires long hours of work to pay for products we are socialized to want. Consumerism promotes wasteful industries like advertising and public relations to psychologically manipulate people and create false needs.

Consumerism underwrites the "American standard of living" that might be creating catastrophic environmental consequences (especially as a model for others). Consumerism offers little compensation for alienating work and political impotence. Consumerism undermines neighborhoods and communities. Consumerism has depoliticized society, turned citizens into shoppers, and reduced politics to another set of market choices. Consumerism could replace political legitimation, allowing even corrupt regimes to survive as long as they deliver the goods.

These criticisms identify serious problems, but they have problems themselves. The standard critiques of consumerism are too monolithic and ahistorical in their condemnation. They don't seem to recognize the pleasures of consumption. They sometimes convey an elitist condemnation of ordinary people. They rely on a simplistic view of consumers as passive and easily manipulated. A better critique of consumerism requires a more historical, nuanced interpretation.

It can be found in *An All-Consuming Century* (Cross 2000), whose title I have modified to frame this discussion. A historian by training but a sociologist at heart, Cross's interpretation of consumerism is guided by two themes. First, consumer society was not inevitable or predestined. It was established by particular people pursuing distinct interests in shifting historical contexts. Consumerism might have saved capitalism, but it didn't happen automatically. It had to be cultivated and then muscled into place. Second, the consumer society that emerged has nonetheless proven durable and adaptable. It matured in both favorable and unfavorable circumstances, and it has survived a number of challenges.

Consumer society emerged in the early twentieth century, as industrialization, urbanization, and mass production created both the productive capacity and the economic demand for such a society. Houses, cars, and appliances moved from the realm of elite privilege to ordinary people. Packaged goods and department stores brought new commodities to the market, and increased leisure time brought people into that market. Even so, these developments did not "naturally" lead to a consumer society. This was when advertising agencies and public relations firms became big businesses by creating needs and linking desires to products. When demand wasn't sufficient, retailers offered the installment plan, so people could buy now and pay later. By the end of the 1920s, a consumer society was already emerging.

With the stock market crash of 1929, life in the United States drastically changed. The Depression could have undermined consumer society, so the fact that it survived is all the more striking. "Nothing speaks more to the power of consumerism than its hold on the American psyche during the Depression and World War II. Despite joblessness and wartime austerity, ordinary Americans held tight to old consuming habits and dreams" (Cross 2000, 67). Even as the economy faltered, people clung to their aspirations. They had help from advertisers who worked even harder to keep those aspirations alive. Marketing became more creative, promotion became more aggressive, and price cuts and bargains kept people buying.

World War II posed yet other challenges to consumer society, but it adapted once again. Although politicians used lofty political rhetoric, many people saw the war as a battle to preserve an American way of life that had come to include material goods and consumerism. Victory was interpreted as a vindication of this way of life. "All challenges to the fairness or rationality of capitalism were dismissed with the promise of a postwar consumers' democracy" (Cross 2000, 84).

After the war, consumerism came roaring back, as pent-up demand met active government promotion of the housing market. Postwar consumerism still emphasized the automobile, but now in bigger, faster, and flashier models. The automobile dovetailed with government support for highways to create suburbs and a whole new market for houses and everything needed to furnish them. With shopping malls, television (as both commodity and advertiser), and youth markets, consumer society appeared to have undergone a full recovery—just in time for its next challenge.

The 1960s brought dissenting voices and movements that had many targets; consumer society was among them. Academics wrote about manipulative advertising. Consumer movements challenged fraudulent practices and demanded government regulation. Environmentalists pointed to the wasteful and ecologically destructive consequences of rampant consumerism and advocated for more rational alternatives. The counterculture posed basic challenges to a society based on instrumental rationality, material consumption, and unrestrained growth. These movements collectively posed big challenges to consumerism. They created important legislation and regulation. They provided a philosophical critique of the "American way of life." Nonetheless, "by the end of the 1970s, not only were political challenges to the consumer market largely marginalized, but the cultural attack on consumerism had proven to be ephemeral and even a boon to a new kind of individualistic consumerism" (Cross 2000, 155). Now consumerism commodified nonconformity. It offered products and images to people who saw their consumption as an act of rebellion against consumption. Marketers happily catered to this kind of "rebellion." Second, consumerism linked consumption and identity even more closely. Like nonconformity, the expressive individualism of the counterculture was rewired so that individuality was now expressed by what one bought. Once again, consumerism survived and incorporated its major challenges.

The twentieth century ends with "Markets Triumphant" (Cross 2000), but the story is more interesting than the outcome. Whereas the 1960s and 1970s saw challenges from the left, the 1980s and 1990s felt them from the right. Conservative critics were incensed by permissiveness and materialism, but never identified the real culprit. In their view, government was somehow responsible for rampant hedonism. The solution was to restrain government spending and unleash market forces to restore discipline in social life. The great irony is that it was the market that promoted the permissiveness that so dismayed conservatives in the first place. The right unwittingly strengthened the very forces they thought they were fighting.

I previously used the expression *capitalism unbound* to refer to the consequences of deregulation. I subsequently found Gary Cross using the phrase "consumerism unbounded" (2000, 232) to conclude his history. In our day, there are few times, spaces, or relations that consumerism has not penetrated. Contrast the quaint reluctance of radio advertising executives in the 1930s to violate the sanctity of the home with the incessant drive to colonize it today through advertising and telemarketing.

Better yet, compare sentimental notions of childhood innocence with the contemporary commercialization of childhood. In *Born to Buy,* Juliet Schor (2004) offers a chilling analysis of how children have been targeted as a niche market of potentially lifelong consumers, if only they can be habituated to buy as early as possible. While marketers work hard to achieve this result, there is increasing evidence of the socially harmful consequences of such efforts on children's well-being and psychological health (Schor 2004, 141–175).

A final example of unbounded consumerism is the peculiar disconnect between consumerism and actual products. As Naomi Klein (1999) documents, consumerism is now less about material goods than about brands, logos, and images that symbolize corporate culture. In yet another example of the resiliency of consumer culture, the identity politics that once challenged corporate capitalism have been co-opted to define niche markets based on age, race, gender, sexual orientation, and the like. The progression from selling goods to marketing brands to branding consumers to commodifying identities nicely exemplifies consumerism unbounded.

Cross's historically nuanced account of consumerism tempers the standard critiques of mass culture, but does not invalidate them. He concludes that the ideology of consumerism has undermined human community, civil society, meaningful politics, and social relationships. Even with its successes, there are potentially catastrophic consequences of continuing the consumerist model for another century. And most poignantly, Cross suggests that in the end, "Americans could not avoid the logic of consumerism—and individualism was progressively reduced to a fashion statement and society to a market" (Cross 2000, 143).

A NOTE ON DOMINATION AND RESISTANCE

When culture intersects with power, it becomes domination. The means of domination include words, symbols, values, images, beliefs, attitudes, and worldviews. The vehicles of domination are mass culture, ideology, hegemony, cultural capital, habitus, and power/knowledge. The beneficiaries of domination are elites whose power is enhanced, obscured, or legitimated. The victims of domination are ordinary people who are deceived, misled, or depoliticized.

In the history of social theory, there have been many versions of this argument. It might be the best explanation we have for why people accept social arrangements that contradict their best interests. Even so, the argument has often been overstated, producing some rather bad sociology.

The early Frankfurt School made eloquent statements about how cultural domination serves elites. Herbert Marcuse claimed that even resistance was absorbed by a dominant culture that was immune to challenge. This seemingly populist argument contained its own elitism. It rested on little research and questionable assumptions. It presumed that ordinary people were passive puppets or cheerful robots incapable of thinking or acting for themselves.

Cultural domination is better understood when we recognize how ordinary people bring agency into the equation. Although not always amounting to resistance, there are many ways people transcend being puppets or robots. We interact with these social forces, often with surprising results. For instance, people are often selective in absorbing media messages. They are not empty vessels. Cultural images might be tools of domination, but people also use them creatively to formulate meanings, fashion identities, and express solidarities.

There are other problems with the "social cement" view of ideology (Thompson 1990) as binding helpless people to omnipotent structures. It obscures subtle ways in which agency becomes resistance. We must distinguish between public transcripts of domination and hidden transcripts of resistance (Scott 1990). Subordinates who show public deference often express private anger, defiance, and resistance. Based on his research, James Scott rejects the idea that people actively embrace values supporting their domination.

The only plausible version of this argument is a "thin" one, where people respond to domination with resignation or quiescence. Even here, cultural domination does not necessarily reduce conflict. Indeed, it can provoke it when elites do not live up to their hegemonic obligations. The strategy of identifying unfulfilled promises embedded in the dominant belief system has fostered resistance and even revolution.

Beyond subtle resistance, there have been more overt challenges to cultural domination. Although today's mass media were socially constructed, they did not have a single builder. Popular political pressures redirected, delayed, or modified the agendas of powerful media elites (McChesney 2000, 2004).

Challenges to consumer culture also modified its course (Cross 2000). Indeed, we are now witnessing explicitly anticapitalist resistance to consumer culture, evidenced by movements for more equitable globalization and sustainable development (Klein 1999). Social movements rarely succeed or fail completely, but they often leave traces on later social practices. Such impacts must be recognized to avoid seeing culture as a monolithic force against a powerless populace.

For all these reasons, cultural domination is best seen as a contested force whose greatest power might be in reification. By depicting a socially constructed process as an inevitably natural reality, culture enlists power to become domination. This is why we need critical sociology to see mass culture as the contested, socially constructed process it has always been. Only then we can de-reify it, identify alternatives, and inform agency.

PART THREE
INEQUALITY AND DIFFERENCE

Chapter 7

The Crucible of Class

The preceding section examined advanced capitalism's major institutions: the corporate economy, the nation-state, and mass culture. In this section, we focus on major social groups and collective identities.

The inequalities of class, race, and gender involve some generic similarities. Each rests upon structures of power and relations of domination. Each involves dominant and subordinate groups, group interests, group formation, collective consciousness and "false" consciousness, and conflict and transformation. At the same time, class, race, and gender have unique features. A comparative analysis reveals both commonalities and differences. This will be the focus of the next three chapters.

Class remains the most conventional inequality examined by sociology. It was central for many classical thinkers. Race and gender, by contrast, were often seen as biologically determined rather than socially constructed. For the white males who defined sociology's classical tradition, it was easy to see class but harder to see race and gender as social facts. Contemporary sociology has finally added race and gender as topics for sociological analysis. Here, the focus is on class; subsequent chapters address race, gender, and their intersections.

MARX'S MODEL OF CLASS FORMATION study

Class for Marx is a dynamic, relational process. Classes emerge and develop over time. Classes bind their members closer together as they distance one class from another. Over time, Marx expected to see increasing solidarity *within* classes alongside increasing polarization *between* classes. Marx called this process class formation or development (Marx and Engels 1848/1948). The logic of class formation is for classes-in-themselves to become classes-for-themselves over time.

As classes-in-themselves, capitalists and workers are necessary if capitalism is to exist at all. Classes-in-themselves are defined by people's relationship to material production. Capitalists own productive property and derive profits and their livelihood from this property. Workers own nothing but labor-power and derive wages and their livelihood from its sale. These differing relations to production distinguish capitalists and workers as classes-in-themselves.

Differing relations to production generate differing relations to consumption. As a general rule, ownership of property yields more income than sale of labor-power; capitalists are wealthier than workers. Hence, distinct lifestyles, consumption patterns, and standards of living further distinguish these classes.

Classes-in-themselves also have conflicting interests. What benefits one class typically comes at the expense of the other class. The tension between capitalists' profits and workers' wages is the most obvious expression of these conflicting interests, because gains for one tend to mean losses for the other. This tension is merely one expression of conflicting interests between capitalism's major social classes.

As classes-in-themselves, capitalists and workers are distinguished by their relationship to production, their relationship to consumption, and their class interests. These, however, are merely categories of people with common characteristics. There is no guarantee that these people will recognize their shared characteristics or feel a collective identity with others in the same boat. The latter are outcomes of class formation; with time, people will recognize their class position, interests, and allies.

The transformation of a class-in-itself into a class-for-itself happens when people act on their class interests. As capitalists seek the cheapest labor and workers seek the highest wages, conflicting class interests become evident. Marx placed particular emphasis on the factory system that capitalists created to control workers, manage costs, and enhance profits. But concentrating workers together in the same time and place had the unanticipated consequence of fostering interaction and communication among workers. The factory system helped workers see that their fate was closely tied to that of other workers and their class as a whole.

These social dynamics promoted class formation. A *category* of people who shared characteristics became a *group* of people who recognized them as a major determinant of their lives. Feminists speak of "consciousness raising" to describe women's growing awareness of how gender shapes their lives. Marx has a similar process in mind when he describes the emergence of self-conscious classes.

Classes-for-themselves arise when people develop a "we-feeling" or collective identity. This identity emerges as people see the effects of class on their social relationships. Consider how class creates segregation; it sorts people into neighborhoods, communities, schools, and social networks with distinct class privileges and disadvantages. When chronic class segregation combines with acute class conflict, class identity becomes socially meaningful as well as objectively real.

These processes also foster class consciousness, which can be seen as a continuum. At a minimum, class consciousness means recognizing that capitalism is a class-divided society. It means identifying one's class position accurately. It further means recognizing one's class interests. It finally means a willingness to fight on behalf of one's class interests. The ultimate expression of class consciousness is revolution; Marx felt this was most likely when objective economic crises were accompanied by subjective class consciousness.

This process culminates with political organization. Collective identity and class consciousness mean little until they fuel a struggle for political power. This requires organization. Whether it takes the form of trade unions, political parties, social movements, or community organizations, classes-for-themselves are most fully developed when they become politically organized (Anderson 1974).

Class formation thus means that both capitalists and workers begin as classes-in-themselves defined by their relation to production, consumption, and class interests. These categories become groups through class conflict that promotes solidarity within and polarization between classes. Class formation brings two classes-for-themselves rooted in collective identity, class consciousness, and political organization.

As a factual prediction, this model runs into trouble. History has not followed the script. The goal of working-class, socialist revolutions has fueled radical dreams but proven all but impossible. The model's real value is not as a prediction but rather as an analytical device and a sociological tool.

For instance, the model generalizes too many forms of group conflict. It fits any situation where categorical identities are hierarchically organized. The identities might be race, ethnicity, gender, nationality, religion, or sexuality. The relation between groups might involve exploitation, oppression, domination, or discrimination. As people act on their interests and conflict emerges, we can expect a shift from "groups-in-themselves" based on categories to "groups-for-themselves" based on collective identity, group consciousness, and political organization. The sharper the conflict, the greater the solidarity within and polarization between groups. Seen this way, the model is a major contribution to the sociology of group conflict.

There is also more to be learned about classes themselves. Before dismissing the model as a failed prediction, recall that it involves two classes. Although the working class hasn't fully mobilized, the capitalist class has. Put differently, Marx wasn't all wrong; he was only half-wrong. Capitalists closely followed the script.

Thus, the capitalist class in advanced capitalism has a strong collective identity and class consciousness. As G. William Domhoff (2002) has shown, this is a highly organized class that uses political strategies to pursue its class interests. The capitalist class is well prepared for "class war," and there are plausible sociological reasons for this. Enormous wealth gives capitalists a huge stake in the existing system and strong incentives to maintain it. They are also a relatively small, homogeneous group, which makes it easier to foster class solidarity. A high degree of capitalist class formation is not a sociological surprise.

The relative lack of working-class formation also has a sociological explanation. Though Marx claimed workers have nothing to lose but their chains, some workers have acquired living standards that include much more than chains. Even modest material comfort seems preferable to revolution and its unpredictable alternatives.

Working-class consciousness has also been blunted by the American dream of prosperity and upward mobility as rewards for hard work. The dream has come true just often enough to sustain the illusion that it is available to anyone willing to pay the price. Thus, although it is easy to see how capitalist wealth provides incentives for class formation, it is harder to see how workers' conditions—real or hoped-for—could promote similar class formation.

The working class is also a majority of the population. Although there might be strength in numbers, it only emerges with organization. Organizing millions of workers is very difficult. The most potent examples of working-class formation have actually been fractions of the working class rooted in social networks in particular industries and communities. Beyond localized instances, the large size of the working class impedes class formation, just as the small size of the capitalist class facilitates it.

The most important obstacle to working-class formation is not size but diversity. Consider the varieties of "work" that "workers" actually do. They are divided among industries. They are geographically dispersed. There are status distinctions between white-collar and blue-collar labor. They are divided between types and levels of skill. Some workers belong to trade unions and labor organizations, and others do not. These differences create inequalities among workers and can foster an "aristocracy of labor," whose members are more motivated to maintain their relative privileges than to challenge the system that provides them.

Workers also come from diverse ethnic, racial, cultural, national, and gender groups. There is no compelling reason to expect class identity will automatically override other identities. Employers have also used this diversity against workers in a "divide-and-conquer" tactic. Through decisions about hiring, firing, promotion, and strikebreaking, bosses set workers against one another along race, ethnic, or gender lines. This further undermines working-class formation.

Differing degrees of class formation for capitalists and workers can thus be explained sociologically. Class formation has also varied over time. Whereas the capitalist class has undergone relatively steady development, the working class has had cycles of class formation and dissolution. The historical record suggests that working-class formation has been neither a one-way street nor a complete failure.

At some moments in U.S. history, the working class exhibited high degrees of class formation. There was intense labor organizing just after the Civil War, during the 1880s, and in the early twentieth century, when workers staged extraordinary strikes that overcame ethnic, cultural, and even racial divides among workers. Working-class formation was evident again in the 1930s, in response to poverty and unemployment caused by the Great Depression.

During the postwar era of "prosperity," unionized workers gained material advantages and became less oppositional. In the 1960s and 1970s, women and minority workers drove class formation, and some white, male workers joined a conservative backlash. By the 1980s, capitalists and their political allies launched powerful attacks on unions that continue to this day. Nonetheless, organized labor continues to recruit nonunionized workers and to explore global initiatives that extend working-class formation beyond national borders.

As an analytic device, Marx's model of class formation defines benchmarks of progress and regress in class development. It will remain useful as long as capitalism generates class conflict.

CLASS OR STRATIFICATION?

Mainstream sociology has developed quite different models of stratification to suggest that class is not the only—or even the most important—kind of inequality. A brief overview will expand our tool kit and clarify the strengths of differing approaches.

Max Weber (1921/1968) argued that social class was only one dimension of social stratification. Whereas Marx saw all history through the lens of class, Weber claimed that different types of stratification are more or less important in different cultural and historical contexts. He identified three types of stratification: class, status, and power.

Weber's understanding of class is close to Marx's. For both, class is about material resources, and the most basic divide is ownership of property. For Weber, however, additional classes emerge around one's relation to markets. Even without substantial property, groups with a positive relation to a market can reap benefits. Almost a century after Weber, computer-savvy entrepreneurs in the Silicon Valley proved his point by capitalizing on scarce skills and parlaying the rewards into great wealth.

Weber also distinguished between class as a category and class as a real group. But unlike Marx, he does not see an inevitable progression from one to the other. He rather sees it as one possibility among others. Finally, alongside two major classes, Weber sees intermediate classes composing a more complex class structure.

Stratification also involves status. Whereas class is about material resources, status is about social honor. Status stratification involves unequal social honor conferred upon different groups in society. Historically, high-status groups were elites defined by religion, literacy, specialized knowledge, or artistic pursuits. More recently, status differences derive from occupational positions and prestige rankings.

The concept of status stratification applies to inequalities based on race, ethnicity, nationality, gender, or sexuality. Like class, status stratification can trigger group formation with strong collective identities and group consciousness. Indeed, status groups might be more likely to develop than classes, because they often share a common culture and language that more readily translates into a "we-feeling."

Class stratification and status stratification coexist and intersect while remaining distinct and independent. Neither is necessarily more central or important than the other. In some societies, one's status will "determine" one's class, and in others, one's class will "determine" one's status.

Power is the ability to achieve one's will despite resistance. Because this ability is unequally distributed, it is a third dimension of stratification. Just as people can be ranked hierarchically in terms of class and status, they can also be ranked in terms of power. However, their locations on individual hierarchies do not necessarily correspond with each other. Pornographers might be wealthy but don't enjoy high status; teachers might have high status without corresponding wealth; police exercise tremendous power with less wealth or status.

Weber's multidimensional approach is broader than Marx's singular focus on class. If we are analyzing societies historically or culturally distant from contemporary capitalism, Weber's approach is crucial. For contemporary capitalism, neo-Marxist approaches become more relevant. Even Weber might agree that in contemporary capitalism, class looms larger than status or power in the overall system of inequality.

Another mainstream approach to stratification is the functionalist tradition (Davis and Moore 1945). It argues that inequality is actually functional for society. Here's the logic. In any society, some positions are more important than others in maintaining the society, and only a limited number of people have the talent to successfully fill these positions. The conversion of natural talent into learned skills requires a costly and sacrificial training period. These functionally important positions must therefore carry disproportionately high rewards, if talented people are to be recruited to fill them.

Thus, social stratification is functional for society, because it motivates talented people to undergo costly training to fill functionally important positions that contribute to social survival. A concrete example: Society needs doctors. Becoming a doctor is costly. Thus, we must pay doctors substantially more than we do people in many other occupations to motivate enough talented people to become doctors. Put differently, greater equality of rewards would be dysfunctional and threaten social survival because we would lose the motivational mechanism needed to fill important positions.

This argument has been extensively criticized from the beginning (Tumin 1953). Determining functional importance and defining "social survival" is quite difficult. Whether talent is scarce is debatable, but it appears to be scarce precisely because stratification denies opportunity to all talented people. The premise of a sacrificial training period ignores situations where these costs are borne by others or other rewards compensate for them. The theory also says nothing about how much inequality is needed to maintain society. If corporate CEOs receiving five hundred times more than the average worker were only paid four hundred times more, would there be a shortage of CEOs, and would society crumble?

For these reasons, this theory is more a defense than an explanation of inequality. Its very language implies that inequality is necessary, positive, and inevitable, because it is "functional." Finally, by focusing on functional consequences, the theory obscures the historical causes of inequality and the role of power and conflict in establishing and perpetuating it.

A final mainstream approach is status attainment models (Blau and Duncan 1967) that measure social mobility and how different factors determine one's position in a social hierarchy. Positions are defined as socioeconomic status (SES), a combined measure of income and occupational prestige. The question is to what extent is a person's SES determined by ascribed factors at birth as opposed to achieved factors they accomplish?

Through a statistical technique known as path analysis (and a cultural bias known as sexism), these models measured correlations between father's education, father's occupation, son's education, son's first job, and son's later job. They found that ascribed factors like father's SES limited sons' social mobility both directly and indirectly. At the same time, early achievement by sons can snowball into greater achievement down the road. Most generally, social class background strongly influences status attainment, with some important variations owing to achieved factors.

This research had an interesting effect. It conceptualized stratification as a tall ladder with many rungs. Any time a son ended up on a different rung than his father, it was counted as social mobility. Because this happened a lot, U.S. society appeared to have high social mobility. But this was more a function of how it was measured than of real movement. By counting even tiny steps as "mobility," the model exaggerated opportunity in the class structure. Whereas the functionalist analysis became ideological by justifying stratification as necessary, the status attainment model became ideological by exaggerating the openness and mobility of the class system.

These mainstream theories make different assumptions than does the Marxist model of class formation. The contrast can be summarized by distinguishing the stratification and the class approach to inequality. By stratification approach, I mean the status attainment model, the functionalist theory, and at least some interpretations of Weber's multidimensional model. By class approach, I mean the Marxist tradition and more recent neo-Marxist variations we will examine shortly. Before doing so, the immediate issue is how do these approaches differ?

First, they have different goals. The stratification approach describes the *distribution* of social resources to various groups. It is geared to questions about what percentage of people possess what percentage of a given resource. The class approach explains both the *production* and *distribution* of social resources. Thus, the labor theory of value explains how material resources are created in the first place and then how they are distributed through the class structure.

Second, they define groups differently. In the stratification approach, classes have differing *amounts* of the same resource like income, sorting people into upper, middle, or lower classes. In the class approach, classes are defined by the *source* rather than amount of income. Income from property defines one class; income from labor designates another.

Third, they suggest different images of inequality. The stratification approach views inequality as a tall ladder with many steps and minute gradations of income, prestige, and power. The class approach views inequality as two qualitatively separate camps with conflicting interests.

Fourth, they differ on the reality of social classes. For the stratification approach, "classes" are arbitrary labels. For example, we could divide the lower class from the middle class at an annual household income of $25,000, but the boundary could also be $28,000 or $23,000. The number of classes and the boundaries between them are essentially arbitrary, because we are dividing the continuous variable of income. For the class approach, classes are real entities with different relations to production and sources of income. They might be more or less developed, but classes are "really out there" as opposed to being arbitrary labels.

Finally, they differ on social mobility. As we saw, the stratification approach makes many fine distinctions, so that even minor changes "count" as instances of social mobility. For the class approach, social mobility means moving from the working class to the capitalist class (or vice versa). Consequently, the class approach detects very little social mobility in a formally "open" class system.

These approaches illustrate how we can look at the same society and see very different things. The stratification lens offers one picture, and the class lens reveals another. This is not a case of "right" or "wrong" but of choosing the approach that suits the questions at hand. Having said that, the questions posed by critical sociology lead us back to Marx's class approach, while at the same time, pointing us forward to important revisions of his basic assumptions.

CONTEMPORARY CLASS ANALYSIS

The vision of a capitalist society polarized into two warring camps has not actually occurred. Updating Marx means addressing the complexity of contemporary class structure in advanced capitalist societies. Critical sociologists insist that class remains crucial; the challenge is to understand how.

Returning to source of income as the root of classes yields a five-class model. There is a class based on income from property, two classes based on combined income from property and labor, a class based on income from labor, and a class-like group defined by lack of income from either source (Anderson 1974).

At the top is a capitalist class deriving its livelihood from property. This includes real estate, raw materials, commercial property, stocks, bonds, and other financial instruments. Such property generates income in the form of rent, interest, dividends, or capital gains. Deriving a livelihood from this income makes one a capitalist, although many hold salaried positions as well. The capitalist class makes up less than 5 percent of the population. Within this group, there is marked inequality of wealth and divisions between "old" and "new" money. Nevertheless, property income sharply separates this class from the rest of the society.

Next is the small business class. It owns income-generating property, but its holdings are small, and its members also work at their business to make a living. Family farms, small shops, and entrepreneurial businesses make up this class. This "petty bourgeoisie" still plays a crucial role in developing and marketing new products. Although sharing some interests with corporate capitalists, the small business class often differs with them over trade, taxes, health care policies, and the like. At any given time, this class makes up roughly 10 to 15 percent of the labor force.

Alongside the small business class is the professional-managerial class. They also receive income from property and labor. Labor income comes from a salaried position, but additional income flows from a direct or indirect link to property. Such rewards are built into top corporate positions whose compensation is padded by fringe benefits, stock options, or bonuses underwritten by corporate profits. This is a class whose interests will be closely aligned with capitalists, because their incomes depend on the profitability of the corporate system as a whole. At any given time, this class also makes up roughly 10 to 15 percent of the labor force.

Below these intermediate classes is a large working class whose income derives from wage-labor. By this criterion, a large majority of the labor force (roughly 75 percent) is working class. Note that there is no "middle class." This category is common in everyday consciousness and political rhetoric, but it has no real place here. The term *middle class* is better seen as an ideological notion making the system appear more equal or open than it really is. Thus, many people who identify as middle class would be defined as working class in this model.

Having said that, this class is extremely heterogeneous, and its diversity is a big obstacle to class formation. This model thus subdivides this class by distinguishing goods- from service-producing jobs and white- from blue-collar jobs. These distinctions define fractions of the working class who differ in specific interests or consciousness.

The blue-collar, goods-producing fraction reflects Marx's image of an industrial proletariat. Historically high in class consciousness and organization, this fraction has been undermined by deindustrialization and the rise of a service economy. Blue-collar service jobs offer a mixed picture. Working in isolation at relatively unskilled tasks does not seem like a formula for class formation, but recent organizing among janitors and hotel service workers partially belies this expectation.

The white-collar, goods-producing sector is relatively small, and the credentials of engineers or technocrats can foster a status identity at odds with class formation. Finally, white-collar, service jobs are a large and increasing sector of the working class. Recent organizing among teachers and health care workers suggest that the collective realities of making a living can override the individual privileges of "white-collar" work. This conception of the working class includes everyone who sells their labor and recognizes varying degrees of class formation in different fractions.

Alongside these four classes is a fifth group defined by a lack of regular income from either property or labor. The chronically poor, unemployed and underemployed people, homeless populations, incarcerated people, disabled or retired workers, and homemakers hardly make up a class. But they are people whose livelihood is at risk in a capitalist society that mainly distributes income through property or labor. To have neither source of income means, at best, dependence on government programs for income substitutes.

The dichotomy of income from property or labor thus generates a five-class model that sees classes as real entities, acknowledges working-class complexity, recognizes groups outside the two main classes, but still sees one's relation to production as fundamental to the class structure of advanced capitalism.

Another revision of Marx's class categories involves contradictory class locations (Wright 1978). In this view, slightly more than half of the economically active population is in the capitalist class, the small business class, or the working class. The remainder is in contradictory locations between these classes. Such locations promote an equally contradictory class consciousness, because their occupants share some interests with both capitalists and workers.

For instance, many managers, supervisors, foremen, or administrators are in a contradictory class location between capitalists and workers. They have authority and control that makes them somewhat like capitalists, but could be fired from their jobs just like other workers. Another example is semiautonomous employees like professors and some other professionals. They have control over their work and schedule like small business owners, but are ultimately dependent on others for their employment just like other workers.

It is difficult to predict the political views and actions of people in contradictory class locations. They are like swing voters that might side with either capitalists or workers, depending on specific issues and circumstances. This model retains the importance of class location while recognizing the complexities between such locations and political interests, consciousness, and conflict.

New forms of exploitation also complicate class structure (Wright 1985). Exploitation involves a transfer of resources where one class benefits from the labor of another class. The exploitation of labor-power remains central to capitalism, but two additional types of exploitation emerge in advanced capitalism.

Skills or credentials are scarce resources that are unequally distributed. The same goes for positions of organizational power and control. People with such assets exploit people without them. Put differently, people with skills, credentials, or organizational power are "overpaid," and those without them are "underpaid."

Multiple types of exploitation further explain complexities of class formation. Thus, some workers are credentialed professionals with organizational power who benefit from two types of exploitation even though they are technically workers. We would expect they would closely identify with capitalists and the system that provides their privileges. Some workers have either skill credentials or organizational power but not both; their political interests are harder to predict. And finally, some workers have neither skill credentials nor organizational power; they have the least stake in a system that exploits them in three different ways.

These insights inform a recent study of class structure revealing that a more polarized class system has emerged in the United States over the past three decades (Perrucci and Wysong 2003, 1–40). In this model, classes emerge from the unequal distribution of "generative capital." This means any resource that can be used to generate more resources. There are four types of generative capital.

Consumption capital means income, which has become more unequally distributed during the past three decades. Investment capital means wealth, which is even more unequally distributed. Skill capital is specialized knowledge and expertise that derives from both experience and education. Social capital is "who you know"; people acquire it by joining elite networks that provide jobs, information, and influence. Each form of generative capital is unequally distributed: A few people have a lot, many people have a little, and some people have essentially none.

Classes are groups with comparable total resources across all types of capital. Having such resources creates economic, social, and political power that enables elites to pursue their interests. Others who lack such resources are preoccupied with basic struggles to survive and attain a fraction of the privileges elites take for granted.

Defining classes this way yields a "double-diamond" class structure. Imagine a small, upper diamond representing a privileged class that is roughly 20 percent of the population. Then envision a larger, lower diamond representing a working class that is the remaining 80 percent of the population. Finally, picture a narrow connection between these diamonds as one rests on top of the other.

Within the upper diamond, there is an uppermost "superclass" of owners and employers composing about 2 percent of the population with a very disproportionate share of generative capital. Below them in the upper diamond is a "credentialed class" of managers and professionals whose high levels of social and skill capital place them in the privileged class.

At the top of the lower diamond, there is a "comfort class" of people with some skill, social, and consumption capital, and perhaps modest amounts of investment capital. Below them is a much larger "contingent class" of wage earners and self-employed. Their incomes are modest, their wealth is minimal, and their employment is vulnerable to fluctuating economic conditions in a globalizing economy. At the bottom of the lower diamond is an "excluded class" of people with weak ties to the labor force.

This model emphasizes two major social classes, recognizes subdivisions within each, sees classes as intergenerationally permanent, denies the reality of a middle class, and underscores conflicting class interests (Perrucci and Wysong 2003).

This analysis also detects class polarization over the past three decades. The domestic stagflation and international competition of the 1970s threatened U.S. capitalists and their profits. They responded with deindustrialization, disinvestment, capital flight, downsizing, outsourcing, shifts from manufacturing to service jobs, shifts from full-time and permanent work to part-time and temporary work, attacks on labor unions, declining wages and benefits, privatization, and attacks on government programs and services. Each strategy illustrates conflicting interests: What capitalists did to maintain profits simultaneously undermined working-class living standards.

Marx's theory of class formation remains important for critical sociology. Neo-Marxist models update the story. Such approaches are nonetheless rather static. Class involves relations as well as structures. Fortunately, other sociological work has examined class relations and complements these models of class structure.

ENRICHING THE STORY

Class models reveal the skeletal structure of social classes, but their robust meaning only emerges with interaction. Marx anticipated class-driven interaction leading people to a collective identity, class consciousness, and political struggle. Although

U.S. history has not consistently followed this script, there have been periods of intense class struggle and interaction that are largely responsible for the right to unionize, the forty-hour workweek, decent wages and salaries, workers' pensions and health care, and many other benefits.

Class is also embodied in daily interaction and experience. Indeed, it is hard to find examples of interaction that are *not* conditioned by class. Class is "there" before we are, in differences in prenatal care across social classes. Our family provides our initial class position, which in turn influences how much education we receive, what adult roles become available to us, what types of work we do, who we marry, where we live, where we shop, how we spend our leisure time, how we respond to stresses that affect our health, what our retirement options are, and the quality and cost of the funeral service that marks our passing.

Class conditions both our experiences and how we make sense of them. What we see as possible or impossible, what we classify as desirable or undesirable, and how we interpret events as opportunities, setbacks, possibilities, or lessons are all shaped by class. Class shapes people's experiences and understandings even when they are not consciously aware of the shaping. Social life often involves a peculiar combination of class-conditioned experiences and class *un*consciousness of this fact.

Put differently, people live in taken-for-granted worlds where their class position subtly and subconsciously shapes what they see as possible in their lives. This is what is meant by habitus: class-specific, taken-for-granted, predispositions to interpret and act in the world in certain ways (Bourdieu 1977; Swartz 1997). Put still another way, classes differ not only in material resources but also in symbolic resources, cultural capital, and habitual predispositions about how to think and act.

Habitus reproduces class structure over time. If Marx's puzzle is why workers have not developed the consciousness to overthrow capitalism, Bourdieu's resolution is that the forces reproducing class are greater than those that might transform it.

Class-specific habitus predisposes some to succeed and others to fail. Through habitus, the class realities of one generation become self-fulfilling prophecies of the next. "In other words, the big structures of economic power that establish and maintain the class system *also* get inside the heads of the individuals subjected to that system" (Lemert 1997, 142; italics in original). Once inside people's heads, the prophecies fulfill themselves. "[T]he powerful work of class structures is the sneaky work of convincing those who fail that they deserve to fail as much as those who succeed believe they deserve to succeed" (Lemert 1997, 144). Even as class struggle seeks transformation of hierarchical relations, class habitus reproduces them.

The reproduction of class structure is also rooted in institutions. Education is a prime example (Perrucci and Wysong 2003, ch. 6). Mass education promised a more egalitarian society through mandatory schooling and greater access to education. Although it is true that more people receive more education with each successive generation, inequality has also increased over the same period.

The combination of more education and more inequality suggests something else is going on. Far from reducing inequality, education actually reproduces social class differences from one generation to the next. At the same time, education also legitimizes inequality by making it appear fair or equitable (Bowles and Gintis 1976).

The myth of education as the great equalizer presumes that everyone receives a similar education, but this is not so. People receive very different amounts and types of education based on their social class background. Educational inequalities mirror class inequalities and reproduce them by transmitting privileges or disadvantages from one generation to the next. Rather than being an equalizer, education is a transmission belt that ensures that most people remain in the same class position over a lifetime.

Class-differentiated education begins early. Privileged classes provide preschool experiences for their children that are beyond the reach of most families. They also send their children to private—and sometimes very exclusive—primary schools and prep schools that are well financed and staffed by highly motivated teachers, providing a rich diversity of educational experiences and individual attention. Most people send their children to public schools that cannot match these experiences. Even public school systems do not provide equal educations. The tradition of local financing based on property taxes means the money available to public school systems reflects the wealth or poverty of its community. This creates dramatic differences in funding per student between affluent, outer-ring suburbs, older, inner-ring suburbs, central cities, and economically depressed areas. There's no grand conspiracy. But it looks *as if* a conspiracy had planned an educational system every bit as unequal as the class system. It would be amazing if such a system did not reproduce the class structure.

By the time students graduate from high school (or not), differences in class, habitus, and cultural capital are ingrained. Reproduction of class structure is then passed on to higher education. It is worth remembering that almost half of high school students never go to college. They come from disadvantaged class backgrounds and are likely to remain there as they enter the job market with essentially no cultural capital.

Those who enter higher education find pronounced class differences. Elite, private, Ivy League colleges and universities are available to the wealthy. Other private institutions and well-ranked public institutions serve children of the professional-managerial and comfort classes. State universities serve children of the contingent class of wage earners and the self-employed. Community, vocational, and technical colleges function as the lowest rung of higher education and correspond to the lowest levels of class structure. The reproduction of class structure that begins in preschool is thus completed in higher education and advanced professional training (for some). At every step, education provides vastly different amounts and types of cultural capital.

The metaphor of education as a transmission belt is too mechanistic. People are active agents in the process. Many people with cultural capital also work hard to maintain class privileges, and others without cultural capital work incredibly hard to overcome class disadvantages. Many educators and institutions are sincerely dedicated to providing as much opportunity as possible. These realities "soften" the reproduction of class, but they don't eliminate it. They also sustain the ideology that education is more equitable than it could ever be under current conditions.

Although class reproduction is subtly woven into educational institutions, the legitimation function of these educational institutions is even more pernicious. There are societies in which people are simply assigned positions based on their parents' position. Wealth, poverty, or something in between is determined by birth. Such practices require legitimation, typically through religious beliefs that promise rewards in an afterlife. In formally open, class systems, it's not supposed to work that way. But it often does, as people inherit their positions through the reproduction of class. In modern societies, such outcomes are legitimated through education.

It is one thing to reproduce class structure; it is another to make it seem fair. Educational institutions do this by claiming to operate as meritocracies. In a genuine meritocracy, rewards are distributed or withheld based on merit. Unequal outcomes are acceptable in a meritocracy as long as they accurately reflect differences in merit. Educational "rewards" take various forms: grades and grade-point averages, promotion between grades, admission into advanced or honors programs, graduation, and acceptance by higher-level institutions.

Schools claim to distribute such rewards based on achieved differences in merit and not inherited differences in status. If true, unequal educational rewards are "fair" according to the principles of meritocracy and the system is legitimate. If false, such claims obscure how the system reproduces inequality. If *believed to be true,* the (false) claim about meritocracy legitimates the reproduction of class structure.

Meritocracies must meet two preconditions. First, accurate evaluation of merit requires equal opportunity. Otherwise it is very difficult to distinguish between genuine merit and unequal preparation. Thus, people with better opportunities might be rewarded for past privileges more than for merit, and people with worse opportunities might be punished for past disadvantages rather than for lack of merit. Imagine a race in which runners begin from different starting lines. If you only consider the finish line when awarding medals, you might be rewarding slower runners who ran shorter distances and penalizing faster runners who ran longer distances. The best way to discover the fastest runner is to have everyone start from the same place. Merit only becomes evident with equal opportunity. Given how preexisting class differences create unequal opportunity, there is no way schools can operate as meritocracies. Such a claim is an ideology that legitimates the reproduction of class structure.

The second precondition of a meritocracy is that it reward skills that are relevant to future performance. It would not be meritocratic to award grades in a high school geography class based on students' eye color or their position on the football team. Grades should reflect knowledge of geography. In particular classes, many dedicated teachers strive to approximate this ideal despite students' unequal preparation. But serious questions arise about general tests of cognitive skills like the SAT or ACT. A classic analysis found that their ability to predict future performance was quite weak, with many high-scoring students later falling short of expectations and low-scoring students exceeding them (Bowles and Gintis 1976). Despite their weak predictive power, such test scores are often gatekeepers for access to higher education. Used this way, they reproduce and legitimate class structure with claims of meritocratic decision making.

Looking at class-as-interaction enriches skeletal models of class-as-structure and reveals tensions between class formation and reproduction. There remain good reasons to expect class formation based on conflicting interests, collective identities, class consciousness, and political organization. There are also good reasons to expect class reproduction based on class habitus, cultural capital, daily experience, and institutional functioning. The tensions between class formation and class reproduction are at the heart of social class in the United States.

FURTHER COMPLICATIONS

Even the best models of class formation and reproduction have limitations. They work best for people rooted in the class system through an occupation. They work less well for students, homemakers, retirees, and others who have indirect or transient links to paid work.

These models also work best for conventional economic production and distribution. But they ignore other forms of socially necessary labor that escape conventional class analysis. Domestic labor is predominantly done by women in households, is not directly compensated by wages, and is crucial to societal survival. Such labor was not taken seriously until feminists challenged class theorists to recognize such labor and the people who perform it.

Finally, class models implicitly assume class is the most basic social identity and type of inequality. In some situations, this might be so. But this should be the conclusion of a careful analysis and not a starting assumption.

Here are some better starting assumptions. People have multiple identities. No single identity is necessarily more central than another. All are lived simultaneously. Each contributes to diverse inequalities. Class formation intersects with other collective identities in complex ways. Race and gender are crucial in these dynamics.

Such assumptions are the bridge leading us to consideration of race and gender in the next two chapters. For now, we conclude with one illustration of the complex intersection of class, race, and gender in advanced capitalist society.

A "pure" capitalist economy would have one large labor market where everyone competes with everyone else for all available jobs. The reality is that capitalist labor markets have long tended to subdivide into at least two sectors. Dual labor market theory provides a more realistic picture.

In this view, capitalist economies have two, largely exclusive labor markets. The primary labor market contains "good jobs." They are relatively high-paying positions with substantial benefits, meaningful opportunities for promotion, high degrees of safety and security, and intrinsically interesting work. Applicants typically require cultural capital in the form of advanced education, credentials, and skills to compete for these positions. The secondary labor market consists of less-desirable jobs that provide lower pay and few benefits. Such jobs "go nowhere," can be dangerous, temporary, or seasonal, and frequently involve boring and repetitive tasks. Less cultural capital is required to compete in this market.

Such dual markets are common in capitalism. If only one race and one gender participated in the labor force, class position and cultural capital would be the major factors steering different individuals into different labor markets.

In the actual labor force of multiracial women and men, additional dynamics come into play. Race and gender interact with class and dual labor markets. The result is that women and racial minorities are disproportionately steered into the secondary labor market, allowing white males to predominate in the primary labor market.

The broad patterns are quite similar, although the specific mechanisms differ. In the case of race, a history of racial segregation and discrimination has concentrated racial minorities at lower levels of the class structure with lesser cultural capital. The combined effects of class position and institutionalized racism effectively bar a disproportionate number of racial minorities from the primary labor market and steer them into the secondary market. The outcomes are evident in substantially higher unemployment and lower income for racial minorities. Such measures have barely changed in recent decades.

In the case of gender, women's disproportionate responsibility for domestic labor makes them less competitive for primary market jobs and full-time, continuous employment. The demands of domestic labor alone are enough to steer many women into the secondary labor force, but other mechanisms operate as well. The entrenched sex segregation in many occupations, along with more overt forms of discrimination, stereotyping, and sexual harassment also channel many women into the secondary labor force and the "pink collar" ghetto. Once again, the result is systematically lower pay, benefits, and job security for women in this market.

The same dynamics that create unfair disadvantages for minorities, women, and especially minority women create unearned opportunities for whites, men, and especially white men. This suggests that groups defined by race and gender have conflicting interests in much the same ways that social classes do. It is time to explore these issues in greater detail.

Chapter 8

The Social Construction of Race

The analysis of social class has been part of sociology from the beginning. Race is different. Although scholars like W. E. B. DuBois (1903) had crucial insights into race relations more than a hundred years ago, sociology was slow to see race as an important subject in its own right.

This gradually changed after Gunnar Myrdal's *An American Dilemma* (1944) placed racial prejudice at the forefront of public consciousness. Along with other work, it helped establish race and ethnic relations as a major subfield within sociology. Group dynamics, racial conflict, prejudice, and discrimination attracted increasing sociological attention.

What really invigorated the study of race was not academic developments but social conflict. As the civil rights movement overturned the most explicit forms of racial segregation and discrimination in the 1950s and 1960s, race became even more central in public awareness and academic study. As the movement evolved from liberal integration to black power to cultural nationalism, different understandings of race emerged. These movement-inspired analyses revealed how race was embedded in social structure.

Current sociological understandings of race thus have a dual legacy. The slowly developing academic study of race has been infused with critical insights from race-based social movements. As we will see in the next chapter, much the same can be said for the impact of the feminist movement in jump-starting sociology's understanding of gender issues.

WHAT IS RACE?

Few things seem more obvious than someone's race. As we interact with others, we unthinkingly place them within familiar racial categories. On rare occasions, someone doesn't easily fit the categories. We might regard them as odd or unusual, but we rarely use such cases to question the categories themselves.

When we "see" race like this, we are also likely to assume race is rooted in biology. The physical differences between races (skin color, facial features, eye shape, hair texture) seem so self-evident as to be beyond question. Everyday consciousness assumes these features reflect well-established biological, physiological, and genetic differences that distinguish races. Well-meaning people might struggle to avoid prejudices and stereotypes, but they are likely to see race as a biologically self-evident reality.

This is a good time to recall Peter Berger's (1963) sociological insight that things are not always what they seem. Beneath the seemingly self-evident biology of race, there are complex social, political, and cultural forces that sustain that appearance. Put differently, race is not biologically determined but rather socially constructed. This implies two seemingly contradictory things. First, racial categories are arbitrary. They have little scientific or biological foundation. They are not "real." Second, these categories nevertheless *become real* through social definitions. As W. I. Thomas noted long ago, if a situation is defined as real, it will be real in its consequences. When the definition is embedded in centuries of institutions and interactions, then race becomes as real as any social phenomenon can be. Race is an illusory biological fiction but a powerful social fact.

There are several reasons to question the biological basis of race. Human beings share almost 99 percent of our genetic composition with higher primates. Put differently, homo sapiens are only 1 to 2 percent genetically different from chimpanzees. If the genetic margin separating two species is so small, the likelihood that there will be consistent genetic differences *within* the category of homo sapiens that sort humans into genetically distinct races is highly implausible.

A second reason to doubt the biological basis of race involves the logic of categories and classification. Such logic makes sense when things fall into mutually exclusive categories based on many relevant traits. It makes less sense if there is a lot of overlap between things in supposedly separate categories. The logic is weakest when there is more individual variation within categories than the average variation between categories. And yet it is this weakest version that applies to race. On any number of physical traits, individual variations within races far exceed average differences between them. When categories persist in such situations, it is because they are based on social definitions rather than on logically compelling reasons or scientifically verifiable data.

A third reason to doubt the biological basis of race involves the history of racial typologies. Systems of racial classification have been proposed for centuries, with none of the logical consistency, cumulative advances, or increasing specificity that define scientific progress. Throughout this history, there has been major disagreement over things as basic as how many races exist. After centuries of work, the only consensus is that the very idea of distinguishing races in biological terms is not scientifically feasible.

A fourth reason to question the biological basis of race involves social and legal definitions. When Southern legislators defined people as "Negro" if one thirty-second of their ancestry was African, this was a social definition and not a biological fact. When Native American tribes use similar measures to determine who is a legitimate tribal member, this is also a social definition and not a biological fact. Because racial definitions vary by place, you can change your race by flying to Brazil where an unusually complex set of racial distinctions will define your race differently from the place you just left (Henslin 2005, 327). Racial definitions also change over time; consider "how the Irish became white" (Ignatiev 1995) in nineteenth-century U.S. history.

One final example: People sometimes defend a biological conception of race based on medical conditions. In the United States, sickle-cell anemia is considered a "black disease." In reality, a predisposition to sickle-cell anemia derives from geography and evolution and not race. In places where malaria was a big threat to human health, a few people had a natural immunity. Through natural selection, they reproduced in greater numbers. However, the same factors creating the immunity also made them susceptible to sickle-cell anemia. Thus, some but not all Africans are susceptible, and some non-Africans from Mediterranean regions and South Asia are susceptible. It is difficult to see how this qualifies as a "racial" disease (Adelman 2003).

It is not physical but social facts that make races "real." This social construction of race is a historical process. People have always noted human differences, but a new discourse of race emerged during European exploration, conquest, and colonization typically dated from the "discovery" of the "New World" in 1492. Thus, Columbus's diaries refer to the "savages" he encountered. With each subsequent encounter between European colonizers and indigenous groups, the discourse of race grew to describe these "others" in racial terms (Winant 2004).

This discourse rested on two premises. The first was that races were biological realities. The second was that races existed in a hierarchy of superiority and inferiority. In these hierarchies, whites, Europeans, or some subgroup of Europeans were inevitably located at the top of the hierarchy. Despite many variations, some races (the people doing the classifying) were always superior to others (the people being classified). The very concept of race is *racist,* because beliefs about superiority and inferiority have always been part of the concept.

The reasons are not a big mystery. European colonization was often brutal and inhumane. It contradicted many social norms, religious principles, and moral imperatives of the colonizers. It required some type of legitimation of the contradiction between values and behavior. Thus the invention of race/racism.

Colonialism only poses a moral dilemma if people are seen as equals. The social construction of race/racism defines the colonized group as inferior or subhuman. The more their humanity is denied, the more brutality becomes acceptable. Consider that few people have qualms about the slaughter and consumption of animals because they are seen as a different species. It hardly occurs to us that this requires a justification. Some versions of racism also suggest that "others" are a different species, so the moral code of the dominant group does not apply. The same logic operates in warfare; it is easier to kill people who are seen as less than human. It is no accident that the most extreme versions of racial thinking culminate in genocide, where others are not only seen as subhuman but as a threat that must be eliminated.

The social construction of race links biology, inferiority, and racism in fateful ways. Like race, racism has many variations. It can provide justifications for enslavement and genocide. It can seek to convert others who have not yet had the benefits of "civilization." It can portray "others" as innocent children requiring protection and guidance. In every version, however, a presumption of racial inferiority is central.

The social construction of race and racism was vital in legitimizing European colonization and conquest. The United States followed suit in the exploitation of African slaves, the conquest of Native peoples, and racist relations with Latino/a and Asian populations. The timing and groups were different, but the history of U.S. race relations mirrors the European model quite closely.

Although race is a biological fiction, there is a social logic to why this fiction arose and how it shapes contemporary society. The challenge of seeing race as a social construction is to balance the seeming contradiction that something arbitrary has been socially constructed into something as "real" as any social fact can be.

RACE VS. ETHNICITY

The social construction of race also becomes evident by contrasting "races" and "ethnic groups." Common sense equates race with biology and ethnicity with culture. Although the link between race and biology is problematic, the equation of ethnicity and culture is sound.

Ethnic groups are distinguished by cultural differences in language, customs, norms, values, and religious beliefs. Although their members might be geographically dispersed, ethnic groups often trace their roots to a distinctive place. Although it is culturally learned, ethnicity "feels" natural to people. Ethnocentrism is a common expression of the "naturalness" or superiority of one's group and way of doing things.

As socially constructed categories, "races" lump together many ethnic groups in the same racial category. Each of the major races typically recognized in the United States (African Americans, European Americans, Latino/a Americans, Native Americans, and Asian Americans) include multiple ethnicities. The most obvious expression of racism is the blatant division between the dominant racial group of European Americans and all other subordinate racial groups.

A subtler expression of racism is that ethnic variations within the dominant racial group are often recognized, whereas variations within subordinate racial groups are not. Thus, in both popular consciousness and much sociological work, ethnicity really means cultural variations among European Americans (Polish, Swedish, Italian, German, etc.) whereas race lumps others into broad racial categories (blacks, Hispanics, Native Americans, etc.). This practice obscures the fact that "white" is also a socially constructed race and that other races have internal ethnic differences.

A long history of unequal treatment has made these arbitrary distinctions into powerful realities. Consider the following contrasts. Members of white ethnic groups typically entered the United States voluntarily, could sometimes conceal their ethnicity, were seen as variations on a common theme of being white, were eventually pressured to assimilate, and had at least some opportunities for integration and upward mobility. Members of racial minorities, by contrast, became part of the United States involuntarily, could rarely conceal their race, were seen as fundamentally different, were subject to strict segregation, and had few opportunities for integration and upward mobility until quite recently. Such differences suggest different models of ethnic and race relations.

For white ethnic groups, the main story is assimilation. However, the melting pot image of assimilation is misleading by implying that all groups change equally as they are "melted" into something new. In reality, there has always been a hierarchy among white ethnic groups. WASPS, or white, Anglo-Saxon Protestants, have been at the top, followed by other Northern Europeans, and then Central and Southern Europeans. Assimilation has not meant blending but rather change by subordinate white ethnic groups. Consider that the United States did not create a new language through assimilation. Assimilating groups gave up native languages and adopted English. Assimilation involved a trade-off in which subordinate white ethnic groups sacrificed ethnic distinctiveness in exchange for admission into mainstream society.

Assimilation involves several stages that begin with cultural assimilation (Gordon 1964). This occurs when a newly arriving white ethnic group learns and adopts the culture of the dominant group. This is the only stage the subordinate group can control. Indeed, they might initially resist this stage, in which case assimilation will not occur. If and when they do initiate the process, control passes to the dominant group.

This is evident in the second stage of structural assimilation. This means acceptance of the subordinate group by the dominant group. Such acceptance initially occurs in secondary groups like the workplace and other public settings. It then involves accepting people as neighbors or in churches and voluntary organizations. It culminates with acceptance into primary groups like friendship networks. At each stage, the subordinate group can initiate contact, but the dominant group retains the power to accept or reject it.

Assimilation then proceeds through other stages that reflect still greater acceptance. Marital assimilation occurs when members of different groups intermarry with increasing frequency and decreasing disapproval. Identificational assimilation occurs when members of the assimilating group switch identities from their original ethnicity to their new nation. This could take generations. Immigrants might retain their Italian identity, while the next generation identifies as Italian American, and subsequent generations identify as American.

Subsequent stages include attitudinal assimilation, indicated by a reduction in prejudicial attitudes about the subordinate group. This often corresponds with behavioral assimilation, evidenced by a reduction in discrimination against members of the group. The process culminates with civic assimilation, signified by the elimination of ethnic conflict.

Although the story of assimilation seems to offer a happy ending, it is shaped by unequal power throughout. The dominant group provides the standard for what assimilation means (becoming like them), and it controls the pace. They retain their dominance because their culture becomes normative for all. The subordinate group pays the cost by relinquishing their ethnic heritage. When the costs seem worth the benefits, groups seek assimilation. Although abstract models oversimplify complex histories, this model accurately describes the assimilation of a number of white ethnic groups in the United States.

Given their different treatment, it is not surprising that the assimilationist model doesn't fit racial groups in the United States. Some insist that with enough time, racial minorities will also assimilate, but this is a dubious claim. The histories of these groups are different, the scope of discrimination is different, and resistance to assimilation has been substantial. Moreover, the persistence of distinctive racial cultures suggests that many people in these groups would not seek assimilation even if it were possible.

Such differences drew many to the model of internal colonialism to analyze racial dynamics. This model rests on an analogy between race relations within a single country and colonial relations between countries. In the analogy, the white power structure in a single country is like the colonial power, and racial minorities in that country are like colonies.

Several parallels lend credence to the analogy. Both relationships begin with forced contact, because colonial powers and white power structures use coercion to establish the relationship in the first place. Coercion might be resisted, but the power imbalance has allowed colonial powers and white power structures to retain dominance for centuries.

A second parallel involves cultural domination. The beliefs and practices of the colonized group or the racial minority are denigrated as primitive or uncivilized. Sometimes there are efforts to convert the subordinate group to the culture of the dominant group, but in all cases the dominant group attempts to undermine the culture of the subordinate group.

Political control is a third parallel. In the colonial situation, extensive staffs of governors and administrators were sent to the colony to run its political affairs on behalf of the colonizing power. With internal colonialism, the dominant group uses both formal and informal political mechanisms to ensure a similar degree of control by the white power structure. The underrepresentation of racial minorities in positions of political power is the tip of the iceberg of political control by the dominant group.

Perhaps the most important parallel involves economic exploitation. This is the driving motive of colonial relations, whether the resources involve cheap labor, raw materials, or commodity markets. With internal colonialism, the role of racial minorities as a secondary labor force with lower pay, fewer benefits, and higher unemployment is merely one indicator of the economic exploitation that is central to this relationship.

Both traditional and internal colonialism create institutional discrimination, as social organizations and practices are built on discriminatory principles. This creates racial inequalities and racially coded practices not just in the economy and polity, but also in housing, education, health care, and criminal justice.

A final parallel is racist legitimation. Systematic beliefs about the inferiority of the subordinate group accompany both forms of colonialism. These beliefs seek to legitimate unequal treatment. At their most powerful, such racist legitimations make colonial domination seem logical, natural, and even beneficial for subordinate groups.

No analogy is perfect, but the history of U.S. race relations more closely approximates internal colonialism than assimilationist integration. What the colonial model underscores is that race relations are rooted in conflicting interests between dominant and subordinate groups. Dominant groups who benefit have a vested interest in maintaining such relations; subordinate groups who pay the price of these relations can be expected to change them if possible.

The question of group interests requires a closer look. The dominant group is really a white power structure of elites who make economic, political, and cultural decisions with far-reaching consequences. This group most clearly benefits from exploitative race relations. The subordinate group refers to racial minorities disproportionately located toward the bottom of class and other hierarchies of inequality. This group most clearly pays the price of racial oppression.

What is less clear are the interests of "ordinary whites." They belong to the dominant racial group but are not in positions of institutional power and do not receive the same material benefits from institutional racism that dominant whites do. This group could define its interests in rather different ways.

On the one hand, ordinary whites may identify with their race. This links them to dominant whites of the same race but of a different class and distances them from racial minorities with whom they might share similar class positions. Historically, this identification allowed even poor whites to claim status on the basis of race; no matter how economically deprived they were, they were still white in a society where that meant a great deal. Ordinary whites can thus derive a social-psychological benefit from their racial identity regardless of material circumstances. But the benefits are more than psychological. Ordinary whites might also derive material benefits from discrimination against minorities if it expands their opportunities at the expense of minorities. By this logic, ordinary whites might see their interests in alignment with powerful whites despite their class differences.

On the other hand, ordinary whites might identify with their class position, which would distance them from powerful whites and align them more closely with racial minorities. This suggests a class alliance across racial lines in which the material similarities of working-class whites and minorities trump racial differences. Such an alliance could challenge racial discrimination, and there is a logic for doing so. Where racial discrimination is high, it allows employers to use a divide-and-conquer strategy that ultimately undermines living standards for both whites and racial minorities (Reich 1981). Racial discrimination thus hurts minorities directly and ordinary whites indirectly. In this scenario, the collective self-interest of ordinary whites is to align with racial minorities and oppose racial discrimination.

The colonial model remains an imperfect analogy, but it frames important questions about the future of race relations. Even without clear answers, it sensitizes us to how group interests shape the social construction of race.

FORMS OF DISCRIMINATION

The colonial model offers a big picture of race relations that rests on many small episodes of discrimination. It is these practices, enacted on a daily basis, that sustain the social construction of race.

Discrimination ranges across many institutions and social arenas. It obviously includes the economy, employment, and political representation. It also includes differences in health, mortality, and life expectancy as a result of differential access to physical and mental health services. It includes deeply rooted patterns of residential segregation that create other problems like unequal access to education. It includes very different probabilities of becoming caught up in the criminal justice system. The effects of discrimination are cumulative, as initial disadvantages become larger inequities over time. Acts of discrimination are the building blocks of racial inequality.

The traditional view of discrimination is that prejudicial attitudes cause discriminatory behavior (Feagin and Feagin 1978). The term *prejudice* means to "prejudge" people on the basis of their group identity. Such judgments often involve negative stereotypes about an entire category of people that are attributed to all its members.

The discrimination that results from prejudice can be explicit, as when people engage in name-calling, racist behavior, or hate crimes. But it can also be subtle or covert. If someone is advertising a job or an apartment and the "wrong" applicant appears, that applicant might be told that the job has been filled or the apartment rented. When the "right" applicant comes along, the apartment or job suddenly becomes available again. In this case, intentional harm is done to someone who might not be aware that they have been the victim of discrimination. Explicit discrimination grabs headlines, but subtle, covert forms are more common and often go undetected. Indeed, it is impossible to know the full extent of discrimination, because much of it is hidden in this fashion. The common thread is a prejudicial attitude. In the traditional model, discrimination occurs when "evil motives" are translated into action.

This model implies that reducing prejudice reduces discrimination. This was part of the logic behind social policies and court decisions favoring integration. It was thought that, with more social contact between groups, people would rethink their prejudices and treat others as individuals and not stereotypes. If prejudice melted away, discrimination would, too. Although the logic seems plausible, there's a problem. By many measures, prejudice in the United States has declined, but racial discrimination has not shown a corresponding reduction.

This prompted a closer look at the traditional view. It became clear that prejudice alone might not lead to discrimination. Prejudiced people need the power to act on prejudice if it is to become discrimination. It also became more evident that discrimination can occur without prejudice. Thus, an employer might have no prejudice against certain people but still refuse to hire them out of a belief that it would drive customers away.

More generally, discrimination limits opportunities for "others" and increases them for discriminators. In such cases, discrimination simply flows from group interest without prejudice. Such discrimination without an "evil motive" can also be an unintentional by-product of institutional policies. As the limits of the traditional model became more evident, sociologists developed another way of thinking about what causes discrimination.

The result was the institutional model in which organizational practices replace prejudice as the major cause of discrimination (Feagin and Feagin 1978). The idea is that social institutions routinely discriminate against many people. In contrast to the traditional model, the institutional model sees discrimination as a normal, routine, chronic outcome rather than a sporadic one. It recognizes that most discrimination is subtle or covert, although overt institutional discrimination still happens, too. It sees discrimination as something that affects thousands if not millions of people, because it is embedded in major social institutions like the criminal justice system or the labor market. Finally, institutional discrimination can be either intentional or unintentional.

Intentional institutional discrimination occurs when there is a conscious goal of unequal treatment. It might be rooted in prejudice, racism, group interest, or some other motive. As with the traditional model, there is an "evil motive" behind such action. Unlike the traditional model, it is not individuals but large organizations that enact these behaviors. In systems of apartheid or legalized segregation, discriminatory purposes are officially proclaimed.

When segregation becomes illegal, intentions to discriminate might no longer be publicly stated but can continue to shape institutional functioning. The redlining of certain neighborhoods as poor credit risks is one example. The use of racial profiling in police practices is another example. The purging of voter registration lists is a third example of intentional, institutional discrimination (Moore 2001). While rarer hate crimes grab headlines, more routine institutional discrimination affects many more people on a daily basis.

Institutional discrimination can also be unintentional. This is indicated by effects rather than motives. Here, we must work backward from discriminatory outcomes to identify the practice or policy that produced them. An example is "side-effect" discrimination that occurs as an unintended by-product of some other practice. Imagine a university that uses an entrance exam to screen applicants. Assume the exam contains no subtle racial biases. Nonetheless, if applicants have been unequally prepared by previous schooling to perform well on this exam, it will produce discriminatory outcomes despite the best of intentions.

A related example is "past-in-present" discrimination where a current practice unwittingly perpetuates prior discrimination. Consider a layoff policy based on seniority. This is not discriminatory in itself. But to whatever extent racial minorities or women have shorter or more episodic work histories as a result of past discrimination, implementing layoffs by seniority will benefit white males and harm minorities and women despite good intentions.

Unintentional discrimination harms many but remains elusive, because it cannot be traced back to a specific person or group with evil motives. In a final twist, it is also possible for "sophisticated racists" who *do* have evil motives to use practices that do not *appear* to intentionally discriminate, knowing that such practices are difficult to identify (Feagin and Feagin 1978).

According to the traditional model, reducing discrimination requires reducing prejudice. According to the institutional model, reducing discrimination requires changing institutions. Whereas the traditional model is "optimistic" that increased social contact will reduce prejudice and discrimination, the institutional model is "pessimistic" that institutions will not simply evolve into less discriminatory behavior. Indeed, the institutional model suggests that if nothing is done, discrimination will continue indefinitely, because institutions are self-perpetuating and because some groups benefit from discriminatory practices.

This is the logic behind affirmative action. It assumes that discrimination will continue unless affirmative action is taken to change the practices that produce it. As a policy, most affirmative action programs involve voluntary efforts to increase the diversity of a pool of qualified applicants. Such policies target informal practices whereby people tend to recruit, hire, or admit people like themselves. By creating policies that require looking beyond familiar social circles when recruiting applicants, affirmative action programs have made modest contributions to reducing discriminatory outcomes.

The persistence of racial inequality in the United States has also prompted a rethinking of the traditional focus on individual prejudice. New research has led one analyst to conclude that in the post–civil rights era, we have entered a time of "racism without racists" (Bonilla-Silva 2003). This argument downplays prejudicial attitudes by suggesting that racism rests on a material foundation of group interests and white privilege. Racism persists because whites derive substantial material benefits from it. Thus, even when whites do not have stereotypical views of minorities, they often perpetuate racism in ways that obscure its victims and beneficiaries.

Where traditional prejudice often assumed biological differences, "color-blind racism" is a more complex racial ideology emphasizing cultural differences. Four distinct frames express color-blind racism (Bonilla-Silva 2003). "Abstract liberalism" uses familiar political discourse about individual rights and equal opportunity to subtly deny structural barriers and implicitly blame victims. "Naturalism" suggests that segregation reflects freely chosen preferences of people to associate with others like them. "Cultural racism" identifies supposedly defective values, beliefs, and practices within minority cultures that are responsible for their lack of progress. Finally, "minimizing racism" acknowledges lingering problems of discrimination while emphasizing how much progress has been made. The implication is that such problems no longer require systemic solutions.

None of these frames sound overtly racist. Indeed, they sound quite reasonable by comparison. They still function, however, as an ideology legitimizing racial inequality. Color-blind racism denies or minimizes institutional barriers and uses the rhetoric of individual opportunity and cultural differences to blame minorities and excuse whites for racial inequality. The emergence of "racism without racists" illustrates how racial meanings and definitions change over time. To analyze such changes, we need to revisit the idea that race is socially constructed.

RACIAL FORMATION

The theory of racial formation sees the social construction of race as a contested process of ongoing conflict (Omi and Winant 1994; Winant 1994, 2004). "[R]ace can be defined as a *concept that signifies and symbolizes socio-political conflicts and interests in reference to different types of human bodies*" (Winant 2004, 155; italics in original). The theory of racial formation also insists on the "reality" of race despite its origins as a social construction.

The challenge is to understand the simultaneous "arbitrariness" and "reality" of race. It arises once race is decoupled from biology. This has often led social scientists to reduce race to some other kind of group and transpose their experiences onto races. This problematic response implies that if race is not about biology, then it is not about anything real. The theory of racial formation maintains that race is not about biology, but it *is* still about something very real. That reality, moreover, needs to be understood on its own terms and not reduced to something else.

One way mainstream perspectives have denied the reality of race is by equating it with ethnicity and using the ethnicity paradigm to analyze race relations. This inevitably turns the discussion back to assimilation. Despite the different histories of racial minorities and white ethnics in the United States, some maintain that racial minorities will eventually undergo the same assimilation as white ethnic groups in earlier decades and centuries. Rather than analyzing race on its own terms, this substitutes the history of ethnic assimilation as a goal for race relations.

This reduction of race to ethnicity is problematic, because it denies the unique features of racial formation (Omi and Winant 1994). It falsely transposes white experience onto nonwhites. It denies ethnic variations within racial groups by equating broad racial categories ("African American") with specific white ethnicities ("Italian"). The ethnicity paradigm also advocates individualistic solutions like upward mobility. The reduction of race to ethnicity thus obscures the distinctiveness of racial oppression and proposes unachievable or undesirable solutions to racial conflict.

An alternative is the class paradigm. This approach reduces race to class or sees the real meaning of race through a class lens. The class paradigm underscores how members of racial minorities are disproportionately located in the working class or lower socioeconomic levels. The logic is that their fates are determined more by their class position than by their racial identity. Moreover, race has reinforced class exploitation by using racial minorities as a secondary labor force and by dividing workers along racial lines. In this paradigm, race is important for its role in a more fundamental set of class dynamics.

Although it illuminates intersections of race and class, this paradigm is not sufficient for understanding racial formation on its own terms. It simply assumes class is fundamental and race is secondary. Moreover, the equation of racial minorities with only one class oversimplifies race and implies that middle- or upper-class minorities face no racial barriers. "It would be more accurate to say that race and class are competing modalities by which social actors may be organized" (Omi and Winant 1994, 32). If so, the class model with its reduction of race to class is insufficient.

A third alternative is the nation paradigm or the internal colonialism model discussed earlier. As we saw, this model emphasizes differences between the assimilationist history of white ethnic groups and the quasi-colonial status of racial minorities. The metaphor of colonial relations has much to tell us about the history of race relations within the United States. As a viable model of contemporary racial formation, however, it has serious limitations.

In a postcolonial world of global mobility, equating races with geographically bounded nations is an increasingly implausible way to think about race relations. There is substantially more interracial contact in contemporary, racially diverse societies than in classic colonial relations. Finally, the nation paradigm obscures increasingly important class differences among minorities by reducing them to a homogeneous, cultural nationality. Although more instructive than the ethnicity and class paradigms, this one also falls short as a way to understand racial formation.

The problem is that each paradigm—ethnicity, class, and nation—reduces race to something else. Each fails to see race on its own terms. The solution is to move beyond these paradigms to a model that sees race as an independently constructed social reality.

This means seeing racial formation as a process in which social, economic, and political forces determine the meaning of racial categories in a given historical context. To emphasize the importance of process, the term *racialization* is coined (Omi and Winant 1994) to refer to the extension of racial meanings to relationships that were previously not classified in such terms.

Consider slavery. Although U.S. planters used African Americans as slave labor for centuries, the practice did not originate for racial reasons. It derived from the economic realities of plantation agriculture. In order to be profitable, such agriculture requires the cheapest possible labor. Planters first used white indentured servants from Europe and then captured Native Americans (Geschwender 1978). Neither group worked out well in the long run. Importing African slave labor gradually emerged as a later alternative in the search for cheap labor. Once the practice was institutionalized, slavery was racialized through racist beliefs and legitimations to justify the use of black slave labor by white, "God-fearing" Christians. Slavery became racialized over time. In other words, "we know that racism did not create slavery, but that slavery created racism" (Winant 2004, 84).

Institutions, practices, and beliefs become "raced" when they are shaped and understood through racial categories. Consider how many urban social problems have become "raced," as popular consciousness and media representations link race with poverty, welfare, gangs, drugs, and crime. These issues involve more whites than nonwhites, but their racialized nature becomes a self-fulfilling prophecy. Thus, people act on racialized beliefs about crime and who commits it, leading to highly disproportionate numbers of racial minorities being suspected, arrested, convicted, and incarcerated for "raced" definitions of crime. The differential penalties for crack cocaine used by minorities and powder cocaine favored by whites is one of the more blatant examples of such racialization.

The most important raced institution is the state. In a racially divided society, the state racializes many social dynamics. "For most of U.S. history, the state's main objective in its racial policy was repression and exclusion" (Omi and Winant 1994, 81). It commenced with the Naturalization Act of 1790 that limited citizenship to free, white immigrants. The pattern continued throughout the nineteenth century as racialized policies of repression and exclusion regulated race relations. A more recent example of state power is the creation of the category "Hispanic" in 1980, racializing a new group of people and embedding the category in state policies, practices, and institutions. States and racial formation are thus closely intertwined.

Racial formation is not just about top-down power. When a collective identity is constructed and used to dominate people, that same identity will eventually become a rallying point for resistance. Whether the identity involves race, ethnicity, gender, nationality, or sexuality, domination provokes resistance. Thus, racial formation is a contested process. People fight back, and even powerful elites cannot completely control racial formation for long. It is more accurate to see racial formation—and the social construction of race more generally—as an ongoing struggle over what race means. Authorities use race to subordinate groups, and racially defined groups use it to resist subordination.

The contested quality of racial formation is evident in recent racial politics. On the eve of the civil rights movement of the 1950s and 1960s, racial formation took the form of domination. White power was the norm, backed up by coercion, segregation, exclusion, and violence. In this period, racial formation was a top-down affair, because of the overwhelming power of whites. Collective resistance appeared futile.

Social changes nevertheless created opportunities to contest racial formation. The disruptions of World War II, the partial integration of the armed forces, the mechanization of Southern agriculture, and migration from the rural South to the urban North all undermined racial domination. When the civil rights movement appeared in the 1950s, it echoed the ethnicity paradigm with themes of individualism, opportunity, and integration. That such a modest agenda provoked such a ferocious backlash is revealing. Simply asking for what whites took for granted amounted to an almost revolutionary challenge to racial domination.

The movement soon transcended the ethnicity paradigm, in part because of the resistance it encountered to its integrationist goals. But the shift was also sparked by "the rearticulation of black collective subjectivity" (Omi and Winant 1994, 98). In other words, black activists made the redefinition of racial identity a central goal. The movement *made* racial formation a two-way street by challenging static notions of race and racial hierarchy. In effect, activists reclaimed the meaning of race from a white power structure and made it their own.

These events transformed the civil rights movement. Activists adopted multiple racial paradigms and diverse political strategies. "Entrists" argued that strategic participation in elections and mainstream institutions could transform the state. Socialists tried to build class alliances across racial lines and link struggles against racism and capitalism. Nationalists encouraged a separatist response of institution-building and cultural pride within minority communities. None met with complete success. The entrist, socialist, and nationalist strategies had the same shortcomings as the ethnicity, class, and nation paradigms on which they were based. Each reduced race to something else and missed the complexity of racial formation. This activism nevertheless shattered older understandings of race and put racial formation center stage (Omi and Winant 1994).

As the movement became more complex, so did the response of the raced state. In some instances, it brutally repressed militant leaders and groups that challenged its authority. More broadly, the state shifted from racial domination to racial hegemony. This meant incorporating oppositional challenges in ways that defused their transformative potential. "Under hegemonic conditions, opposition and difference are not repressed, excluded, or silenced (at least not primarily). Rather, they are inserted, often after suitable modification, within a 'modern' (or perhaps 'postmodern') social order" (Winant 1994, 29). Although hegemony might be less violent than outright domination, it amounts to a more complex system of racial control.

Racial hegemony has sparked competing racial projects on both sides. On the reactionary side, the far right still equates race with biology and advocates violence to prevent all forms of "race mixing." The new right translates old-fashioned racism into code words that are not explicitly racist but nonetheless trigger racist attitudes and actions among those who know the code. The neoconservative right uses egalitarian language to advocate individualism and reject group-oriented solutions. They use the rhetoric of a color-blind society while ignoring the historical legacy of being a color-conscious society. This is the most sophisticated defense of the white power structure. It uses familiar, liberal ideas to argue for illiberal ends. It exemplifies "racism without racists" advocating "color-blind racism" (Bonilla-Silva 2003).

On the progressive side, pragmatic liberalism appeals to group identities to mobilize political support for racially progressive policies, including affirmative action. It advocates pluralism and tolerance and attempts a difficult balancing act between advancing minority rights and maintaining social peace. Finally, radical democrats seek full acceptance of racial difference and identities in the name of autonomy. They seek democratization of the state and redistributive policies to foster racial equality (Winant 1994).

Racial formation is thus a dynamic, contested set of social and political meanings. The current diversity of racial politics—consisting of at least five distinct and competing racial projects—testifies to the fluidity of racial formation and the social construction of race.

THE CONSTRUCTION OF WHITENESS

It is intriguing that whites attribute "race" to "people of color" but don't see "white" as a "color." It's as if race applies to people who differ from the norm but not the group that is the norm. Given this, it is important to turn the microscope back on the dominant group and its construction of whiteness.

Like other socially constructed racial categories, whiteness emerged historically. Consider how "the Irish became white" over decades of conflict and eventual assimilation in the United States. More pointedly, this is the story of "how the Catholic Irish, an oppressed race in Ireland, became part of an oppressing race in America" (Ignatiev 1995, 1). When Irish immigrants first arrived in the United States, they were perceived as an inferior race by Anglo-Saxon powers on both sides of the Atlantic. However, rather than joining with other subordinate races, the Irish distanced themselves from minorities and aligned with whites. They pursued the classic assimilationist trade-off: "In becoming white the Irish ceased to be Green" (Ignatiev 1995, 3). This suggests that assimilation means moving toward the dominant group and away from minorities, because the dominant group is defined precisely by its distance from racial minorities. Until a group made both moves, assimilation was unlikely.

The Irish example fits a broader template of how whiteness was created through an amalgamation of initially diverse ethnicities. This history falls into three periods (Jacobson 1998, 13–14). From the founding of the country into the mid-nineteenth century, citizenship was confined to "free white" immigrants, implicitly meaning Anglo-Saxon and sometimes other Northern European peoples. From the mid-nineteenth century to the early twentieth century, immigration from Southern, Central, and Eastern Europe challenged the equation of whiteness and Northern European descent. During this period, a complex racial politics initially defined these immigrants as inferior races at the same time that they sought a broadening of the definition of "white" to include them. It has only been since the 1920s that ethnic differences were downplayed and a more generic white identity was forged. This period "redrew the dominant racial configuration along the strict, binary line of white and black, creating Caucasians where before had been so many Celts, Hebrews, Teutons, Mediterraneans, and Slavs" (Jacobson 1998, 14).

By mid-twentieth century, whiteness became the dominant racial norm. This proved short lived, as "it is no longer possible to assume a 'normalized' whiteness, whose invisibility and relatively monolithic character signify immunity from political or cultural challenge" (Winant 2004, 50). As race-based social movements recast their own racial subjectivity, white identity also became more self-conscious.

As white dominance was challenged, it triggered "grievances of the privileged." Some whites claimed they were under attack "simply for their race." Others decried a world in which minorities seemed to get advantages withheld from whites through "reverse discrimination." Still other whites lamented the lack of a distinct and vivid white culture they could identify with just as other races identified with theirs. Such defensive responses imply that although whites are still dominant, such dominance can no longer be taken for granted.

These responses also belie the ongoing privileges of the dominant group. White privilege means that despite recent challenges to the racial order, it continues to be organized in ways that benefit the dominant group. Such privilege is often invisible to those who benefit, while being highly visible to those who pay the price.

This is nicely captured in Peggy McIntosh's (2005) efforts to teach about male privilege in women's studies courses. Her female students quickly grasped the concept and readily supplied examples. Her male students conceded that women faced certain disadvantages but denied their male privilege. To understand this denial, McIntosh examined her own dual status as a white woman. As a woman, she could readily see male privilege. As a white, she had difficulty seeing her racial privilege, just as men had difficulty seeing male privilege. The broader pattern is that privileged groups rarely recognize their own privileges and perceive any challenge to them as victimization. Such complaints are not simply disingenuous; they reflect a real inability to see how whiteness and maleness continue conferring privileges even in a social order undergoing challenge and reformulation.

These privileges come in two categories. "Unearned advantages" are "positive" privileges that should not be abolished but made available to all. The privilege of not being a crime suspect simply on the basis of one's race is an unearned advantage for whites that should ideally be an unearned entitlement for all. "Conferred dominance" involves "negative" privileges that need to be abolished to create racial equality. Discrimination that benefits dominant groups at the expense of subordinate ones fits this type; it should be abolished in any society seeking racial equality (McIntosh 2005).

These are now the goals of a "new abolitionist racial project." Proponents of this movement identify white privilege as the lynchpin of white supremacy and see rejection of privilege by whites as essential to creating a just racial order. Advocates put a positive spin on the epithet "race traitor" by countering that "treason to whiteness is loyalty to humanity" (Winant 2004, 63). As this racial project unfolds alongside others described earlier, it is difficult to deny that we are in a period of highly contested racial formation.

Understanding race requires looking beyond taken-for-granted appearances. It also requires a multilayered analysis of domination. Critical sociology is tailor-made for both tasks. It illuminates both the social construction of race and the challenges seeking to deconstruct racial hierarchies in the name of a more egalitarian society.

Chapter 9

Gendered Selves and Worlds

Gender bias is the oldest form of social inequality. It exists in all societies, including those in which class and race inequality have been minimal or nonexistent. Indeed, gender inequality might have provided the model for later inequalities of class and race.

A challenge in analyzing gender is separating universals from variations. Here are two universals: Every society has a gender division of labor. In no society for which there is reliable data have women been the dominant group. Here are two variations: The tasks assigned to women and men have differed from one society or historical period to another. The degree of gender inequality has differed greatly from near equality to extreme inequality.

A further challenge in studying gender concerns the nature-nurture question. Sex differences in size, strength, and ability to reproduce are important biological realities. But differences in size and strength are averages; some women are bigger and stronger than some men, despite the average difference. Moreover, physical differences are increasingly insignificant when compared with social power. Lots of big, strong people find themselves in subordinate positions compared with dominant group members who are smaller or physically weaker.

Differences in reproductive biology appear to be the basis of gender inequality, but appearances can be deceiving. Women's reproductive capacity has been the core of their power in some societies and the basis of their enslavement in others. We must be careful in interpreting "biological" realities, because social definitions and cultural meanings are much more important. Like race, gender is socially constructed, despite its seemingly biological basis.

In contrast to racial or class inequality, gender inequality involves intimate relations between individual members of dominant and subordinate groups. Stratification usually means segregation. Indeed, integration was once thought to be a solution to racial inequality. Gender inequality shows that close interpersonal bonds can coexist with substantial differences in group power.

The complexities of gender are explored through several paths in this chapter. First, we will look at variable meanings of gender across time and space. Second, we will analyze contemporary gender relations at the micro and macro levels. Third, we will review leading feminist perspectives on gender. Finally, we will review some recent sociological understandings of gender in social life.

A LITTLE HISTORY

Contemporary images of marriage are highly romanticized. A decidedly different view can be found in a provocative if speculative history of social evolution that views marriage as a "world-historical defeat" for the female sex (Engels 1985). The reasons involve the connections among gender, family, property, and the state.

Friedrich Engels hypothesized that the earliest human societies did not have private property, rigidly defined families, or formal political authority. They allowed unregulated sexual relations and indiscriminate mating. Jealousy and possessiveness were unknown. Because paternity was uncertain, descent was traced matrilineally, and women had status and power as a result.

As societies produced a surplus, everything changed. Private property was invented. Class systems developed. States emerged to protect wealth. More restrictive forms of marriage arose to restrict female sexuality. It was only through such restrictions that men could establish paternity and transmit property to their legitimate offspring. The new standard of female monogamy was accompanied by possessiveness and jealousy, as women became another form of property.

The "world-historical defeat" of the female sex was a shift from sexual permissiveness between equals to patriarchal domination between unequals. Although some of these speculations about early societies are dubious, Engels was correct that many were more sexually permissive and egalitarian than later societies. Moreover, although property inheritance is merely one factor in social evolution, the link between controlling private property and restricting female sexuality remains a provocative hypothesis about the social construction of gender.

A more empirically rigorous analysis shows that social evolution moved from hunting and gathering societies to simple and advanced horticultural societies, to pastoral and agrarian societies, and finally to early industrial and postindustrial societies (Chafetz 1984). In the first two, sex stratification is quite low. It increases to very high in pastoral and agrarian societies and remains high in early industrial societies. Only in postindustrial societies does it decrease somewhat. Echoing Engels, this analysis finds the greatest sex equality is in the earliest human societies and inequality increases with social evolution. Unlike Engels, the analysis finds that there is some progress toward equality in postindustrial society.

Variation in sex stratification over time is due to several factors. Higher degrees of gender differentiation (where men and women are seen as complete opposites) are associated with higher degrees of sex stratification. Ideological or religious support for sex inequality is also associated with higher degrees of sex stratification.

The most important factors are the organization of work and family. Family structure involves lineality, locality, and the division of household labor. Work organization involves the sexual division of labor, especially who performs the most highly valued productive activities. Work organization also involves how easily workers can be replaced, the "attention span" of work, the degree of sex segregation, and ownership and control of the means and products of production.

The most succinct conclusion is that the degree of sex stratification depends on the extent to which women contribute to producing valued social resources and control the output of such production. When they do both, sex stratification is quite low. Whey they do neither to any significant extent, sex stratification is quite high. Because women's capacity to do either depends on the organization of work and family, these institutions are largely responsible for variations in sex stratification.

The contemporary lesson is twofold. Increasing sex equality in postindustrial society will require changes in work organization and family structure. Work issues include pay equity, affirmative action, comparable worth, reducing sex discrimination and segregation, and increasing participation in valued work. Family issues include fertility control, reproductive rights, child care, and household divisions of labor. When changes in both arenas enhance women's opportunity to produce and control valued social resources, sex equality will increase. Until then, progress will be difficult.

The history of industrialization in the United States exemplifies these generalizations and illuminates contemporary gender arrangements. Changes in the economic functions of the family have had a major impact on the social construction of gender.

In the period before industrialization, the family was a unit of production (Strasser 1982). From colonial times to the mid-nineteenth century, families produced most of what they needed and consumed most of what they produced. They were relatively self-sufficient. Everyone in the family had productive roles and made essential contributions. Power differences and divisions of labor certainly existed, but they were mitigated by the family's dependence on everyone's productive contribution.

Industrialization undermined family production. It brought larger, more efficient units of production outside the household in workshops, plants, factories, and offices. It shifted productive work from within to outside the family. It separated home from workplace. It replaced subsistence production with an economic market and increased the demand for wage-labor.

As families lost their productive function, they acquired another economic function. They became responsible for the reproduction of labor-power needed by an industrializing economy. This was literally true, because families raised the next generation of workers, often with the assistance of "factory schools" that trained children for industrial labor. It was also figuratively true on a daily basis. Separated from harsh workplaces, the family became a retreat where workers could rest and replenish before returning to work. Families were still vital to economic production, but their output was no longer subsistence goods but labor-power itself.

The reproduction of labor-power remained crucial into the early twentieth century. After World War I, mass production and new technology slowed the demand for labor and increased the need for markets. Families acquired a third economic function as units of consumption. Houses, cars, appliances, furniture, clothing, durable goods, and food became commodities marketed to families. The family thus went full circle from a unit of production to reproducing labor-power to a unit of consumption.

Industrialization is often equated with progress, but it had contradictory and even negative impacts on families and family members. Industrialization meant "downward mobility" for men, even as they remained the dominant gender. When productive work moved outside the home, men went from self-employed to someone else's employee. The 1870 census was the first to find more people working for others than for themselves; it was a turning point from self-employment to wage-labor. Working for someone else was a status "demotion" that made workers highly vulnerable to circumstances beyond their control.

Changes for women were even more dramatic. Many women lost their productive roles in the household. They continued to work extremely hard within households, but the social definition of this work changed from productive labor to domestic labor, or housework. Consistent with Janet Chafetz's cross-cultural analysis, when women were no longer responsible for the production of socially valued resources, their status declined and gender inequality increased. Though industrialization eventually simplified domestic labor, it devalued the work and the people who did it.

Children underwent a parallel status decline, as their productive role also evaporated. Industrialization converted women and children from productive economic assets into dependent economic liabilities. Industrialization decentered the family and undermined the productive roles of a bygone era.

These changes created "separate spheres." The public sphere involved productive work and commercial relations, and the private sphere contained family life and emotional relations. Each acquired meaning from its contrast with the other. As a "haven in a heartless world" (Lasch 1977), home and family were romanticized as emotional, nurturant, and supportive. They contrasted sharply with work and marketplace, stereotyped as cold, rational, and competitive arenas shaped by the survival of the fittest. Because men and women prevailed in separate spheres, this reinforced very different gender roles. Masculinity was equated with the cold, competitive, rational traits of the public sphere, and femininity was equated with the warm, supportive, emotional traits of the private sphere. The history of industrialization shows that our gender stereotypes have little to do with nature and much to do with historical circumstances and cultural definitions (Strasser 1982).

A historical lens on gender is essential. Whereas common sense sees biological determinism, a historical perspective reveals the social construction of gender.

THE SEX/GENDER SYSTEM

Sociologists came late to the study of gender. Through the 1960s, gender was submerged in family sociology and analyzed by a functionalist approach that endorsed conventional gender arrangements. A rare exception was Helen Hacker's (1951) discussion of "women as a minority group." It was the revival of the feminist movement in the later 1960s that placed gender on the sociological agenda.

Sociologists struggled to overcome their own gendered preconceptions. Consider the problematic term *sex role* that was popular in the 1970s. Because *sex* refers to biology, the term *sex roles* implies that gender is biologically determined. The term *role* is also problematic, because it comes from functionalism, where roles are defined as reciprocal and complementary expectations about people's behavior. To analyze gender as a role presumes that gender relations are automatically harmonious and complementary. Even common sense suggests otherwise.

These problems led to a new concept: the *sex/gender system. Sex* refers to biological differences of genitalia, reproduction, and secondary sex characteristics. *Gender* refers to culturally learned differences. *System* refers to all the social mechanisms that link cultural notions about gender to biological sex differences and make gender a major axis of social structure. Put differently, the sex/gender system links cultural notions about femininity and masculinity to female and male bodies. Although recognizing biology, this concept takes a social constructionist approach to gender as primarily determined by social, historical, and cultural factors.

A constructionist view can even apply to "biological" sexuality. Consider the sexual diversity among human beings. Some people are born with ambiguous genitalia. Some people have an identity different from what their body indicates. Some people are attracted to members of the same sex, or to both sexes. This diversity is obscured by a powerful cultural norm that insists that there are two—and only two—"opposite" and heterosexual sexes. The power of this cultural norm is evident every time an infant's genitalia are surgically altered or whenever forms of sexual desire are defined as deviant or normative. Even at the level of biology, we are more diverse than our cultural categories recognize. It is an exercise of social power when such dualistic categories trump the messier matters of biology.

Although it is intriguing to ponder how sex is socially constructed, it is abundantly evident that gender is so constructed. In our society, culture creates, emphasizes, or exaggerates gender differences. Consider simple examples from everyday language. Casual references to the "opposite sex" imply sexes are mutually exclusive, with no common characteristics. References to "male" and "female" hormones obscure the fact that we all have the same hormones (in differing proportions). Popular culture suggests that women and men are from different planets, because their communication styles are so different. You can easily construct your own examples from all the advertising that exaggerates gender differences between presumably opposite sexes.

These dynamics even distort the science of sex and gender. Most research on sex differences finds average group differences. Less often reported, however, is the range of variation within each group. Typically, the variation within male or female scores is far greater than the average difference between them. When graphed, the results form two bell curves almost superimposed on each other. The small distance between the peaks of each curve reflects average difference between groups, and the extensive overlap of the curves from one tail to the other indicates major similarities. So why do we interpret such findings as "proving" difference rather than similarity? It would seem that the cultural emphasis on difference even intrudes on the interpretation of scientific findings (Epstein 2007).

This cultural lens also creates a bias about what is a significant finding. Differences—no matter how small or trivial—are regarded as important findings. When no differences are found, studies might be dismissed as flawed efforts that failed to produce a meaningful result. In such cases, intriguing findings are dismissed, because cultural bias overrides scientific evidence. Such biases can also influence the publication process and dissemination of results. When this occurs, the "scientific record" becomes an expression of cultural biases rather than a corrective to them (Epstein 2007).

The causes of sex and gender differences remain open questions. To the extent that our culture exaggerates them, we must ask why. The social construction of race suggests an answer. Defining groups as different (especially when biological factors are seen as causing differences) quickly leads to unequal treatment of those groups. In the social construction of race, the definition of difference led to the institutionalization of inequality. The same dynamic operates with gender. Indeed, societies with high gender differentiation have greater sex stratification (Chafetz 1984). It is not difference—real or fabricated—that is the problem. The problem is the social response to difference that interprets it as a license for inequality.

The sex/gender system is fundamental to social organization. Its effects are evident at the micro level in gender socialization, identity formation, and interaction rituals. Its effects are evident at the macro level in the "gendering" of institutions that perpetuate conventional practices of sex and gender. Like race, gender is constructed to make it appear to be a natural rather than a social arrangement. The more "naturalized" it appears, the more entrenched gender inequalities become.

This begins with the social construction of gender identity. After determining it is healthy (and sometimes before), the first thing people want to know about a newborn baby is its sex. The universality of the question is revealing. It's important because even newborns are quickly assigned a gender. It's important because people bring different expectations and interactions to babies based on their sex. Infant girls are handled more gently and delicately than are infant boys, beginning gender socialization that continues for a lifetime and establishes our most fundamental social identity.

The scripts are familiar enough. Femininity means emotion, nurturance, domesticity, dependence, passivity, cooperation, submissiveness, and appearance. Masculinity means reason, emotional distance, public sphere involvement, independence, action, competition, dominance, and achievement.

These scripts construct differences that foster inequality in at least two ways. First, the traits in the masculine script are qualities generally valued in our culture; linking masculinity to them amounts to preferential treatment in the allocation of gender. Some of the traits in the feminine script are not valued or are actually *devalued* in our culture; femininity becomes devalued through its distance from core cultural values. Second, *if* men and women follow the scripts, dominance is perpetuated as men become adept at using power and women are trained to accept subordination. Gender conformity reproduces gender inequality.

How much these scripts are changing is unclear, but two observations are in order. First, there have been more challenges to, and changes in, the feminine script than to or in the masculine one. It makes perfect sense that women as a subordinate group would be more likely to resist gender conventions (even while proclaiming "I'm not a feminist…") because they pay their price. It also makes sense that men as a dominant group are less willing to change and more inclined to defend traditional arrangements that provide their privileges.

Second, it is an old sociological truism that the power of a norm is revealed by the social reaction that occurs when it is violated. If gender scripts have been significantly undermined, then people should no longer react strongly when others deviate from gender scripts or even borrow from the script of the "opposite sex." There are cultural niches where "gender bending" is not only accepted, but applauded. But there are many more places where gender deviance is still being policed through the societal reactions it provokes.

Such policing often involves accusations of homosexuality. This suggests that the sex/gender system also involves social control of sexuality. Such control is em-bodied in three norms. The first is the norm of heterosexuality itself. Although it remains unclear how biology and culture shape sexual orientation, it is abundantly clear that our culture promotes heterosexuality and represses homosexuality. There is a related norm of romantic love as an adjunct to heterosexuality. Taken together, these norms link erotic desire and emotional bonds to the "opposite sex." Because gender scripts deny some traits to both genders, the "opposite sex" might indeed become attractive as a gateway to traits denied to one's own gender. In this way, the creation of "oppositeness" and promotion of heterosexuality go hand in hand.

A second traditional norm regulating sexuality links it to reproduction. This norm is rooted in several religious traditions, and its strength varies with them. In some respects, U.S. culture has changed quite a bit by linking sexuality to pleasure rather than, or in addition to, reproduction. At the same time, religious traditions repressive of sexuality have had a major resurgence. Opposition to homosexuality, abortion, contraception, "premarital" sex, and sex education suggests that control of sexuality remains a major battleground.

A third norm regulating sexuality is male dominance. At the extreme, some men engage in sexual assault, coercion, harassment, or victimization, and such behaviors might not be taken seriously unless the victim fits a certain profile. More generally, men retain disproportionate control of social resources that provide control over sexual activity as well. On the other hand, challenges to male dominance have established reciprocity and female sexual pleasure as important alternative norms. It remains to be seen whether such challenges will be co-opted into more subtle male dominance or lead to more egalitarian arrangements.

A third dimension of the sex/gender system is the gender division of labor. The historical pattern ties men to public sphere activities and women to the domestic sphere. Even so, women's status varies, depending on the locus of a society's most productive and valued work. Industrialization increased the separation of spheres and intensified gender inequality. Such inequality persists in households with a male breadwinner and female homemaker.

Throughout the twentieth century, more women joined the labor force. Paid employment would seem to undermine inequality, as women gained material resources and the status associated with productive work. On the other hand, this participation occurred in a distinctively "gendered" way that has undercut such gains.

The gendered nature of paid work takes several forms. For many married women with (or planning for) children, labor force participation is secondary to child rearing, and paid employment is in addition to unpaid domestic labor. This is evident in the temporary, part-time, or flexible work arrangements where many women are concentrated. The result is often a "double day" of tasks in both spheres.

It might appear that unmarried or childless women can escape this dilemma and pursue a more stereotypically masculine career path. This is often posed as a "choice" that women are "free" to make, which is a half-truth. The gendered reality is that women must often "choose" between alternatives that men can unproblematically take for granted. Put differently, the gender division of labor allows men to combine careers with fatherhood much more easily than women can combine careers with motherhood. This is not to say that many women don't do both, but the gender division of labor makes it difficult for women and routine for men to do so.

Setting family aside, the workplace is also a deeply gendered institution. Full-time women workers still earn substantially less than their male counterparts. Pay equity legislation is important, but the more important problem is occupational sex segregation. Laws requiring equal pay for equal work mean little when people do different work, and that is what segregated labor markets ensure. Although a few women can be found in virtually all occupations, they remain concentrated in those reflecting traditional gender scripts—hence, women's predominance as nurses, secretaries, clerical workers, teachers, sales clerks, waitresses, maids, and other "pink-collar" positions. Such occupations make up a secondary labor force whose work is often temporary or part time, whose pay is lower, whose benefits and health care might be minimal or nonexistent, and whose opportunities for advancement are quite limited. When occupational sex segregation combines with discrimination and periodic sexual harassment, the outcome is a profoundly gendered workplace.

A fourth dimension of the sex/gender system is the gendered nature of *all* major social institutions. Thus, women predominate in elementary education and lower-status positions, and men prevail in higher education and higher-status positions. Although not an explicit part of the lesson plan, students learn about gender by observing who has status and power in these institutions. Studies of classroom practices and curricular representations of gender show that educational institutions still perpetuate gender difference and inequality (Sadker and Sadker 1994).

The political system is also profoundly gendered, as evidenced by the under-representation of women in political office and the difficulty they encounter in fund-raising. Hillary Clinton is the first viable female presidential candidate in the United States, but it is doubtful she would be without her marriage to a former president (talk about social capital!). It's not about qualifications; gender inequality means that even highly qualified women face obstacles men do not.

The result is that a majority of the population is politically underrepresented along gender lines. The political agenda also reflects gendered interests in more subtle ways. "Male" issues of business, taxes, trade, war, and crime prevail over "female" issues of welfare, health, and education. A thought experiment is suggestive. If women made up more than 75 percent of the political leadership and controlled all branches of government, how different would the political agenda be? The difference you can imagine suggests the gendered nature of politics as usual.

The family might be the most profoundly gendered institution of all. Beyond obvious examples, consider caring for elderly parents and relatives. These are almost automatically seen as women's responsibilities, even when men are more closely related to the people in need. Women who already experience a double duty of domestic and paid labor often also care for dependents at both ends of the life cycle.

Every social institution rests on gendered assumptions. They are woven into the fabric of social life in explicit, subtle, and unconscious ways. The pervasiveness of these assumptions has two important consequences. First, their cumulative effect is to "naturalize" gender differences. Because similar assumptions and practices seem to be everywhere, it is hard not to see them as natural rather than socially constructed. Second, the pervasiveness of these assumptions and practices reproduces gender inequality with surprising ease. Like the institutional discrimination that perpetuates racism or the unthinking habitus that reproduces class, there is a momentum to institutional sexism that maintains it indefinitely unless explicitly challenged. As macro-level patterns and micro-level interactions recreate one another, the result is to make gender inequality look like the most "natural" thing in the world.

FEMINIST FRAMEWORKS

Academics were slow to develop a sociology of gender, but women have always lived the politics of gender. Like other subordinate groups, they have acquiesced when necessary and resisted when possible. Individual resistance is common; collective resistance is rarer. Since industrialization transformed women's lives, however, there has been an ongoing women's movement.

When people resist inequality, they become theorists of how it operates and how it can be dismantled. This is why some of the best sociology has been inspired by challenges to inequality; this warrants a closer look at theories developed by feminists as they resisted gender inequality.

A woman's rights movement emerged in the 1840s and 1850s, advocating equal rights feminism. The theory invoked familiar Enlightenment ideas in the U.S. political tradition; it became radical by proposing their extension to women. It assumed women and men were fundamentally equal and basically similar. Their common humanity was seen as more important than their differing biology and gender. From these premises, gender inequality was an illogical set of institutional arrangements demanding major change. Although equal rights feminism seems tame now, in its day it posed a radical challenge to quasi-feudal gender arrangements.

Equal rights feminism might have been logically compelling, but it did not recruit large numbers. In the latter half of the nineteenth century, social feminism attracted more adherents. It emphasized differences between female and male temperaments. Social feminism was closer to conventional opinion on sex and gender. Indeed, there was a danger that social feminism would reinforce rather than challenge traditional gender stereotypes. Political activists were nonetheless adept at using difference in the service of equality. Combining equal rights and social feminism, they argued that to whatever extent men and women were equal, women deserved the vote just like men; to whatever extent they were different, women needed the vote so all could benefit from their unique perspective. In this way, two seemingly contradictory theories of gender were linked to the same cause.

First-wave feminism ended when women won the right to vote in 1920. Tensions between competing views of gender quickly resurfaced. In 1923, the Equal Rights Amendment (ERA) was introduced into Congress for the first time. Advocates saw it as a logical extension of equal rights feminism that would expand opportunity and curtail discrimination against middle-class and professional women. Social feminists saw it differently. They argued that an ERA would jeopardize protective labor legislation that limited the hours and conditions under which women worked. Social feminists defended this legislation and wanted it extended to men rather than denied to women. The first ERA debate thus highlighted tensions between different theories of gender in the feminist movement.

For almost fifty years, feminism survived "the doldrums" (Rupp and Taylor 1987) as a skeletal network rather than a mass movement. Second-wave feminism emerged in the late 1960s as part of a cycle of new social movements. The revival of feminism as a mass movement stimulated new theories of gender inequality.

Second-wave feminism arose in two forms. College-educated, professional women advocated liberal feminism. *The Feminine Mystique* (Freidan 1963) was a classic statement of this stance. Based on interviews with white, middle-class, suburban homemakers, Freidan identified the "problem that had no name" as the feminine mystique, meaning women's identities were defined through relationships with others (primarily husbands and children). Freidan's solution was for women to develop vocations or avocations that would provide an identity independent of such relationships. For all practical purposes, this was interpreted as a call for women to seek careers as a path to independence.

Liberal feminism advocated equal opportunity for women by unraveling gender segregation and discrimination. A simple example was classified ads in separate columns titled "help wanted—female" and "help wanted—male." The ads symbolized the structural reality of sex-segregated occupations with major differences in pay, benefits, and advancement. Liberal feminism emphasized the public sphere, but also supported access to contraception and abortion. Although not dwelling on "personal politics," liberal feminists knew that efforts to expand occupational opportunities would mean little if women didn't control their reproductive lives.

Liberal feminism resembled equal rights feminism. It envisioned gradual, cumulative reforms in social institutions that would improve women's opportunities and allow them to demonstrate their inherent equality with men.

Alongside liberal feminism, a younger generation of college women with experience in other social movements developed another version of feminism. Radical feminism identified gender oppression as the most fundamental source of social inequality. Advocates argued that gender oppression was the oldest form of inequality and that class or race inequalities were modeled on gender inequality (Lerner 1986).

Radical feminism saw male dominance, or patriarchy, as the defining feature of social orders past and present. Some versions borrowed Marxist imagery and defined women as a "sex-class" needing to overcome "false consciousness" and male-identified behavior to arrive at a revolutionary feminist consciousness and overthrow patriarchy. For this approach, the moderate reforms of liberal feminism were inadequate to the goal of fundamental change. A more basic revolutionary transformation was required if women were to achieve true liberation.

Radical feminists recognized patriarchal control of material resources, but they also explored other forms of male domination. They pioneered the politics of the body by reframing rape as a crime of violence rather than a sexual aberration. This politics of the body identified a sexist continuum rooted in the sexual objectification of women that included harassment, assault, and battering as mechanisms of patriarchal control. This wing of the movement was largely responsible for establishing rape crisis centers and battered women's shelters to serve women and cultivate feminist consciousness.

Radical feminists were also keenly interested in how patriarchy shaped personal life. The 1960s slogan that "the personal is political" found new shades of meaning in this context. Whereas professional women brought feminism into the boardroom, radical women brought it into the bedroom, putting intimate, emotional, and sexual relations under feminist scrutiny. They challenged conventional female socialization as creating "internalized oppression." In this context, consciousness-raising groups had a life-changing impact for many women by reframing "personal" problems as threads in a larger mosaic of patriarchal control. Such reframing recalled the sociological imagination as a translation of "personal troubles" into "public issues" (Mills 1959).

Liberal and radical feminism coexisted in the late 1960s and early 1970s. Where liberal feminism was an individualist, reformist, and integrationist response to institutional inequalities, radical feminism was a collectivist, revolutionary, transformative challenge to patriarchal domination. Despite their differences, these approaches had an important limitation. They both spoke with a white, middle-class accent that presumed certain class and race privileges while enunciating feminist grievances. Recognition of these limitations led to broader forms of feminist analysis that considered multiple dimensions of social inequality.

Socialist feminism focused on the intersection of capitalism and patriarchy. In such "dual system theories," capitalism generates class inequalities to the benefit of capitalists, and patriarchy spawns gender inequalities to the benefit of men. Each system reinforces the other, creating a complex challenge for social change activists.

The gender division of labor assigns different tasks to women and men; it also creates male control over female labor of many different sorts. This division of labor operates in two social spheres, producing benefits for men and capitalists at the expense of women.

In the private sphere, the division of labor assigns women a disproportionate share of the domestic labor required to maintain families and households. Men benefit, because this creates surplus time they can devote to their careers or simply enjoy as "leisure." Another intriguing feature of domestic labor is that it is unpaid. Capitalists and capitalism benefit because unpaid labor subsidizes overall economic profitability. To appreciate this, ponder the market value of domestic labor and the economic implications of paying women an appropriate wage for this labor (in addition to paying "breadwinners" their market value). Women's domestic labor is thus a crucial if invisible underpinning of a profitable capitalist economy.

In the public sphere, the gender division of labor creates entrenched patterns of occupational segregation and gender discrimination. Men benefit, because this reduces competition for desirable careers and wages. Capitalists benefit, because labor market segregation and discrimination create a secondary labor force whose labor can be purchased more cheaply. Once again, women pay the price of these double benefits to men and capitalists.

Capitalist patriarchy is pernicious because it is self-sustaining. The realities of this system make it logical for individual families to make "choices" about earning money and maintaining families that reproduce the very system that creates the problems in the first place. The implication is that systemic change in both public policies and private practices are necessary to achieve gender equality.

Whereas socialist feminists addressed both class and gender, cultural feminists reasserted the centrality of gender differences. Whether derived from nature, nurture, or some combination, differences were crucial to cultural feminist politics. Whereas some versions of feminism had emphasized similarities between women and men, cultural feminism stressed women's distinctive nature (Black 1989; Donovan 1985).

Cultural feminism saw women as nurturant, emotional, intuitive, relational, and supportive. It argued that childbearing gave women special insight into the needs of dependent and vulnerable people and a natural propensity to care for them. Some cultural feminists saw women as "natural" pacifists and envisioned a woman-led world free from conflict and violence. Grander versions of the theory suggested that women and men had very different ways of thinking, knowing, and understanding the world.

While seeming to accept gender stereotypes, cultural feminism used them to very different purposes. Rather than seeing women's qualities as weakness or inferiority, cultural feminists asserted their desirability and superiority. As in nineteenth-century social feminism, women's pacific nature was seen as the solution to problems created by a male dominated world. If male rationality, logic, competitiveness, and aggression caused many of the world's problems, then female emotion, intuition, nurturance, and cooperation held the key to solving them.

Cultural feminists thus resisted integration or assimilation into male-dominated worlds and institutions. They advocated a separatist strategy and "women-only" spaces, affirming women's distinctive nature. Cultural feminists created women's culture in alternative institutions like feminist bookstores, women's health cooperatives, women's music festivals, feminist spirituality gatherings, and the like. They symbolically expunged men by identifying as "wo*myn*" rather than "wo*men*." Although lesbians were important in many kinds of feminist politics, they had a strong affinity with cultural feminism. Both supported "women-identified women," whether expressed emotionally, sexually, or politically.

In reasserting gender difference, cultural feminists saw gender as the most fundamental social divide. Like earlier forms of feminism, this had strong appeal for white, middle-class women, for whom gender was the only basis of unequal treatment. It had less appeal for working-class women or women of color, whose life experiences were shaped by multiple inequalities. Cultural feminism ran the risk of an essentialist view of group differences in which one identity is linked to fundamental essences or universal natures. The more one looks at multiple systems of inequality and how gender is refracted through the lenses of class, race, nationality, ethnicity, and religion, the more problematic the premise of a single, universal, female essence becomes.

NEW PERMUTATIONS

The feminist frameworks just reviewed analyze women's position, how it differs from men's, and how the difference becomes inequality. Such insights provide a bridge between feminist movements and feminist sociology. Dorothy Smith (1987, 1990) has been one of the major architects of that bridge.

Smith develops a sociology from the standpoint of women. Although this might sound like a modest step, it fundamentally challenges gendered knowledge and mainstream sociology. The idea is that women have a particular standpoint in society that gives them a distinct way of understanding the world. Although Smith acknowledges class, race, and ethnic variations, she observes that gender persists in rooting most women in domestic, familial, household, and relational tasks and activities. Women thereby experience life's material realities directly. As they prepare food, clean dirt, diaper babies, bleed monthly, and nurse elders, these experiences create a distinct perspective.

This standpoint reflects specific, particular, and localized events, people, and experiences. It is attentive to detail, context, biography, and relations. Precisely because this standpoint and knowledge differ from that of men, it has been ignored, marginalized, or seen as invalid or distorted. In calling for a sociology from the standpoint of women, Smith seeks to validate these experiences and knowledges as deserving more study than they have traditionally received.

This means more than just including something previously excluded. It also challenges the "objective knowledge" that marginalizes women's standpoint. Here's the crucial part. Everyone occupies a standpoint. This includes men. There is no "objective" location encompassing everything and providing universally true and valid knowledge. There are only standpoints and only knowledges from those standpoints.

Men's standpoint connects them to public, political, economic, or institutional tasks and activities. This standpoint also fosters a certain kind of knowledge. Unlike the particular, concrete, and local knowledge that emerges from women's standpoint, men's standpoint generates knowledge that is abstract, categorical, and general. Whereas women's standpoint involves specifics and details, men's standpoint favors categories and generalities.

Women's standpoint might thus describe a neighbor as "Jane who has trouble with words and gets confused but loves old-time jazz and butterflies." Men's standpoint might describe the same woman as "a case of primary progressive aphasia with early onset degenerative dementia." The former provides specifics about a particular person, and the latter reduces her to abstract categories.

These are not just differences. A hierarchy is involved. Knowledge from men's standpoint is privileged, whereas knowledge from women's standpoint is marginalized. The general is seen as better than the specific, the universal is preferred to the local, the categorical is thought more accurate than the particular. The cumulative result is that knowledge from the standpoint of men is seen as valid, objective, and true, and knowledge from the standpoint of women is seen as partial, subjective, and anecdotal (at best). Knowledge from men's standpoint thus creates the illusion that it transcends all standpoints by being objective, and knowledge from women's standpoint—if acknowledged at all—is seen as limited.

Standpoint theory validates the supposedly subjective knowledge of women and delegitimizes the allegedly objective knowledge of men. Smith describes this hierarchy of gendered knowledge as "relations of ruling." These relations sustain patriarchy, white supremacy, and capitalist dominance by using certain kinds of abstract knowledge as a form of social power. This knowledge is embodied in texts that classify the world in categorical terms. As we saw in the social construction of race, those who do the categorizing end up with power over those so categorized.

Relations of ruling are embedded in bureaucracies that ignore particular or situational aspects of people so as to place them in general categories and process them accordingly. These relations are also embedded in science, to the extent that it classifies specific phenomena into abstract types in pursuit of "objective" knowledge. To the extent that sociology sees itself as a science in this way, it is subject to Smith's critique as yet another expression of relations of ruling that convert knowledge into power by obscuring its own standpoint.

This analysis of relations of ruling recalls Habermas's (1987) image of an abstract system colonizing an everyday lifeworld and Foucault's (1980) idea that knowledge quests are simultaneously power grabs. What Smith adds is that these dynamics involve gender. We thereby need a feminist sociology rooted in the standpoint of women to challenge such power and gender hierarchy.

Standpoint theory also informs black feminist thought or Afrocentric feminism (Collins 1990). Consider again how mainstream feminism has always had a white, middle-class bias. In some respects, it is only logical that women who are relatively privileged in class and racial terms would develop a feminism that addresses their particular disadvantages of gender. But this feminism offers little to women of color.

A parallel problem exists in much Afrocentric thinking. Although insightful about racial inequality, these ideas have been male dominated and inattentive to problems women encounter arising from the intersection of racial and gender oppression.

Put somewhat differently, the standpoint of (white) women can critique patriarchy, and the standpoint of (male) minorities can expose racism, but both do so one-dimensionally. Neither addresses how multiple oppressions work together. This is where the standpoint of women of color becomes crucial. With rare exceptions (think Oprah), such women live at the intersection of racial oppression, gender hierarchy, and class inequality.

This logic builds on insights of standpoint theory. It is an irony of power and privilege that when the world works in your favor there is little incentive to really understand it. When the world works against you, you must figure it out if only to survive it. Thus, although dominant groups have obvious forms of social power, subordinate groups often have a better understanding of how power is actually exercised (and can be resisted). Their standpoint reveals more about power than that of the dominant group.

In addition, whereas dominant standpoints foster abstract, general, categorical knowledge, subordinate standpoints provide local, particular, experiential knowledge. This was Smith's (1987) insight about women, and it is echoed in Patricia Collins's (1990) study of women of color. Their standpoint trusts knowledge gained and passed on through direct experience. Such knowledge has been marginalized by mainstream institutions, but it has been kept alive in folk traditions, women's culture, family customs, community storytelling, and black music.

These points combine with the standpoint of women of color to make a powerful argument. If a subordinate standpoint reveals the intricacies of one form of power, then a multiply subordinate standpoint reveals not just single dimensions of power but also how they coexist and intersect. What white women or black men experience one- or two-dimensionally is experienced three-dimensionally by working-class women of color.

It follows that some of our best insights about power should come from the standpoint of women of color and the consciousness and knowledge deriving from that standpoint. This stance underscores that *all* people have multiple identities and are located in multiple systems of inequality. These identities and locations always shape who and where we are in the social landscape.

The result is a social structure Collins (1990) calls a matrix of domination. Everyone is located somewhere in the matrix, and most people have combinations of privileges on some dimensions and disadvantages on others. Thus, even "privileged" white males can experience class disadvantages; affluent, male, African American attorneys encounter racial discrimination; and white, female CEOs confront gender stereotypes.

What the matrix illustrates is that most people are both "oppressors and victims." This means that a majority of people have an interest in undermining the matrix as a whole, thereby dissolving their disadvantages along with those of others. The matrix is sustained when people think in terms of only one identity. This creates a dynamic of divide-and-conquer, in which the common interests of most people are obscured by the particular interests of single identities. In this way, the standpoint of women of color enriches our understanding of not just gender inequality, but of all types of social inequality.

Most versions of feminism assume that gender is socially constructed into something "real" through socialization. As a "real" identity, it is used to oppress women, but that same identity is crucial in mobilizing women to resist oppression. But what if gender is not as "real" as we think?

This is one of the challenges posed by Judith Butler's (1991) poststructuralist analysis of gender. It highlights a paradox of feminist politics. Struggling against patriarchy seems to require the category of "woman" to recruit people to the struggle. However, using the category in this way creates problems. "Woman" has very often been interpreted in ways that exclude some women from the category and the struggle (working-class women, women of color, lesbians, or Third World women). Generic categories like "woman" obscure major differences among the people so categorized. Moreover, the very use of the category "woman" implies there is a core identity shared by all female persons. What if this is not true?

In Butler's view, using the category and identity of woman—even to challenge gender hierarchy—ends up perpetuating that very hierarchy. It does so by reinforcing the idea that there are two, unalterable, core genders. Although one gender might struggle against the other, the premise of two core genders remains unchallenged.

The unintended effect of rallying around such an identity is thus to reinforce a binary gender order that "allows" only two, fixed genders. It also sustains the notion that heterosexuality is the only acceptable relationship between these two fixed genders. It finally maintains male domination with its rigidly dualistic conception of what kinds of people exist in the world. Appealing to "woman" as a core identity has the unintended consequence of shoring up a gender order based on compulsory heterosexuality and male dominance.

For Butler, gender is not a core identity as much as it is a kind of performance. Where mainstream feminism sees socialization as creating a core gender identity, poststructuralist feminism speaks of materialization as learning how to perform gender. We learn to embody gender by moving, speaking, acting, emoting, and desiring in ways that signify that we are a particular gender. When these performances succeed, we receive social support. As we and others trade and support such performances, we collectively create the illusion that genders exist as core identities.

This illusion sustains gender hierarchies that police who people can be. It accepts those who perform gender appropriately and marginalizes those who don't.

As a result, deviant gender performances like cross-dressing, or dressing in "drag," become highly subversive because they threaten to expose how *all* versions of gender involve performances. If gender is a performance that can be revised and changed, then it is much more fluid and ephemeral than even many feminists have presumed. The biggest challenge to patriarchy therefore comes not from rallying around gender categories but from dissolving them altogether.

Postcolonial feminism provides a final instance of new gender understandings (Mohanty 2003; Spivak 1996, 1999; Trinh 1989). Women in Africa, Asia, and Latin America developed such perspectives through a familiar route. On one hand, they were left out of male-dominated theories of national liberation and struggles against colonialism. On the other hand, they found little of relevance in mainstream, Western feminism that grew out of very different social conditions. As with U.S. women of color, these cross-pressures led postcolonial women to develop a feminism that reflected their specific experiences.

Postcolonial feminism involves yet another dual struggle against patriarchy and colonialism. It rejects any Western version of feminism that reduces political struggle to gender alone, because this oversimplifies the problem and might alienate women and men who need to work together against postcolonial powers. It also rejects any independence platform that equates political struggle with nationality alone, because this also oversimplifies the problem and tends to reinforce traditional male dominance.

Postcolonial feminists must thereby navigate a complex political terrain. At times they might support traditional customs that preserve indigenous cultures against Western pressures to change. Doing so, however, risks reinforcing the patriarchal aspects of those customs while also attracting criticism from Western feminists for not challenging male dominance more directly. At other times, they might challenge native practices in the name of gender equality and risk being ostracized by their own people for becoming too "Western" and adopting colonial values.

Postcolonial feminism clarifies the standpoint of mainstream, Western feminism. The latter has always been tempted to speak in broad or even universal terms about gender. Postcolonial feminists have shown how such tendencies lead to biases about cultural differences just like traditional colonialism. Perhaps most important, postcolonial feminism has challenged the Western bias that women in developing nations are basically powerless to respond to their situation. The activism of postcolonial feminists demonstrates again that wherever there is power, there is likely to be resistance as well.

Standpoint theory, intersectionality theories, poststructuralist feminism, and postcolonial feminism are some recent trends in the analysis of gender. More generally speaking, feminist theory provides a fitting conclusion to our look at class, race, and gender, because it grew by asking who is left out of mainstream theories. This logic applies to all types of inequality. Thus, the limitations of even the best class theories become evident when women's contributions to social production and reproduction in households (as well as wage-labor) are considered alongside the male-dominated market production that has heretofore defined class theory.

The result has been not just new theories but new ways of theorizing. In its striving to be inclusive, its sensitivity to those at the margins, its analysis of rich relations between seemingly separate spheres, its refusal to claim a totalistic understanding, and its relentless critique of myriad forms of power, feminist theory is a strong template for a critical sociology seeking to challenge all forms of inequality.

PART FOUR
SELF AND SOCIETY

Chapter 10

The Emergence of the Individual

A popular magazine in the United States is simply titled, *Self.* It caters to young women, and contains a familiar mix of fashion, beauty, and relationship advice. But the underlying message seems to be "it's all about you." The paradox is that each reader is encouraged to cultivate a unique self, based on the same mass-marketed advice being read by millions of others. This is merely one example of the glorification of the individual in U.S. culture. Individualism is a hallmark of modernity, but it is nowhere more pronounced than in the United States.

The pursuit of individualism can undermine bonds with others and create profound loneliness. Yet, we often seem incapable of thinking beyond ourselves. Some time ago I co-taught an experiential course based on a wilderness canoe trip. The goal of the course was to build a utopian society during our seven-day adventure. We asked our students what utopia meant to them. To a person, they said utopia would be unrestricted individual freedom to do whatever they wanted. The notion that such freedoms might clash, or that larger norms might be needed, or that utopia might mean being connected to others did not occur to these otherwise bright students.

The sociological imagination offers a closer examination of such taken-for-granted notions. Historical and comparative lenses are especially helpful in seeing the distinctiveness of familiar social worlds. This is why Alexis de Tocqueville's (1853/1969) commentaries on early U.S. society are so highly prized. As a Frenchman looking at U.S. life, he could clearly see what was becoming invisible to Americans themselves: that their lives were increasingly organized around the principle of individualism, with both positive and negative consequences.

All this makes it hard to grasp that "individuals" did not exist until relatively recently. Nevertheless, a classic sociological argument makes exactly this claim. Although societies have always contained people, the notion that people are "individuals" with unique functions, personalities, and temperaments is historically new. In this sense, society preceded the individual, who only emerged through a long process of social evolution that eventually led to the individualism that has become a taken-for-granted part of contemporary consciousness.

FROM "WE" TO "I"

Emile Durkheim's (1893/1964) take on individualism is part of a broader study of social evolution. It rests on a dichotomy between traditional and modern societies. For most of human history, people lived in traditional societies. People in such societies were undifferentiated; they were very similar to one another. Because of these similarities, the modern notion of the individual standing apart from or opposed to the group had no meaning. The tribe or clan was the basic social unit, and people were utterly subordinate to such units.

Some of these societies underwent technological and demographic changes that jump-started social evolution. The domestication of animals, the rise of agriculture, and the development of communication and transportation systems promoted settlement, migration, and the growth of stable and sedentary populations in villages and eventually cities. The combined effect was increasing population size, as societies accumulated the resources to support larger numbers.

Some societies also expanded geographically, allowing their increasing numbers of people to spread out over new lands and territories. Eventually, however, societies encountered limits to geographical expansion while populations continued to increase. The result of population growth and geographical limits was an increase in moral or dynamic density. More people interacted with more other people, and with greater frequency, on a daily basis.

Increasing dynamic density posed a danger that the struggle for survival would intensify and bring increasing competition and conflict. Indeed, some societies undoubtedly succumbed to these pressures and disintegrated.

In other cases, societies survived through a new social invention known as the division of labor. Rather than competing to do the same things, the division of labor allowed people to specialize in different activities. Specialization reduced competitive pressures as people sorted themselves into distinct slots in the division of labor. Such specialization also created a new interdependence among people doing different things and fulfilling different functions.

Modern societies thereby evolved with the division of labor. It solved the threats posed by increasing dynamic density, conflict, and competition by creating functional interdependence and cooperation between people's activities. With a sufficiently complex division of labor, modernizing societies could continue to expand while also reducing conflicts over scarce resources. The division of labor was thus the central survival mechanism of social evolution.

Durkheim underscored the contrast between traditional and modern societies at either end of the evolutionary process. He was especially interested in different kinds of solidarity in each society. Traditional societies had mechanical solidarity. This meant that the parts of the society were homogeneous or identical to one another; there was little interdependence between them. There was also a low degree of dynamic density. Mechanical solidarity thus linked similar units together. Think of a chain consisting of identical links. Because they are all the same, some links can be removed without destroying the chain; it simply becomes shorter than before.

Social control in traditional societies was based on punitive law and repressive sanctions. Deviance was seen as a grave threat to moral order. There was a powerful collective conscience holding the group together. It consisted of collective sentiments, emotions, norms, values, and morals. People saw themselves as group members rather than independent individuals. This collective conscience was so strong that virtually any deviance was a serious challenge to group integrity; that is why it was dealt with so harshly. The collective conscience thus sustained mechanical solidarity in traditional societies. It created solidarity based on what people thought and believed by ensuring that everyone thought and believed the same things.

There were no "individuals" in traditional society because of the functional similarities in what people did; there was simply no basis for differentiation. The collective conscience insisted that people's identities were collective and not individual; who you were was a function of your tribe or clan and not of any unique, personal characteristics. Finally, if people did "express themselves" as different, it was likely to be taken as a deviant challenge to group solidarity, for which they likely received harsh treatment. In some circles, it could get you declared a witch and burned at the stake.

If there were people but no individuals in traditional societies, and if such societies make up the vast majority of human history, then it follows that the individual is a recent social invention. It is a by-product of modern societies.

These societies have survived by organic solidarity. This means that the parts of society are heterogeneous, or different from one another. Because of these differences, there is a high degree of interdependence among the parts. There is also a high degree of dynamic density. Organic solidarity links different units together. Think of a complex molecule consisting of unique elements. Because of the differences, removing even one element jeopardizes the entire molecule, because there are no functional substitutes to play the same role.

Modern societies have a correspondingly different type of social control; with some exceptions, it is based on cooperative law and restitutive sanctions. Many forms of deviance are seen more as technical violations of rules than moral challenges to society itself. Perpetrators are more likely to pay restitution or undergo rehabilitation than to suffer harsh punishment. As before, Durkheim uses types of deviance and punishment as a lens through which to study larger questions about social solidarity.

In modern societies, the different response to deviance suggests a change in the collective conscience. It is less important, less central, and less collective than before. Indeed, in modern societies there might be multiple collective consciences coexisting alongside one another. Such plurality means that no one belief system is supreme over all others, and that none can provide a universal source of solidarity. Moreover, modern belief systems acknowledge the individual by recognizing inalienable rights, personal freedoms, and individual dignity. With social evolution, the collective conscience declines as the value of the individual increases.

This might seem to imply that modern societies have less solidarity, but they have an alternative to the collective conscience. The division of labor is modern society's functional equivalent of the collective conscience. The division of labor provides the organic solidarity that unites modern societies. Whereas traditional societies were held together by the normative integration of what people believed (and they all believed the same things), modern societies are held together by the functional integration of what people do (and they all do different things).

The fact that people do different things in the modern division of labor promotes the emergence of the individual. Individualism began when people differentiated their productive activities and occupied distinct niches in the division of labor. Once it took hold, individualism expanded its meaning from what people do to who people are. Thus was born the contemporary notion of the individual as a unique bundle of personality traits that distinguish one person from another.

Even today we can catch glimpses of the contrasts Durkheim discusses. Traces of past worlds still exist in immigrant communities, in the cultures of indigenous peoples, and in intentionally isolated communities like the Amish. Other examples can be found where religious fundamentalism provides an overriding belief system and an unambiguous moral compass for a strongly integrated community of people. Such examples illustrate Durkheim's hypothesis that traditionalism and individualism don't readily mix; when they do, look for conflict between traditional collective identities and modern individual ones. Such battles are further testimony that individualism is not "natural" but rather a product of social change and evolution.

Durkheim was a modernist who saw the emergence of the individual as a healthy development. The same individualism that would have been deviant in traditional societies was normal in modern ones. Moreover, Durkheim was a strong political supporter of individual rights and liberties. Nevertheless, he was also aware of the potential problems that arose with the new emphasis on individualism, and he detailed such problems in his subsequent work.

TOO MUCH OF A GOOD THING?

Durkheim's study of suicide (1897/1951) is a cautionary tale about individualism in modern society. It can quickly become too much of a good thing. More broadly, Durkheim's study of suicide made the case that social facts always shape individual phenomena. For Durkheim, individual explanations of human behavior are almost always inferior to sociological explanations.

Suicide was a good example. Nothing seems more personal than the decision to take one's own life. If anything is best explained in psychological, individual terms, it would appear to be suicide. But not for Durkheim. He finds the most intriguing aspect of suicide to be variations in suicide rates across different groups, times, places, and circumstances. He proceeds to argue that suicide rates are a social fact that can only be explained by other social facts. The larger point is central to sociology itself: What appears as an individual event requiring a psychological explanation when observed "up close" is often a social reality requiring a sociological explanation when placed in a larger social context. Put differently, Durkheim puts the individual in their place by showing that even seemingly personal decisions are conditioned by social factors.

The point is that suicide rates vary inversely with the degree of integration in modern society. In other words, the less integrated a group or a society is, the higher its suicide rates. The formula was reversed in traditional societies: The more integrated the group or society, the higher its suicide rates. The seeming contradiction reflects the difference between the two societies. In traditional societies with mechanical solidarity, the potential danger is that integration becomes too strong and poses a danger to people that leads to suicide. In modern societies with organic solidarity, the potential danger is that integration is too weak and poses a danger to individuals that also manifests itself as suicide.

The link between integration and suicide has two dimensions. Cohesion refers to social bonds that link an individual to others, to larger social groups, and to a sense of belonging or membership. Regulation refers to rules, guidelines, values, and codes of conduct that help individuals orient themselves and make decisions through a strong moral compass. A low degree of integration could arise from either insufficient cohesion or inadequate regulation; both lead to higher rates of suicide.

Egoism arises with insufficient cohesion. It is "excessive individuation" in which a normal process of individual development goes too far so that the individual is no longer connected to others in a socially meaningful way. Put differently, the argument is that belonging keeps us grounded so that we avoid dangerous or self-destructive behavior. Groups with high cohesion and a sense of belonging will therefore have lower suicide rates than groups with low cohesion. Members of groups with little cohesion are especially prone to egoistic suicide.

Durkheim's evidence concerned suicide rates in different religious faiths. It was initially a puzzle that Protestant groups, regions, and countries had substantially higher suicide rates than their Catholic counterparts. The mystery dissolved with a closer look at the structure of their respective religious beliefs. Protestantism involves a direct relationship between the individual and God, with relatively little emphasis on connections among Protestants or on religious community. In Catholicism, on the other hand, there is a much stronger connection to religious community and to others who mediate one's relationship with God. Protestants were thus more prone to egoism, and correspondingly had higher rates of egoistic suicide.

Anomie describes insufficient regulation. To be anomic means to be without the norms, rules, or guidelines that normally orient people and guide decisions. When a group lacks strong normative guidelines, its members are more likely to engage in dangerous or self-destructive behaviors. Such groups will have higher rates of anomic suicide.

Durkheim's evidence here involved rapid changes in economic conditions like financial crises or unexpected prosperity. When such changes happen quickly, they create anomie because the rules, regulations, and rhythms of "normal" life no longer apply when people become suddenly poor or rich. Rapid economic fluctuations produce higher rates of anomie and higher rates of anomic suicide. The argument is especially persuasive because it works in both directions. It's not surprising that people who suddenly become impoverished are more likely to commit suicide. It *is* surprising that people who suddenly become rich are also more likely to commit suicide. The key variable is not the material fact of wealth or poverty; it is the social fact of anomie that is the better predictor of suicide rates.

In traditional societies, the dangers are reversed. Group cohesion can be so powerful that people become completely submerged in the group and offer their lives "too easily" through altruistic suicide. Alternatively, social regulation might be so overwhelmingly controlling that people succumb to fatalistic suicide. There are thus four types of suicide, but they are all related to whether social integration is too strong (in traditional societies) or too weak (in modern societies). In all cases, suicide rates are a social fact best explained by the degree of social integration.

Although suicide provided a dramatic focus, the logic applies more broadly. High rates of anomie or egoism are correlated with many different kinds of deviant, self-destructive, or antisocial behavior. After all, group cohesion and normative regulation don't just deter suicide; they minimize many undesirable behaviors. When they fail, we can expect not just higher suicide rates but higher rates of crime, delinquency, addiction, and the like. Many social problems stem from insufficient social integration.

Several theories of deviance (and its treatment) flow from these insights. To take one example, consider the importance of the group in programs like Alcoholics Anonymous. Recovery depends on attending meetings where social cohesion and bonding with others is a key element. By the same logic, people in recovery are encouraged to have a "sponsor" they can contact if they are in danger of returning to self-destructive behavior. It is connections with others that deter the problematic behavior.

Durkheim himself suggested that to combat egoism, we need small and intermediate size groups to provide people with membership and belonging. He felt this was especially important as modern society moved toward massive social institutions that dwarfed individuals. To deter anomie, Durkheim advocated moral, ethical, and civic education to balance individual freedoms with social obligations.

Durkheim's work reveals the potential dangers of (excessive) individualism. He would not have liked my students' image of utopia as a world of unrestricted freedom. To the contrary, he claimed that "it is not true ... that human activity can be released from all restraint" (Durkheim 1897/1951, 252). His view was that without social restraint, people become slaves to self-destructive impulses. To be without social restraints is to have no immunity against such impulses. It is society that rescues us from this fate by providing the cohesion, regulation, and integration that allows people to control their impulses and achieve relative freedom.

Durkheim really puts the individual in their place. Society precedes individuals. It existed for a long time without "individuals." And even with the emergence of the individual, social cohesion and regulation remain necessary to avoid self-destructive tendencies. In a culture that has come to glorify the self, Durkheim's work provides a healthy corrective for how to think about the individual in modern society.

A NOTE ON ADOLESCENCE

The emergence of the individual changes the life cycle in modern society. Once again, a phenomenon that seems natural and even biological—what we call adolescence—proves to be a social construction.

Indeed, childhood itself is more a social status than a biological reality. In traditional societies, "childhood" was not a distinct stage in the life cycle. Children were treated simply as small adults. They assumed adult roles and responsibilities as soon as they were physically able to do so. The transition from dependent young to adult roles was very quick.

This is true through the Middle Ages in Europe. Paintings from that era show young people dressed in the clothing of adults and involved in adult activities (Aries 1965). Although not the conscious intention of the artists, the message in these paintings seems to be that there was no "childhood" in the Middle Ages. For all practical purposes, children were just small adults.

It was modernization in general and industrialization in particular that created "childhood." As we saw previously, industrialization transformed the family from a unit of production into a unit of consumption, and it transformed the economic roles of family members. Men became breadwinners working outside the home for someone else. Women became homemakers doing unpaid domestic labor. And little people became "children" in the modern sense. Like many women, they lost productive roles and were transformed from economic assets into economic liabilities or dependents.

Gender and childhood were altered by these developments. Masculinity became tough and competitive, and femininity became domestic and maternal. Because women and children shared the domestic sphere, similar conceptions were transposed to children. The reason we think of children as innocent, vulnerable, and needing protection derives from this historical period and the connections between childhood and domesticity. Before then, when small people functioned as adults, they were just as likely to be perceived as tough, aggressive, scheming, or vicious. In both cases, conceptions of people derived from the worlds they occupied. When the worlds changed, so did the conceptions.

The loss of children's economic role left a gap that was filled by formal education. What began as the "factory school" evolved into modern schooling dedicated to meeting the distinct needs of (newly invented) "children." The rise of this child-centered institution reinforced the ideas that children were different, they inhabited a unique world, and they needed protection, nurturance, and guidance if they were to develop into fully competent adults.

If childhood is a social construction, this is even truer of *adolescence*. The term was invented in the early twentieth century to designate a stage between childhood and adulthood. Adolescence might seem to combine the disadvantages of both, but it is here to stay. A major function of adolescence is to allow people the opportunity to explore and establish individual identities. In traditional societies, such identities would not need to be "established" as an individual achievement. Identities were rather derived from the kinship structure, and people moved quickly through initiation rites to adulthood.

Contemporary adolescence has replaced two- or three-day initiation rites with years of identity exploration. Moreover, adolescence now leads not to adulthood but to young adulthood. With extended education, later marriage, deferred child rearing, and later career starts, many people do not assume fully adult roles until they reach their thirties. Many people thus ease into adulthood at biological ages that practically defined elders in traditional societies. It is not that people's biology has changed (although life expectancy and control of disease has changed). It is rather that new social constructions have arisen, dividing the life cycle into more intermediate stages in keeping with the demands and opportunities of industrial and postindustrial society.

The timing and nature of these developments are entirely consistent with Durkheim's observations about the emergence of the individual. In traditional societies, identities derived from group membership. They did not have to be "found," "explored," or "tried out." They were simply there.

In modern societies, the division of labor created social differentiation among people that in turn created the individual. Identities are now only partially fixed by birth, kinship, or geography. An increasingly large part of our identities is individually achieved rather than collectively assigned. As individualism and identity have become major life tasks, modern societies have developed more numerous stages in the life cycle to accommodate such challenges.

INDIVIDUALISM AND ITS DISCONTENTS

Although the individual is a hallmark of modern society, the greatest emphasis on individualism is in the United States. Since de Tocqueville (1853/1969), individualism has attracted both praise and criticism. Such reactions reflect the time and place of the observers. Whereas de Tocqueville was struck by the contrast between European hierarchy and U.S. egalitarianism, more recent sociological observers have identified other dimensions of contemporary individualism.

An example is provided by David Riesman's *The Lonely Crowd* (1950). Like William Whyte (1956) and C. Wright Mills (1956), Riesman was concerned with how large-scale organizations were turning people into anonymous, faceless cogs in the social machinery of contemporary society. In contrast to Durkheim's worries about egoism or excessive individuation, these critics were lamenting the loss of individuality and rise of overconformity in mass society.

Riesman analyzed changes in prevailing social character over time. The dominant social character in preindustrial societies, not surprisingly, was the "tradition-directed" person who conformed to social norms with little friction, because traditional people were highly subordinate to the collective.

With modern society and the emergence of the individual, the "inner-directed" person appeared. They internalize clear goals and values early in life through strong socialization by family members and authority figures. Once in place, these values firmly guide conduct, producing a highly individualized personality that stays on track. Inner-directed persons are not very susceptible to external influences that contradict their inner-direction; they tend to ignore such pressures and follow their own path.

By the 1950s, however, this inner-directed person was giving way to the "other-directed" person. They are less influenced by families and more susceptible to peer groups and the surrounding environment. They are predisposed to seek acceptance, to fit in, and to value social approval. Whereas the inner-directed person is mostly unaffected by external influences, the other-directed person seeks it out as a guide to conduct. In Riesman's metaphors, inner-directed people have psychological gyroscopes that keep them on track, and other-directed people use radar to pick up social cues and respond accordingly. To expand the metaphor, inner-directed people move in a straight line determined by their internal gyroscope. Other-directed people, by contrast, bounce around like a pinball in response to external influences.

Riesman lamented the loss of (inner-directed) individualism in the mass society of his day. Whereas Durkheim feared too much individualism in modernity, Riesman felt there was not enough. As a preferable alternative, he called for an "autonomous" individual to emerge that would overcome the drawbacks of both inner- and other-directed character types (Kivisto 1998, 109–113).

Soon after Riesman's critique of other-directedness, the political protest and counterculture of the 1960s provided a very different social backdrop for Philip Slater's take on individualism in *The Pursuit of Loneliness* (1970). The book criticized U.S. culture's obsessions with technology, violence, competition, scarcity, and hierarchy; within this context Slater offered intriguing comments on individualism.

Three human desires are deeply frustrated by the individualism of U.S. culture. The first is a desire for community, which has been the norm for much of human history and has only recently been overturned with the modern emphasis on individualism. The second is a desire for engagement to address social and interpersonal problems, which is frustrated by the detachment that accompanies modern individualism. The third is a desire for dependence and shared responsibility, which again is difficult to meet given the emphasis on individualism.

There is a perverse circularity built into our brand of individualism. It leads us to minimize, avoid, or deny the interdependence at the root of all human societies. It is expressed in our quest for privatized means of living by owning our own home, car, and a complete, private, repertoire of technological gadgetry. The result is the pursuit of loneliness: "We seek more and more privacy, and feel more and more alienated and lonely when we get it. What accidental contacts we do have, furthermore, seem more intrusive, not only because they are unsought but because they are unconnected with any familiar pattern of interdependence" (Slater 1970, 7).

Having constructed such traps, we can't escape them because we fall back into the "individualistic fantasy that everyone is, or should be, different—that each person could somehow build his entire life around some single, unique, eccentricity." (Slater 1970, 8). Although it might appear that we freely express our individuality, the standards are set by the larger culture so that "everyone tends, independently but monotonously, to pursue the same things in the same way" (Slater 1970, 9). In an ironic twist, the pursuit of individuality reinforces mass conformity.

Our "independence training" contrasts even with other modern societies that have a healthier balance between independence and interdependence. It also has serious emotional consequences. When independence is equated with individualism, then individualism can only be achieved through emotional detachment from others. Such detachment, in turn, breeds indifference and competitiveness toward others, accompanied by lingering guilt about these qualities. U.S. individualism thus traps us in a snare of social and emotional difficulties.

Many of these dilemmas are evident in middle-class child rearing techniques that prevailed in the mid-twentieth century. Dr. Spock—the pediatrician, not the Vulcan—advised permissiveness, individualism, and female domesticity. The advice built on the assumption that every individual is unique and has a positive potential that can only develop under the right circumstances.

Such assumptions place considerable burdens on children to "develop their potential" or be regarded as a failure. It also magnified the importance of proper child rearing, reinforcing women's domestic role and making child care a full-time—though individualized and privatized—activity for middle-class women. As Slater notes, "We are a product-oriented society, and she has been given the opportunity to turn out a really outstanding product" (Slater 1970, 67). The political and cultural climate of the 1960s thus illuminated numerous dilemmas arising from our brand of individualism.

A decade later, yet another critique equated individualism with narcissism (Lasch 1979). It "describes a way of life that is dying—the culture of competitive individualism, which in its decadence has carried the logic of individualism to the extreme of a war of all against all, the pursuit of happiness to the dead end of a narcissistic preoccupation with the self" (Lasch 1979, 21).

Christopher Lasch roots this malaise in post-1960s politics, when he claims Americans gave up on public, political issues in favor of purely personal preoccupations. This inward turn was accompanied by a waning of history. The past was no longer seen as a coherent model for living in the present, just as the anticipation of a predictable future also fell by the wayside. One aspect of the narcissism Lasch discusses is thus an overriding orientation to a present divorced from both past and future.

The self is now guided by a therapeutic sensibility that rejects the notion of a public or social good to pursue purely personal well-being, health, and security. Echoing Riesman's shift from inner- to other-directed personalities, Lasch sees the narcissistic personality as heavily invested in maintaining high self-esteem, while at the same time being dependent on others to validate it.

This therapeutic sensibility might identify real problems, but it offers self-defeating solutions. "Arising out of a pervasive dissatisfaction with the quality of personal relations, it advises people not to make too large an investment in love and friendship, to avoid excessive dependence on others, and to live for the moment—the very conditions that created the crisis of personal relations in the first place" (Lasch 1979, 64–65).

The narcissistic personality combines a grandiose conception of the self with an inner emptiness and loss of faith in any meaning system beyond the therapeutic sensibility. It nevertheless persists because it resonates with larger social institutions. "For all his inner suffering, the narcissist has many traits that make for success in bureaucratic institutions, which put a premium on the manipulation of interpersonal relations, discourage the formation of deep personal attachments, and at the same time provide the narcissist with the approval he needs in order to validate his self-esteem" (Lasch 1979, 91).

Rather than becoming more social and cooperative, people have simply become more adept at manipulating others for their personal benefit. In a claim that seems to describe many parents' involvement in their children's sports teams, Lasch notes that activities "ostensibly undertaken purely for enjoyment often have the real object of doing others in" (Lasch 1979, 128). Thus, the manipulation favored by the narcissistic personality is an understandable response to the degradation of social life in which pleasure and play have been taken over by self-interest, unrestrained competition, and psychic survival at all costs.

Such personality types predominate in part because of changes in the family and child rearing. In Lasch's view, traditional parental authority has been undermined by government bureaucracies, capitalist markets, and mass media. Deprived of authority, parents have become dependent on experts for advice. And the advice has shifted from clear prescriptions to vague exhortations to trusting feelings as the main guide in childhood socialization. This "cult of authenticity" allows volatile emotions to overrule traditional guidelines and reasoned judgments; it was meant to restore parental confidence but in fact has helped to undermine it.

"The decline of parental authority reflects the 'decline of the superego' in American society as a whole" (Lasch 1979, 305). Narcissistic personalities emerge because social conditions discourage the establishment of a strong super-ego with internal behavioral controls. This critique of "permissive" child rearing is most intriguing when Lasch notes that "the decline of authority does not lead to the collapse of social constraints. It merely deprives those constraints of a rational basis" (Lasch 1979, 316).

Narcissistic personalities have difficulty forming attachments, while also needing recognition and affirmation. The combination puts great strains on personal relations. As much as people might desire intimacy, narcissism frustrates these desires, because narcissistic personalities are wary of commitments and more attuned to manipulating emotional states than to fully experiencing them.

In the end, Lasch traces narcissism to the new paternalism of capitalist society. It stimulates needs and dependence, but it also creates personalities that cannot fulfill those needs or escape that dependence. In Lasch's dark imagery, individuals become their own worst enemy, because narcissistic personalities preclude real satisfactions.

Speaking from different historical contexts, Riesman, Slater, and Lasch demonstrate how individualism has been a battleground of conflicting social forces throughout much of the twentieth century.

HABITS OF THE HEART

Lasch's critique of narcissism is entertaining to read. He rails against contemporary culture like an old-time preacher. He has some dazzling insights. At the same time, his argument relies on isolated examples, catchy metaphors, and literary references. It lacks systematic evidence.

Such evidence can be found in *Habits of the Heart* (Bellah et al. 1985), a widely acclaimed study blending theoretical ideas with empirical research to offer fresh insights about individualism in contemporary U.S. society. This work picks up almost a century after Durkheim to examine modern versions of old dilemmas of individualism.

Echoing Durkheim, the authors agree that individualism has grown inexorably through U.S. history. Their concern is that this growth might have become cancerous by destroying the social bonds that moderate the harmful effects of individualism. To examine these issues, they focus on the relations between public and private life, the need for a balance between the two, and the ways in which individualism either establishes or undermines that balance.

Echoing my students cited at the beginning of this chapter, the "first language" of U.S. individualism defines freedom as being left alone by others. However, "[w]hat it is that one might do with that freedom is much more difficult for Americans to define" (Bellah et al. 1985, 23). Moreover, this notion of freedom means that "it becomes hard to forge bonds of attachment to, or cooperation with, other people, since such bonds would imply obligations that necessarily impinge on one's freedom" (Bellah et al. 1985, 23).

Their tone is more measured than Lasch's, but this is a familiar story. As people seek lives they think they want by maximizing individualism and freedom, they create conditions that make it very difficult to be connected to others in ways that are also important. This is not just a personal problem of loneliness or alienation; it also erodes the collective fabric required for social health.

Examining U.S. character in historical context reveals two major forms of individualism. Utilitarian individualism is rooted in rational self-interest and economic calculations about success in a competitive environment with others. This form of individualism implies sturdy self-reliance on one's own skills and resources. It is the kind of individualism long associated with the entrepreneur as a social type; more recently, utilitarian individualism fits the role of the manager in a highly rational-ized and bureaucratic society. Such individualism can lead to success measured by the accumulation of material resources, but it also connotes a coldly self-centered orientation to the world.

Whereas utilitarian individualism is about the rational calculation of self-interest, expressive individualism is about the exploration of emotional life. For this type, self-expression is more important than self-interest. Historically, expressive in-dividualism has been associated with romantics, artists, musicians, poets, and others whose lives are centered around emotional aspects of self and the human condition. In the modern world, expressive individualism is symbolized by the therapist.

Both types of individualism persist, because they correspond to the functional divide in modern society between public and personal life. The utilitarian version of individualism fits well in the economic and occupational spheres of public life and their orientation to competition and success. The expressive version of individual-ism fits well in family roles and social relations of personal life with their emphasis on sentiment and emotional exploration. As social types, we are like instrumental managers in the public sphere and expressive therapists in the private sphere.

Whereas the utilitarian individual is explicitly self-interested, the expressive individual seeks fulfillment through relationships with others. This would appear to counteract the destructive aspects of individualism, but the picture is more compli-cated. With expressive individualism, "its genius is that it enables the individual to think of commitments—from marriage and work to political and religious involve-ment—as enhancements of the sense of individual well-being rather than as moral imperatives" (Bellah et al. 1985, 47).

Put differently, expressive individualism seeks relationships with others as long as they meet personal needs—and not a moment longer. Individualism still trumps the relationship because its rationale is fulfilling individual needs. This type of individualism treats "normative commitments as so many alternative strategies of self-fulfillment. What has dropped out are the old normative expectations of what makes life worth living" (Bellah et al. 1985, 48). In different ways, both types of individualism subordinate collective duties and social obligations to individual interests and personal needs.

Consider the iconic U.S. quest of finding oneself. Self-reliance is often thought to arise through leaving home and community; the irony is that these are the roots of whatever self we possess in the first place. This could be why later in life, many people gravitate to "lifestyle enclaves" of people with similar values and interests that provide self-validation through connections with people like themselves. Al-though radical individualism implies that we only find ourselves by leaving others, it is more accurate to say that "we find ourselves not independently of other people and institutions but through them. We never get to the bottom of our selves on our own" (Bellah et al. 1985, 84).

Love and marriage offer a microcosm of the cross-pressures between indi-vidualism and commitment. Marriage traditionally has been a practical, economic arrangement between groups rather than a romantic one between individuals. The transition from one to the other has transformed marriage into a vehicle of personal fulfillment. Marriages therefore become endangered when they no longer deliver such fulfillment. Because marriage and family also remain the central social institutions for the reproduction and socialization of children, the cross-pressures between marriage as a personal satisfaction and family as a social institution symbolize the tensions between modern individualism and social commitments.

Contemporary individualism also pursues therapy as a vehicle of self-discovery. Although not as harshly critical of the therapeutic ethos as Lasch (1979), Robert Bellah and his coauthors describe how seeking self-discovery leads people away from connections with others. Self-actualization is sought as a purely personal matter, and institutional arrangements are seen as beyond one's control. In these ways, therapy unwittingly encourages accommodation to such institutions rather than a sense of agency that might change them through collective action. Finally, therapeutic advice seems to endorse expressive individualism, but it is heavily influenced by instrumental calculations of the costs and benefits of different paths to fulfillment. It is another example of modern culture's elevation of individual needs above collective engagements that might actually fulfill such needs.

Turning from private to public life, the effects of individualism are no less evident. There are many ways people get involved in larger public communities. Often, however, such involvement means associating with people like oneself; it is another version of using others to reinforce one's individuality. People do express concern about the decline of community in their interviews. However, it is difficult for them to respond effectively, because the norms that support communities and foster public involvement have withered in the face of an individualistic ethos.

Similar tensions arise around citizenship. The U.S. ethos of individualism does not equip people to respond effectively to the macro level of society. "If the culture of individualism has difficulty coming to terms with genuine cultural or social differences, it has even more difficulty coming to terms with large impersonal organizations and institutions" (Bellah et al. 1985, 207). Social order is complex because of the interactions of many interdependent groups. Individualism keeps people from understanding this order clearly. Perhaps that is why politicians and mass media so frequently reduce complex issues to simple narratives of heroic or evil people; such narratives resonate with individualism in ways that more complex stories never could.

Religion has traditionally provided unity and integration, so it is an especially interesting arena for understanding U.S. individualism. U.S. history reveals a privatizing of religion, reducing it from cultural obligation to individual preference. The social fact of a religious community that precedes and imposes itself upon the individual (for better and worse) now seems quite foreign. In the individualistic United States, we choose a religion in the same way we choose lifestyles, candidates, cars, and toothpaste in a market of competing brands.

People's responses to the dilemmas of individualism are nevertheless quite complex. The very people who fiercely defend individualism also express dissatisfaction with its consequences and a desire for stronger connections with others. In other cases, people can't think "outside the box" of individualism and yet recognize that it comes with a heavy price in the deterioration of public life and community norms. As the most individualistic culture in the world, U.S. society is thus one of the best places to examine the tensions between individualism and the longing for broader social connections.

On these issues, there is a gap between common sense and the sociological imagination. The former embraces ontological individualism, or the "idea that the individual is the only firm reality" (Bellah et al. 1985, 276). The sociological imagination, by contrast, favors ontological "relationism," or the idea that groups and individuals are interdependent so that individuals only become real in the context of the group. Even mainstream sociology is implicitly critical of common sense by debunking the surface appearance of individualism and revealing its inescapably social roots.

As a final example, consider the ideal of the "self-made man." Although the phrase resonates with U.S. consciousness, it is sociologically nonsensical. People can only be collectively made. No one changes their diapers, invents their language, finds their food, cultivates their mind, acquires their skills, or develops their identity in isolation from others. The most basic sociological insight on this question is this: We are social before we are individual (Lemert 1997). Durkheim demonstrated this on a social evolutionary scale, but the same truth is replayed in the life of every person who emerges from a web of social ties to become an individual in modern society.

Chapter 11

How We Become Who We Are

The previous chapter traced the history of the individual. We learned that the individual is a late arrival who appears only with the rise of modernity. All societies contain people, but only modern ones have individuals.

This chapter traces the biography of the individual. Here, the individual arrives late in a different sense. We become individual only through socialization. We begin this process utterly dependent on others. Only after extensive social support do we develop self-awareness, become individuals, and acquire identity. In both historical and biographical terms, individuals only emerge through social connections with others. We are always social before we are individual (Lemert 1997).

When we ponder what makes one person different from another, there are at least two types of answers. A psychological answer seeks unique traits to explain personal differences. A sociological answer examines the relationships people have with others. Here individuality arises not from something internal, but rather from our external ties to others. A classic version of this idea sees the individual existing at the center of a "web of group affiliations" (Simmel 1908/1955).

A modern variant is the sociograph. You can construct your own. Draw a small circle in the center of a piece of paper to symbolize you. Now draw spokes radiating out to other circles that represent the people in your life. Your relationships with those people differ in many ways: the length of time you have known them, the closeness or intensity of your bonds with them, and the like. Imagine drawing spokes in differing colors, thicknesses, or lengths to capture such nuances.

If you took this exercise seriously, the resulting sociograph would be different from those constructed by others. Sociographs illustrate how no two people occupy the same location in a web of group affiliations. Put differently, we all have unique locations in social networks.

A sociological perspective thus explains the uniqueness of individuals not by focusing inward on personal traits but rather by focusing outward on social networks. We differ from others because we occupy different locations in different networks. Even individuality is not "personal" as much as it is "social."

Take the exercise a step further. Imagine moving to some other circle in your sociograph and constructing that person's sociograph. Their web would include you and some people you know in common, but it would also include people who aren't in your web. Now imagine constructing a sociograph for everyone in your sociograph. As the number of spokes multiply exponentially, the circles representing individuals become less prominent than the ties linking them together. Indeed, the circles representing people come to look like fleeting interruptions in a flow of social forces and connections between them.

The imaginary exercise dramatizes how individuals don't exist apart from social ties with other individuals and groups. Moreover, individuality itself (even with its connotation of uniqueness) is best seen as a product of our distinctive ties with others rather than a purely personal set of traits.

In what follows, we explore how individual selves emerge through social processes. The exploration begins with C. H. Cooley's looking-glass self and proceeds to the synthesis of George Herbert Mead. We then examine symbolic interactionism and identity theory. The chapter closes with observations about how human beings are reflexive actors who bring self-awareness to every situation they encounter.

COOLEY'S CONTRIBUTIONS

Charles Horton Cooley made two vital contributions to understanding how selves emerge through a social process. His work anticipates that of George Herbert Mead, who inspired the symbolic interactionist tradition, which remains sociology's best guide to unraveling questions about self and society.

The first of Cooley's (1998) contributions concerns the role of primary groups in social life. Primary groups involve intimate, face-to-face interaction with others. Within primary groups, we know others and are known to them as whole people, because our involvement is ongoing, all-inclusive, and central to our sense of self.

People also belong to secondary groups, but their connections to such groups are less personal, less intimate, more formal, and often shorter lived than with primary groups. In the sociograph you imagined a moment ago, your primary group consists of the people with whom you have the strongest (and often longest) bonds. They are probably the people closest to you in the sociograph. Farther away from you and your primary group, there are probably other nodes and networks that represent your secondary groups.

The vast majority of people begin their lives within a primary group of family members and perhaps others who are regarded as "family." For better or worse, whether "functional" or "dysfunctional," such familial primary groups are the first and most important social group through which most of us are socialized and develop a sense of self and individuality.

As our self develops, we venture out and join other groups. On the first day of school, we become members of a secondary group of other students. What might start as a frightening social encounter with strangers often develops into another primary group. As we come to know, interact, and play with the same circle of kids, we might form increasingly intimate bonds that become primary relationships.

In adolescence, such peer groups often become more primary and intimate than our family groups. When young people feel as if their friends understand them in ways their parents no longer do (and when parents feel the same way), it is a good indication of multiple primary ties (and tension between them). A more intense emotional tie might then arise, as a romantic partner displaces both the peer group and the family. And somewhat later, we might marry one of those partners and begin a family that will become our next primary group.

Throughout the life cycle, our web of group affiliations consists of shifting combinations of primary and secondary groups. But primary groups remain central to who we are. Our sense of self is intimately connected to these groups. In somewhat different sociological language, primary groups are crucial reference groups; we refer ourselves to these groups to judge who we are, what to do, how to act, and where to find validation for the people we have become. For all these reasons, our webs are held together by our thickest social ties to primary groups.

Cooley's second major contribution is his notion of the self, which is closely tied to primary groups. The key point is simply that there is no self or individual apart from our relationships with other people. "From Cooley's vantage point, then, the self is a social product, a product 'produced' largely in the primary group. It is a product best labeled a 'looking-glass self,' in that a child obtains an identity only with the realization that his or her picture, idea or image of himself or herself 'reflects' other people's picture of him or her" (Reynolds 2003, 63–64).

Imagination is crucial to Cooley's notion of the self. To say that we live in an imaginary world sounds like a put-down. But imagining involves basic processes of thought and cognition; to imagine is to think about the world, about people in the world, about our impressions of them, and about their impressions of us. In this sense, we inevitably live in an imaginary world, because we routinely try to understand the world by thinking about it. These processes are central to how we construct, maintain, or undermine our sense of self and identity.

When we combine primary groups and imagination, we can see the logic in Cooley's "looking-glass self." A crucial part of our imaginary lives involves speculation about the thoughts of others. The thoughts of others, in turn, contain impressions about who we are (and we're pretty disappointed if they don't). It is through this interactive process that we arrive at our sense of self.

This self has three components. First, we imagine how we appear to others. Second, we imagine how they evaluate our appearances. Finally, we construct a sense of self, based on our imaginary understanding of how others evaluate us (Reynolds 2003, 64). Put more succinctly: I am who I think you think I am.

Although the term *looking-glass* sounds quaint, the metaphor of a mirror still makes the point. Without others to reflect who we are back to us, we would have no reliable means of arriving at a sense of self. Common sense might dismiss this as "imaginary," but sociological insight says that this is all we have to base a self on.

We can even dispense with the metaphor. We use real mirrors when we want to assess, modify, or repair our physical appearance. The mirror is essential to get outside ourselves and see ourselves from the perspective of other people. In parallel fashion, our self only becomes known to us through the perspective of other people.

Cooley claimed we also develop strong, emotional responses to the selves that we construct through the looking-glass process. The emotions Cooley regarded as most central were pride and shame. When our judgments of others' judgments about us suggest we are viewed positively, then our self incorporates pride in who we are. When our judgments of others' judgments about us suggest we are viewed negatively, then our self incorporates shame about who we are. For Cooley, the looking-glass self was as much about emotional responses as cognitive processes (Scheff 2005).

Popular culture often tells people to "be positive" and "feel good about themselves," as if this could be accomplished by sheer will. More sociologically informed advice would say surround yourself with people who are positive about and feel good about you. Easier said than done, but if Cooley is right, our self-feelings do not arise on their own and cannot long exist in contradiction to the feelings we imagine others have about who we are.

MEAD'S SYNTHESIS

Building on the work of Cooley and others, George Herbert Mead formulated a distinct perspective on self and society. Mead wrote little but was a gifted lecturer at the University of Chicago. Upon his retirement and death in 1931, his students assembled his ideas into a sociological classic titled *Mind, Self and Society* (Mead 1934/1962).

Mead's work synthesized ideas prevalent in late nineteenth- and early twentieth-century social thought. Georg Simmel's web of group affiliations is one element. So is Max Weber's insistence that we can only understand social action if we see it from the perspective of the actor. Cooley's looking-glass self plays an obvious role. William James had also studied the social self. Mead also drew on the work of John Dewey, who approached mind not as a physical structure but as a process of interpretation and meaning. Finally, W. I. Thomas had discussed the "definition of the situation" and demonstrated that situations defined as real will be real in their consequences. The imagery of social actors imposing definitions on the world around them and acting on those definitions was central to Mead's work.

Mead's synthesis put him at odds with other sociological approaches. Many versions of sociology analyze social structures as static entities, but Mead saw society as a dynamic process of change and fluidity. For Mead, the social world is less like still pictures and more like a movie playing at multiple frames per second. Moreover, although some versions of sociology explain the world through casual relationships of independent and dependent variables, Mead saw social elements as interrelated and interdependent. Each part gained its meaning from its relationship to others and to the whole, so it is difficult to isolate elements that can be analyzed as cause and effect.

Having said that, Mead is clearly in the sociological camp by recognizing that society precedes and shapes the individual. Although grammatically awkward, a more conceptually accurate title for Mead's book might have been "Society, Mind, Self and Society," to suggest the priority of society as a social environment in which minds and selves develop in individuals who only then become competent social actors.

Mead's exploration of minds and selves develops some of the core ideas of interactionist sociology. The first challenge is to understand the development of individual minds. Mead's concern is not with the physical structure of the brain but with the social process of the mind. The focus is not neurons and synapses but rather consciousness and meaning.

Mead begins with behaviorist logic but quickly moves from static psychological behaviorism to symbolic social psychology. He defines a gesture as any action that serves as a stimulus and provokes a response. The response becomes a stimulus for the initial actor who then responds to it, which in turn becomes a new stimulus for the second actor. In this way, a conversation of gestures is an interactive spiral of stimuli and response between two or more actors.

Whereas behaviorists applied this logic to all human behavior, Mead thought conversations of gestures were primarily found in the nonhuman animal world (which is the basis for much behaviorist research going all the way back to Pavlov's salivating dogs). Such nonhuman animal behavior is largely rooted in instincts, meaning that animals are pre-wired to act in certain ways and do not rely on symbolic interpretations to do so. Mead's favorite example was a dogfight in which the behavior of each dog becomes a stimulus provoking an instinctive response in the other dog, leading to an escalation of barking, snarling, flattened ears, bared teeth, biting, and the like.

Mead departed from behaviorism by arguing that the vast majority of human action—and certainly the most sociologically interesting action—could not be understood as instinctual, unthinking patterns of stimulus and response. Humans differ from other animals because they formulate, interpret, and attribute *meaning* to actions and to people in their environment. This is why a boxing match is very different from a dogfight. Unlike dogs, boxers interpret, imagine, anticipate, and deceive as part of their strategy. It is this complex mental world—even in the brutality of the boxing ring—that qualitatively distinguishes human *action* from animal *behavior*.

To capture human action, Mead proposed different terminology. In contrast to the simple gestures of animals, human interaction involves significant symbols. Simple gestures become significant symbols when they meet two requirements. First, they carry a specific meaning. Second, that meaning is shared within some community of people. Although this might sound obtuse, the best example is right here on the page. Human languages are vast collections of significant symbols known as words, which in turn can be put together in larger, meaningful units like phrases, sentences, paragraphs, and even books. Physical gestures (handshakes, applause, the finger) can also be significant symbols if they carry a specific, shared meaning.

Significant symbols arise from interaction, because it is only through interaction that they achieve significance. Consider that the meaning is in the response. If you utter a phrase that elicits immediate recognition, the odds are it is a significant symbol that carries the same meaning for others as it does for you. If your phrase is met with a blank stare, the odds are it's not a significant symbol, because it is not calling up a similar meaning in those around you.

Here's a simple example. I live with a cat that freaks out when someone rings the doorbell. After an especially traumatic episode, I tried a stopgap measure of taping a small piece of paper over the doorbell. To me, the paper meant "don't ring the doorbell—knock instead." The next day, a delivery person rang the doorbell (traumatizing the cat). The day after that, someone selling something I didn't need rang the doorbell (further traumatizing the cat). Neither person interpreted the paper over the doorbell in the way I intended. It was not a significant symbol, because there was no shared meaning between me and my visitors. The day after that, a neighbor came to borrow something and gently knocked on the door. In this instant, the piece of paper became a significant symbol, because she assigned the same meaning to it that I did and acted accordingly. She did so because she had also tried to keep people from ringing her doorbell and disturbing her child's afternoon nap.

The simple example illustrates several larger points. Significant symbols are not static; they emerge through interaction only when it becomes evident that people assign the same meaning to some part of their environment. Moreover, what is a significant symbol to some people might not be a significant symbol to other people. This is most obvious when speakers of different languages attempt to communicate; it is a struggle to find even a minimal set of significant symbols so they can understand one another. But even within the same language group, there are subcultures of people who speak distinctive sublanguages known to them but not to outsiders. Indeed, the identity of many subcultures depends precisely on who "gets it" (that is, shares their significant symbols) and who doesn't have a clue.

This demonstrates the social roots of individual minds. Here's the logic. "Mind" is shorthand for the process of thinking, involving consciousness and meaning. Thinking is really an internalized conversation of significant symbols. The focus of our thought could be anything: how to spend the weekend, whether we should call an elderly relative, pondering the motivation behind a friend's snide comment, or whatever. Regardless of the topic, to think is to have a silent conversation with oneself about that topic. Whereas interaction is an externalized conversation of significant symbols with others, thinking is an internalized conversation of significant symbols with ourselves.

Mead implies we cannot think without significant symbols; they are the building blocks of the internalized conversations that compose thinking. But if the symbols that compose thinking are significant, this means they carry a shared meaning. Such shared meanings can only arise from interactions with others. The conclusion seems obvious. Humans are born with a physical brain but not a social mind. Minds are only acquired through social interaction with others. That social process provides us with the shared meanings of the significant symbols that allow us to think. When it comes to minds—as with so much else—we must first be social before we can be individual. Sociologically speaking, socialization makes us human by developing the capacities that distinguish us as a species.

Mead's argument might seem convoluted, but it resonates with common sense. Imagine encountering someone on a city street who is babbling incomprehensibly. What conclusions do we draw about their mental state? Now imagine that people who speak this person's language appear, and they have an animated discussion in Norwegian about how to find the subway station. We are likely to revise our opinion of their mental state when we recognize that they share meanings and a language with a group of people (just not us). But if no one ever comes along who understands our urban babbler, we are likely to conclude that they have "lost their mind." Even everyday language links making sense, shared meanings, and having a mind.

For Mead, the distinctive qualities of human interaction emerge from our ability to create, learn, and communicate significant symbols. They allow us to interpret stimuli and respond in meaningful ways. They allow us to develop abstract concepts that go beyond immediate experience and classify experiences into categories. This allows imaginative reflection on past experiences and future possibilities rather than learning only through trial and error. In the end, this makes intelligent action possible, as we use significant symbols, shared meanings, and abstract concepts to learn from the past, interpret the present, anticipate the future, and link them all together.

If minds only emerge through a social process, the same is true for selves. We are not born with a self but rather acquire one through socialization. Cooley's looking-glass self is an early statement of this position, and Mead builds on it.

The self has two components; one is there from the beginning. The "I" refers to impulses to act toward the world. This inborn "I" is later joined by a socialized "Me" to form a fully developed social self. Selves thereby involve interaction between the "I" and the "Me."

Although the impulses of the "I" are channeled by the socialization of the "Me," it never disappears. The "I" persists as an active subject; it is the part of us that acts in the moment. The persistence of the "I" even in the mature self means that people are always capable of spontaneous, creative, unpredictable actions. The self is never completely determined by larger social forces, because we always retain the capacity to act back upon those forces.

To have a self means to see oneself as an object. It is the capacity to be self-aware or self-conscious. The "I" can never achieve such awareness because it is always acting in the moment. It is the "Me" that provides this self-awareness. The "Me" only develops through "taking the role of the other." This is Mead's version of Cooley's looking-glass self. The underlying idea is quite similar: We arrive at a sense of self by imaginatively taking the role of other people in our social environment. From their perspective, we are an object in their world. When we imaginatively adopt their perspective, we are able to see ourselves as an object. We develop self-awareness.

Once again we must be social before we can be individual. Until we interact with others whose roles we imaginatively take, we cannot develop a concept of ourselves as an object. We need others whose roles we take to provide the mirrors that tell us that we have a self and who we are. Immersion in sustained interaction with others is the only way we develop a mind and a self; it is the way we become human.

To have a self is to be capable of observations, judgments, and feelings about the self that only become possible by taking the role of the other. If we act in ways that surprise others (and ourselves), this demonstrates the capacity of the "I" to act in novel ways. If we explain such action by saying "I'm not myself today," we are displaying a fully developed self. The statement is logically ludicrous but sociologically sensible. We are saying that some momentary action is inconsistent with a well-established sense of who we are based on a long process of role taking. Only the "Me" can offer such observations about the self.

The "Me" is thus the perspective of others internalized by the self. The "Me" is a developmental product of interaction that emerges in stages. As infants in the pre-play stage, we are incapable of getting outside ourselves and taking the role of others. Infants are all "I" and no "Me." As young children, however, we begin to develop both a mind and the ability to take the role of the other. In the play stage, we take the role of significant others in our social environment. These are specific people who are familiar to us. As we play, we model their behavior and imaginatively see the world from their perspective. This is the earliest version of seeing ourselves as an object; by imaginatively seeing ourselves through the eyes of our parents or primary caretakers, we begin to develop a sense of self.

As we become more skilled at role taking, we enter the game stage and simultaneously take the roles of multiple others in more complex situations. The famous example is playing baseball, but any team sport will do. To play such games well, each player must anticipate the actions of everyone else on the team. By anticipating their actions in different situations, good players align their actions to fit with overall team strategy. Such game playing presupposes an ability to take multiple roles that only emerges over time. This is why young children can handle some interactive play but are incapable of more complex team games.

As we progress from taking the role of significant others to multiple others, we eventually take the role of the generalized Other. This is not a particular person or group but rather the larger society and its norms and values. Returning to Cooley's language, the development of the self proceeds by switching mirrors. As very young children, it is particular, significant others who provide the mirror that tells us who we are. As older children, it is multiple others who provide that mirror. As socialization continues, the mirror becomes all of the attitudes, values, and beliefs that compose our society itself. The constant is that we look outside ourselves to know who we are. The variable is which "others" are most central in reflecting our self back to us.

The ability to take the role of the generalized Other signals a fully developed self. This "Other" is initially outside us, but it becomes incorporated inside us in the form of the "Me." The mature self combines the acting "I" and the socialized "Me." Because the self requires a "Me" and the "Me" requires taking the role of the other, the self only emerges through social interaction with others.

The development of mind and self go hand in hand. The internal conversation that composes the mind can only occur with a corresponding self-awareness that signifies a self. Both emerge through interaction with others that provides shared meanings and role-taking opportunities. Although later sociologists have pursued many variations on these themes, Mead's synthesis provides a vital sociological understanding of the relationship between self and society.

SYMBOLIC INTERACTIONISM

Mead's student Herbert Blumer took the lead in publishing Mead's (1934) ideas. Blumer also coined the term *symbolic interactionism* to underscore the importance of symbolic meanings in interpreting human action. The phrase sounds awkward, but conveys much about the assumptions of this approach.

Blumer (1969) subsequently claimed that symbolic interactionism could be summarized in three basic premises. The first is that human beings act toward things on the basis of the meanings things have for them. What is important is not the things but rather the meanings that we (and others) attach to them.

This seemingly subtle distinction makes a big difference. Consider the contrast between psychological behaviorism and symbolic interactionism. Behaviorists explain what we do as responses to stimuli in the environment. The environment determines behavior by providing stimuli that mechanistically lead us to seek rewards and avoid punishments. The stimuli, response, rewards, and punishments are assumed to be transparently self-evident to both the organism and the behaviorist. There is no need to explore the subjective "black box" of the mind; behaviorism rather seeks an external explanation linking behavioral responses to environmental stimuli.

This makes sense if people respond directly to things. It makes much less sense if they respond to the meanings of things, as Blumer claims. Interactionism sees action as a process of self-indication. Actors select which aspects of their environment are meaningful for them. Because they assign meanings to their surroundings, it could be said that actors determine their environment rather than the other way around. Because meanings vary across persons and situations, we must examine how minds shape meanings. Interactionism thereby seeks an internal explanation of action by linking minds, meanings, and actions.

The first premise establishes that meanings are central. The second is that meanings are derived from social interaction. This locates meanings between two polar opposites. They are not purely objective qualities attached to things in the same way in all times and places. But they are also not purely subjective choices of individuals outside interaction. Meanings are rather intersubjective accomplishments of social interaction. Like Mead's significant symbols, objects acquire meanings as a result of ongoing social interaction.

This premise explains variability in the meanings of objects over time and across groups. Why do people disagree about the appropriateness of Indian mascots for sports teams? How do people interpret the meaning of the Civil War in the South and the North? What does the word *gay* mean to different generations of people? When is graffiti a marker of gang affiliation, and when is it art? What does it mean to have a tattoo or a piercing? Such meanings are not fixed and objective; neither are they purely subjective and idiosyncratic. It is interactions in different groups that define the "same event" like the Civil War as a humiliating defeat or a glorious victory. Both meanings are "true" in different social worlds that sustain those definitions through interaction.

The variability of meanings reflects the pragmatist heritage of symbolic interaction in which things acquire meaning by how they are used or how people interact with them. Thus, a tree has different meanings and becomes a different object for the botanist, the timber company, and the poet. Take another example. A woman nursing an infant is interacting in a way that defines her breasts as nourishment and nurturance. That same woman making love with her sexual partner is interacting in a way that defines her breasts as erotic stimulation and gratification. That same woman undergoing an exam by her doctor is engaged in an interaction that defines her breasts as potential sites of disease and malignancy. Same woman, same breasts—but drastically different meanings arise from different interactions with different people.

The ways that interactions create and sustain meanings also establish the definition of the situation. Such definitions are intersubjective, cultural creations that provide cues about what to expect and how to behave in a given situation. Differing definitions of the situation create different meanings in "objectively" similar situations. A woman who bares her breast in public to nurse her infant might meet with acceptance, whereas a woman who does so in a strip joint might be condemned or even arrested (depending on local ordinances). A male doctor examining a female patient is engaging in behavior that could be construed as sexual assault in other settings, but is regarded as normal as long as the medical definition of the situation is maintained.

Blumer's third and final premise is that meanings are handled and modified through an interpretive process. This means that even when meanings are well established (and especially when they are not), people still tailor them to the specific situation at hand. This work begins with the process of self-indication in which people "create" their environment on the basis of intersubjective meanings.

The process continues because no two situations are exactly the same and general meanings must be adapted to specific settings. People are active throughout this process. "The actor selects, checks, suspends, regroups, and transforms the meanings in the light of the situation in which he is placed" (Blumer 1969, 5). This process of interpretation is a formative one in which meanings are used, revised, and modified as the actor fashions action that will be meaningful to all concerned.

Blumer's formulation of symbolic interactionism puts it at odds not only with psychological behaviorism but also with more structural approaches in sociology.

Blumer insists that concepts like structure, system, function, or institution are really shorthand abstractions for people interacting with one another. Although the shorthand is convenient, it becomes a trap when we speak as if these abstractions act or even exist apart from the interactions that sustain them. For Blumer, good sociology avoids structuralist abstractions by focusing on the meanings and interactions that create, sustain, and modify social patterns.

IDENTITY THEORY

Interactionist theory provides sociology with its best understandings of identity. The starting point is that the self is the ability to see oneself as an object, evidenced by self-awareness or self-consciousness. This awareness originally emerges from, and subsequently depends on, interactions with other people.

We move from self to identity by asking what kind of object we see ourselves to be. If self is the object, identity is the meanings attached to that object. Identity emerges when meanings are attached to the object we call the self.

Blumer's first premise is that it is not objects but their meanings that are important. This applies to identity as follows. Everybody acquires a self. We couldn't interact with people if they didn't have a self through which to organize interaction. What is of interest in interactions is not the generic selves everyone possesses, but the particular identities or meanings of those selves. This is how we identify ourselves and others; who people are is a function of the meanings or identities linked to selves.

Blumer's second premise is that meanings arise through interactions with others. They are intersubjective accomplishments. The same applies to the meanings we call identities. Just as Mead's symbols become significant when they call up the same meaning in others as they do in us, identities become real when there is a shared understanding about who someone is. "One's identity is established when others *place* him as a social object by assigning him the same words of identity that he appropriates for himself or *announces.* It is in the coincidence of placements and announcements that identity becomes a meaning of the self" (Stone, cited in Vryan, Adler, and Adler 2003, 368; emphasis in original).

Take an extreme example. I might believe, and then announce to the world, that I am the second coming of Christ. If I persist in this claim, I will be dismissed as a nutcase. If I convince a small band of devoted followers of my claim, we will all be dismissed as mentally unstable (but perhaps dangerous because of our numbers). But if I somehow convince hundreds, then thousands, and finally millions of people around the world of my identity claim, and they relate to me as if I am that person, then don't I become that person? If my announcements and others' placements concur, does that not become my identity? In less extreme cases, the process is clear: Identity emerges when an actor's announcements and others' placements coincide.

Blumer's third premise is that meanings are handled and modified through an interpretive process as people tailor meanings to fit specific situations. Applied to identity, this means that we continually reinterpret, select, check, regroup, suspend, and transform our understandings of who we and others are as part of ongoing inter-action. For example, we understand that people (including ourselves) have different identities in different situations. When we encounter them in a certain situation, we selectively present some of our identities and expect them to do the same. If everyone enacts identities appropriate to the situation, interaction will proceed smoothly.

Each of Blumer's premises about meaning thus applies to identity itself. Inter-actionism also distinguishes several types of identities, including social, situational, and personal identities (Vryan, Adler, and Adler 2003, 367–372).

Social identities arise when we announce and others place us in positions within social structures. Identities based on class, race, gender, religion, or sexual orientation exemplify social identities. They are broad social categories that link us to others with similar traits and separate us from those with different traits. Social identities shape how people are enabled or constrained by social order; differing opportunities emerge from the statuses granted to or withheld from these identities.

Situational identities arise when we engage in face-to-face interactions with oth-ers and organize our action through situationally appropriate roles and definitions of the situation. Although they might be repetitive and patterned, situations are relatively short lived. When we attend a baseball game, we become a fan; when we go on vaca-tion, we become a tourist; when we leave for work, we become a motorist or commuter. We thus acquire a situational identity in a particular context. The ways we enact this identity are constrained by cultural norms and situational definitions, but there is always room for some individual creativity in enacting situational identities.

Personal identities arise when we construct biographical narratives about who we are. They distinguish us from others in the same positions or situations. Thus, part of my story is that when I was an undergraduate, I made my living (and more) as a drummer in a rock-and-roll band. Even though I stopped playing when I went to graduate school more than thirty years ago, it is part of who I am, because it is who I once was. Moreover, it helps establish my distinctiveness: Not many college professors are former rock drummers, and not many rock drummers become college professors (and it's probably just as well that they don't).

Situational identities like baseball fan, grocery shopper, or wedding party member are short lived and don't necessarily reveal much about who we are. Social identities are more permanent because they are difficult or impossible to change, although people can either embrace them or hold them at arms' length. Personal identities are more lasting in a different way, because they rest on a person's accumu-lated biography. Although we can distinguish different types of identity, the basic principles of identity theory still apply. Identities of all types are meanings attached to the self that emerge through announcements by self and placements by others.

Like all meanings, identities are socially constructed, maintained, and transformed. Most identity transformations are gradual, developmental transitions through the life cycle. Even though parenthood or retirement might feel sudden to the individual, they are routine in that they happen to many people and it is possible to anticipate and plan for them in advance. Other, less common identity transfor-mations are quick and radical in nature. When prisoners of war are brainwashed or people undergo a conversion experience, they might renounce former identities and embrace radically different ones very quickly.

Another type of identity transformation involves "suspended identity" (Schmid and Jones 1991). This occurs when people must leave one identity behind while adopting another identity. If they intend to reclaim their former identity, it is not so much terminated or transformed as it is suspended. It's as if they hang that identity in the closet until they can wear it once again. When citizen soldiers are called up as army reservists or National Guard troops, they suspend their citizen identity and adopt a soldier identity. Unlike regular army troops, however, they are likely to see their citizen identity as the "real" one, which is temporarily suspended during military duty.

A classic case is people who go to prison. Before going to prison, people have a "pre-prison identity." Like the civilian anticipating becoming a soldier, these citizens anticipate becoming a prisoner as they move through the criminal justice system. A common response is self-insulation by minimizing contact with others, avoiding conflict or violence, and avoiding any situations that might undermine their pre-prison identity.

Despite these resolutions, inmates cannot take their pre-prison identity with them, nor can they live in complete isolation. They have to create a prison identity to relate to staff, guards, and other prisoners. Short-term inmates see this prison identity as temporary and situational, although they worry that it might displace their pre-prison identity. While serving time, inmates experience a dualistic self. They try to sustain a pre-prison identity, which is temporarily suspended, privately held, and rarely affirmed. They simultaneously enact a prison identity, which is self-consciously learned, enacted for self and others, and affirmed through prison interactions.

Toward the end of their sentence, prisoners develop a release identity that sets aside their prison identity and revives their suspended identity. Like earlier stages, this involves much self-talk about who they really are, how they might have changed, and how they can become the person they used to be. Upon leaving prison, former inmates acquire a post-prison identity that distances them from their prison experience and helps restore their suspended identity (Schmid and Jones 1991).

Prison thereby poses a particular identity challenge. Although most of us will not go to prison, all of us undergo processes of identity formation, maintenance, and transformation. Interactionist theory provides powerful tools for understanding them.

PEOPLE AS REFLEXIVE ACTORS

Interactionist theory underscores how human action is guided by reflexivity. People are conscious of the meanings of selves, others, and objects in their world, and they use this knowledge to organize actions and pursue goals. The premise of reflexivity is shared by other theoretical perspectives as well.

As we saw in chapter one, there is a debate in sociology over the relationship between structure and agency. Structure-based approaches emphasize large social patterns that seem to dwarf individuals. Agency-based approaches stress individual choices and seem to deny the weight of external factors. Neither approach is completely satisfactory; the challenge is to strike a balance between the two.

One attempt is structuration theory (Giddens 1984). It rejects a view of structures as merely external and constraining forces that exist on their own. Rather than structures, it speaks of "structuration processes" as a way of linking structure and action. Here, structures are no more than the outcomes of past actions and the means for organizing current ones.

Seen this way, structuration processes sometimes constrain action because they are obstacles to what we want to do. But they can also enable action when they provide resources and means to pursue goals. Rather then seeing structures as external, controlling forces, we should see structuration processes as providing opportunities to act (within certain limits). Moreover, when people act, they unintentionally reproduce (and sometimes transform) those very structures.

This approach assumes people are reflexive actors. People in society "are vastly skilled in the practical accomplishments of social activities and are expert 'sociologists.' The knowledge they possess is not incidental to the persistent patterning of social life but integral to it" (Giddens 1984, 26). In other words, people routinely use practical consciousness in daily life to monitor their actions and the actions of others and to align both. This consciousness contains much practical knowledge about how things work in a particular society and culture.

People also incorporate sociological knowledge into practical consciousness; ideas like self-fulfilling prophecies, unintended consequences, or group-think have migrated from social science to everyday consciousness. It is difficult to appreciate the importance of this practical consciousness, because it becomes second nature once we're socialized. But if you've had any experiences with other cultures or languages that made you feel "dumb," it underscores how "smart" you are about your own culture and language and how unconsciously you call upon knowledge of it to do things.

Another way of describing reflexivity is sociological competence. "This seemingly native, highly practical, virtually ubiquitous capacity sustains us individually, but it also contributes mightily to our ability to form and keep social relations with others. Without it, social life would be impossible. Without it, every time we entered a new and different social situation, we would be forced to learn anew what to think of it and how to behave. But, most of the time, we understand what is going on and where we fit in" (Lemert 1997, 5). Like linguistic competence, sociological competence seems to be an inherent capacity to understand the social world. When it is matched with socialization, we use it in an almost effortless way.

Although acquiring sociological competence is *almost* effortless, it nonetheless requires practice. Charles Lemert (1997) draws on Pierre Bourdieu's (1977) notion of habitus to understand how sociological competence is sustained through practice. The concept of habitus underscores how much of social life involves habitual actions that once had to be learned but then became second nature—things that we do unthinkingly, and usually quite competently. Like Giddens's structuration, Bourdieu's habitus is where agency and structure meet and their seeming contradiction is resolved. Habitual practices simultaneously result from social rules (structures) and individual flourishes (agency) that produce action (Lemert 1997, 44).

From another angle, habitus is the intersection between actions experienced as novel by the individual while simultaneously conforming to social patterns. This is most evident when we first learn things that have yet to become habitual. The first time we drive a car, have a sexual encounter, or work at a job, the event is new to us but part of a larger pattern that happens in roughly similar ways for millions of people. The awkwardness that characterizes each of these original experiences demonstrates that these competencies must indeed be learned and practiced. At a certain point, driving, sex, or working are accomplished with much less awkwardness, signifying that we have learned and habitualized them. We have acquired sociological competence.

In everyday life, we focus on immediate concerns. We rely on sociological competence and acquired habits. It rarely occurs to us that our actions help sustain the society around us. Nonetheless, habitual actions performed by socially competent actors do precisely this. Giddens's structuration, Lemert's competence, and Bourdieu's habitus all point to the same conclusion. Social order rests upon the reflexivity of actors who use existing structures to do things while simultaneously (if unintentionally) sustaining, recreating, and transforming those very structures. Without reflexivity, social order itself would be impossible.

CONCLUSION

Interactionist theory provides rich insights into mind, self, identity, and reflexivity. It is a good example of humanistic sociology. As such, it is critical in two ways. First, it is critical to an accurate understanding of the complex, dialectical connections between self and society, structure and agency, and micro and macro levels of society.

Second, it is critical by revealing that things are not always what they appear to be (Berger 1963). If we want to see past appearances to underlying realities, this theory is like a backstage pass in the theater of social life. Consider individualism one more time. As noted earlier, U.S. culture is probably the most individualistic in human history. If any culture assumes we are individual before we are social, it is ours. Interactionist theory is thus critical to seeing all the ways we are unavoidably social before we can become individual (Lemert 1997).

The third sense of critical sociology explicitly examines power, domination, exploitation, and oppression. Here, interactionism has been largely silent. It critically examines U.S. individualism, but it uncritically accepts U.S. egalitarianism.

U.S. culture has always emphasized its distance from European traditions, where rank, status, class, and distinction are crucial. U.S. ideology describes a "classless" society where everyone gets a chance and no one is held back by artificial social barriers. Although not necessarily embracing these specific ideas, interactionism's image of society also downplays vertical hierarchies and emphasizes horizontal life-worlds. The interactionist image of society is multiple social worlds of distinctive meanings and identities coexisting alongside one another. It implicitly sees society as a pluralistic conglomeration of such worlds.

What is lacking in this image is the role of power in social life. Although it is true that different social worlds construct different meanings, it is also true that some worlds have the privilege and power to make their meanings normative while marginalizing others. The meanings central to interactionist theory are often hier-archically organized so that some groups benefit at the expense of others.

This is nicely captured in the notion of ideology as meaning in the service of power (Thompson 1990). Interactionism has provided a rich vocabulary for analyz-ing meanings in social life, but it will only reach its fully critical potential when it examines the relationships between meaning and power.

Chapter 12

The Sociology of Everyday Life

Symbolic interactionism provides our best answers to questions about self and society, but other approaches broaden the questions and enrich the answers. This chapter examines sociologies of everyday life, including phenomenological sociology, the social construction of reality, ethnomethodology, and dramaturgical sociology. It concludes with final reflections about the self in a postmodern social world.

PHENOMENOLOGICAL SOCIOLOGY

Philosophers have long debated *ontology* and *epistemology.* Those are fancy words for questions about what really exists in the world and how we can have reliable knowledge of it.

Here's a real-life example: Imagine driving on a winding, two-lane road late at night. Just beyond your headlights, you see an ambiguous shape at the side of the road. In an instant, you convince yourself that it is a deer about to jump into the road. As you brake and approach, you realize there's no deer. It's simply a bush, backlit by the moon. Your mind tricked you into seeing a deer and believing it was real—but only for an instant. Philosophers ask whether such mind tricks occur more often and last longer. If so, how do we know what is real and that our knowledge is reliable?

These questions were at the heart of a philosophical debate between John Locke and Immanuel Kant. Locke maintained that an external, objective world exists independently of all observers. Moreover, that objective world has an inherent order to it. Finally, people are blank slates, or passive observers of that world. We perceive an orderly world because we use our senses to grasp the objective world and its inherent order. For empiricism, order is *out there* and people learn about it as they interact with the world.

Kant took a rationalist or idealist position. He agreed that we have perceptions of the world around us, but thought they are chaotic and fragmented. They only become orderly because *we* organize them into meaningful patterns. Rather than blank slates, we are born with innate categories like time, space, motion, and causality. We use these categories to impose order on fragmentary sense impressions of the world. This is why we "see" a deer that isn't really there.

In contrast to empiricism, Kant argued that we can never know for sure about the external world and whether it is orderly. People might believe they live in an orderly world, but only because their mental categories create order for them. For rationalism, order is *in here* because people impose meaning on otherwise chaotic perceptions.

Edmund Husserl elaborated this position at the end of the nineteenth century by developing phenomenology. Like Kant, Husserl emphasized how mind creates order. Everything we know about the world is filtered through mind and consciousness. Our mind is the source of intentions, which in turn create a meaningful world. It is our purposes or goals that impose order on the world.

Like Kant, Husserl believed that an orderly world is an accomplishment of our minds. However, we are not necessarily aware of this accomplishment. In everyday life (what Husserl called the lifeworld), we rely on a natural attitude of taken-for-granted assumptions. Here's the interesting twist. The natural attitude makes us into naive empiricists who take an orderly world for granted. The natural attitude provides a sense of order, but obscures how it comes from us rather than existing "out there."

The natural attitude means we assume that an objective world exists, that it has meaning and order, and that it is intersubjectively shared with others who experience it in much the same way we do. The natural attitude just seems like common sense. In reality, it tricks us into thinking that order is in the world instead of in our minds. Based on these misguided assumptions, we plan, act, and find our way in the world.

This philosophical detour has taken us from Locke's empiricism through Kant's rationalism to Husserl's phenomenology. Let's get back on the main road of sociology with the guidance of Alfred Schutz (1932/1967). In the early twentieth century, he developed a phenomenological sociology indebted to Husserl's idea of intentionality and Weber's emphasis on subjective meanings.

Schutz agrees with Husserl that the natural attitude is crucial in everyday life. Schutz, however, sees this common sense perspective as a fragile and delicate construction. He asks how we maintain this attitude in the first place. We return to sociology by examining how social interactions sustain the natural attitude. Put differently, how do we convince ourselves and others that we live in an objective, orderly, shared world?

The most basic way we do this is by *assuming* reciprocity of perspectives. We assume that "the experiences I am having here and now are similar or identical to the experiences you are having here and now; if we traded places, our experiences would be essentially the same."

This assumption is like the default setting for social interaction. It gets it started. However, even though we assume reciprocity of perspectives all the time, it is not necessarily true. The room we experience as cold might be warm to others; the poem that brings us to tears might leave others untouched; the music we find jarring could be someone else's favorite song. So it sometimes turns out that our perspectives are *not* so reciprocal after all.

When interaction breaks down in this way, the focus often shifts to consciously creating the reciprocity that people have just realized is missing. When we question others, express feelings, share impressions, or argue positions, it can narrow the gap between perspectives. Reciprocity is thus the unstated assumption of all social interaction, and it often becomes its explicit goal when people realize it is lacking.

The impression that we live in an orderly world is also maintained by stock knowledge. This is the common sense stuff "everybody knows." Stock knowledge becomes so familiar that we forget we once had to learn it. Once we do so, it becomes "second nature" and unquestioned. This knowledge and the way it gets embedded in everyday life makes our world appear natural, normal, logical, and inevitable. It makes it easy to see the world as an orderly place and hard to see how we create our impression of an orderly world.

Much the same may be said for recipes, or cultural knowledge of "standard operating procedures" for accomplishing everyday goals. The metaphor of a recipe suggests a basic set of ingredients while allowing for variations once people learn the recipe. Like stock knowledge, recipes are learned but eventually become second nature. As we unthinkingly resort to familiar routines to accomplish things, this also reinforces our sense of a naturally ordered world.

We also sustain a sense of order in the world through typifications. Like Kant, Schutz claims that we use mental categories to organize our experiences into coherent patterns. Unlike Kant, Schutz's typifications are not innate but learned.

Typifications are essential to everyday life. Here's why. Every person and situation we encounter is unique, at least in the details. If we were constantly attuned to the unique aspects of each person or situation, we would be mentally overwhelmed. Life would be an endless series of new events, and lessons from the past would not apply to the present. We manage this potentially dizzying complexity through typifications. We understand unique people or situations as instances of broader types of people or situations that we already know.

We grasp a complex world by sorting it into typifications and using them to understand particular people and situations. Typifications are like the definition of the situation. Once we know the definition of the situation—or once we find appropriate typifications through which to understand a situation—we know what to expect, what norms are in effect, how to behave, and the like.

Like stock knowledge and recipes, typifications are learned. They are a bit like stereotypes. We have typifications of corporate CEOs, movie stars, truck drivers, welfare recipients, lawyers, plumbers, and soccer moms. We have typifications about fraternity parties, funerals, weddings, football games, and jury trials. When we impose these typifications on people or events, it frames who or what they are.

It also sustains a belief that the world is already organized along certain lines when the organization actually derives from typifications in our minds.

These ideas reinforce each other. The assumption about reciprocity of perspectives includes the assumption that people share stock knowledge, recipes, and typifications. The cumulative effect is to create the impression that we live in an "objective reality." Put differently, we convince ourselves that the order we detect in the world really exists out there rather than being the product of our minds. This is how we sustain the natural attitude.

Whenever these beliefs guide interaction to a smooth conclusion, it becomes easier to believe in an objectively ordered, intersubjectively shared world. Even so, the natural attitude remains a fragile construction. Its assumptions are not necessarily true. Every life contains moments when they break down. We might learn in the most unpleasant ways that others don't share our perspective, that our stock knowledge is no help, that our recipes led to unintended and unwanted outcomes, or that our typifications don't fit and have left us clueless.

As a final illustration, consider what happens when people have an existential crisis and fundamentally question their world. Others typically provide reassurances through Schutz's techniques. We tell people in a crisis that we once went through the same thing—invoking reciprocity of perspectives. We use typifications by saying they're going through a phase, or they're in the third stage of grief, or any other cultural category that draws the person back into a world of reciprocal meanings. And if we can't rescue them, we use yet another typification of "mental illness" that allows us (and perhaps them) to understand their lack of reciprocity with us. Such moments reveal how the natural attitude is a mere hypothesis and how the order in our world is socially constructed rather than objectively given.

THE SOCIAL CONSTRUCTION OF REALITY

Schutz's phenomenological sociology inspired the social constructionist theory of Peter Berger and Thomas Luckmann (1966). People construct many realities, but the reality of everyday life is fundamental. Although arbitrary and relative, we experience it as certain and absolute because of our assumptions about it. Through stock knowledge, typifications, and recipes, we define subjective experiences, intersubjective meanings, and objective structures as fundamentally real.

Language is central here. It is a repository of shared meanings and cultural typifications. Relevance structures are also central. Combining typifications and intentionality, relevance structures orient us and provide meaning in given situations.

Relevance structures mean people in the same objective space often live in different subjective worlds. Every day people gather in hospital emergency rooms, but they bring different relevance structures to it as accident victims, overworked surgeons, medical residents, claims adjustors, triage nurses, and janitorial staff. What is "real" about the situation depends on whose relevance structure is in play. Relevance structures impose different meanings for different people.

The social construction of reality occurs through three interrelated processes. Externalization means that human purposes and intentions motivate actions that create a particular social world. Externalization means society is a human product.

Objectivation means that these externalizations seem to become independent, freestanding realities. They appear to have a life of their own and to exist without the intervention of people. Objectivation means that society is an objective reality.

Internalization means that this seemingly objective world is retrojected into our consciousness. Through socialization, we acquire an internalized understanding of this socially constructed world. Internalization means people are also a social product.

All three processes occur simultaneously. Consider any organization, school, church, business, or other enterprise. Trace its history back to its origin. Before that point, it had no reality outside the intentions of people who created it. As they did so, the organization took on a life of its own. It now might seem like a self-sustaining entity. People encountering the organization now are likely to do so in objectified ways that make it appear to stand apart from human action. Multiply this example across all social organizations, and you get a sense of how reality is socially constructed.

The metaphor that people are the authors of their social worlds bears further examination. In everyday life, many people feel as if they can't even control their personal lives, much less be the authors of the social world around them. Moreover, power differences mean that some people are in a much better position to construct social reality than other people. And finally, even if the world is the product of our intentions, it is also filled with unintended and unanticipated consequences. So the metaphor requires several caveats. Most basically, no one "authors" the world with a blank sheet of paper. Everyone inherits a preexisting world; through internalization that world becomes theirs before they can even have the tools to write their own world.

The world we inherit is institutionalized. Institutions emerge when people do habitual, repeated actions over a long time. Through habit and repetition, shared and reciprocal typifications emerge that became peoples' stock knowledge and recipes. By the time someone new comes along (and we were all new once), this world appears to exist on its own despite its creation by social actors.

Take a small but revealing example. On the first day of a new class, people make a decision about where to sit in the classroom. On the second day, there might be some reshuffling, but many people return to their original seat. By the fourth or fifth meeting, such decisions become routinized; people arrive and sit in "their" seats without even thinking about it. If people don't claim familiar seats, it feels awkward; it might even be seen as deviant if someone takes "someone else's" seat. In this mundane example, a type of social reality has been externalized from people's intentions, objectified as an external order, and internalized back into people as normative expectations. If you were there at the beginning, you know this "reality" is the collective product of intentional decisions. But by the end of the semester, it will feel like a taken-for-granted, natural order of things.

Society as an objective reality thus emerges through institutionalization. Over time, institutions also acquire legitimations that provide rationales for why things are the way they are. Such legitimations can draw on tradition, mythology, theology, philosophy, or science. When the power of legitimations is added to that of institutions, it is remarkable that we are able to see society as anything other than an objective reality that imposes itself on us from "out there."

If there is any circumstance that might help us see that reality is socially constructed, it is when realities collide. If people only live in one culture, they are especially likely to see it as objectively real. But when people are exposed to several cultures with different institutions and legitimations, they are more likely to see them as relative, socially constructed realities.

Modernity and relativism are thus intimately connected (Berger and Luckmann 1966). Modernity involves the conscious coexistence of multiple societies, cultures, institutions, and legitimations. Reality has always been socially constructed, but it might be easier for more people to see it that way since the dawn of the modern era.

THE ETHNOMETHODOLOGICAL TURN

The second offshoot of phenomenological sociology is ethnomethodology. Most closely associated with Harold Garfinkel (1967), ethnomethodology refers to the practical methods ordinary people use in everyday life to make sense of the social world around them. Whereas Schutz was interested in how people sustain the natural attitude, ethnomethodology explores the actual techniques people use to convince themselves and others that they live in an objectively ordered world.

People use procedures to produce interaction. These procedures can be directly observed, but they can also be accessed through people's descriptions of their interactions with others. Ethnomethodologists are interested in accounts people give of encounters with others, because they reveal how people collectively construct order.

Studying accounts and procedures reveals the indexicality of meanings or the importance of context. Meanings don't derive from words or gestures alone, because virtually all words and gestures carry multiple meanings. If all we had was the word or gesture, we wouldn't know which meanings are in effect. We decide among multiple meanings by considering words and gestures in the context in which they are used.

This is another version of the argument that order is not "out there" but rather "in here" as actors judge context to find meaning. Put differently, the explicit parts of communication are just the tip of the iceberg; what is literally said indexes an implicit context of understandings that is crucial to finding meaning.

Meaning also derives from reflexivity in social interaction. Consider again that social life is a sequence of unique events. No two situations are exactly alike. To the extent this is true, it poses a challenge for people. How do we make sense out of an unending sequence of new situations?

This is where reflexivity comes to the rescue. When we enter a situation, we interpret it as a particular instance of a more general category. Because we know about the category, we know what meanings to transpose from the category to the situation. Yet again, we find the experience meaningful, not because order is "out there" but rather because we impose order on it using such categories.

Reflexivity resembles Kant's innate categories that impose structure on ambiguous perceptions and Schutz's typifications that place experience in familiar categories. What is crucial is that these mental categories do not have any objective reality; they are not "out there." They are rather tools that help convince us that there is an objective world out there, and that we understand it.

The belief that we live in an orderly world is an artful accomplishment of social actors rather than a passive recognition of external reality. Another way ethnomethodologists make this point is through conversation analysis. Careful scrutiny of the tiniest conversational details reveals how meaning only emerges from people's active search for it.

Consider how much of what people "understand" in a conversation is not actually said. We often "read between the lines" to form an interpretation. Indeed, what is not said might be more significant than what is said. Moreover, understanding often depends on sequence. Two statements can mean different things when presented in different order, so we attend to sequence to determine meaning. We also rely on people's biographies to interpret what they say. Even so, we sometimes find no meaning until something "clicks" that allows us to retrospectively understand previously meaningless comments. Each aspect of conversation reveals the importance of context in finding meaning and how meanings are socially constructed.

Ethnomethodological analysis is challenging because these techniques are largely unconscious and taken for granted by skilled social actors. When we are good at using them, we create meaning without even realizing it. To expose these processes requires some clever interventions into everyday life.

Consider an experiment that college students were told was designed to explore the value of brief therapy (McHugh 1968). Student volunteers were asked to describe a problem they were having and then ask questions of a therapist who would only respond with a "yes" or a "no." Students were then asked how they interpreted the advice and whether it was helpful. Unbeknownst to the students, the therapist's "answers" were randomly predetermined in a deliberately meaningless sequence. Although somewhat artificial, the experimental design ensured that there was absolutely no "meaning" on one side of the exchange.

Despite the therapists' meaningless input, students constructed "meaningful" interpretations out of their responses. Indeed, the experimenters were surprised by how many students completed all the questions and even claimed to have benefited from the therapy. Some became quite angry when they were debriefed and told that the "advice" they had just received was meaningless. Although this situation is contrived, it illustrates how people enter interaction with such a strong expectation of meaning that they often find it even when it isn't there.

Another way to see these practices is by "making trouble." You can make trouble in any situation by simply challenging things everybody takes for granted. The typical result is that the interaction quickly breaks down and people become upset and angry. The fact that social reality can be disrupted so readily is further evidence that it is a delicate, collaborative social construction. When we act in ways that undermine social reality, it proves to be not very real after all.

The ease with which social order can be disrupted underscores the importance of the techniques people routinely use to create and maintain it. A basic technique is *doing* reciprocity of perspectives. Schutz claimed this is something we assume; Garfinkel sees it as something we *do*. Indeed, we do it every time we nod or otherwise indicate understanding or agreement with someone in everyday interaction. Here's the interesting part. Sometimes we do reciprocity of perspectives even when we don't understand or agree with the other party. We thereby use techniques that imply reciprocity and a shared world even when they do not exist.

The same is true of the "et cetera principle." This refers to situations where people begin a story or an explanation but don't complete it on the assumption that the other person has enough information to do so on their own. When we rely on this principle, we rarely learn whether their version would actually match our own. But we are likely to assume it would, especially if they do reciprocity of perspectives by indicating that they know exactly where this story is going and there's no need for us to spell out every detail.

Despite such techniques, there are times when social order breaks down in obvious ways. Additional techniques are then used to repair the damage. These involve apologizing, explaining that we didn't mean to do something, or otherwise providing a rationale for disruptive actions. When others respond with empathy and reciprocity of perspectives (saying they've made the same mistake, etc.), the breach in social order has been repaired. In all these ways, ethnomethodology understands society as something social actors accomplish by using "folk" methods in everyday life.

SOCIAL LIFE AS DRAMA

Phenomenological sociology views people as agents who actively construct social worlds and their meanings. The same is true of dramaturgical sociology. The metaphor here is that the world is a stage and that people are players on it. Dramaturgical sociology literally sees people as actors in social life.

This approach is well summarized in *The Presentation of Self in Everyday Life* (Goffman 1959). The starting assumption is that people deliberately create and enact a certain type of self in every situation. Like all good acting, we try to create a *persona,* or an image of ourselves, as a certain kind of person. A major goal of self-presentation is impression management. When done successfully, performances are believable. The combination of self-presentation and audience validation means that we become the self that we are performing.

Ordinary people recognize this. We don't have to be trained sociologists to know that people try to make a good impression, that how they appear and who they really are might be different, and so on. So in everyday life, we are both performers and audiences for other performers. In both cases, we are keenly interested in authenticity.

When a performance seems authentic, we might say that "what you see is what you get" or that someone is "for real." We sense no gap between their performance and who they really are. We might conclude that there is no performance here and that we are seeing the "real person." These are the most effective performances of all.

This underscores the importance of judging performances. Doing so involves distinguishing between two kinds of expressions. Expressions *given* are aspects of a performance that are intended by the performer. Expressions *given off* are harder to control and slip through the performance. When there are contradictions between expressions consciously given and unconsciously given off, we tend to believe the latter and to judge the performance as unconvincing.

When a defense attorney has her client get a haircut and wear a suit to court, this is an attempt to control expressions given and create a good impression of the defendant. If the defendant leers at women jurors and uses obscenities on the witness stand, these expressions given off contradict those given by the suit and the haircut. Jurors are likely to conclude that the leering and obscenity are better clues to who this person is than the suit and haircut.

Many performances involve idealizations, where people present themselves in the best possible light or in socially desirable ways. To be effective, they can require tight control to prevent damaging information from slipping through and undermining the performance. Other performances might involve misrepresentation, where actors deliberately present themselves in a deceptive manner ("I'm your friend first and an insurance salesman second"). Still other performances involve mystification that creates social distance between the performer and audience, generating a feeling of awe. There are also demystified performances, as when rock stars, politicians, or celebrities wade into the audience to mingle with ordinary people.

Certain generic elements like fronts and props are found in many performances. Some fronts are spatial. The location of people in a suite of offices is a front supporting a performance about who's in charge: The person in the corner office farthest from the door you entered. I don't have a corner office, but my office is filled with thousands of books that support my performance as a professor (whether I've actually read them or not). The deliberate disorder of a teenager's bedroom is yet another front that supports the performance of a rebellious self.

Fronts can also be personally embodied. Clothing, grooming, and adornment are always crucial to self-presentation. As different as they might be, the suits and skirts of the business world and the piercings and tattoos of youth culture are both fronts supporting certain performances. Some fronts make explicit identity claims; slogans on clothing, buttons on backpacks, stickers on bumpers, and customized license plates are common examples.

Some performances involve teams and require the cooperation of several performers. When doctors and nurses do surgery or the staff of a formal restaurant opens for business, they are staging a collective presentation. Even if most team members hit their marks, the performance can still be undermined by the missteps of one or two team members.

Teams must therefore maintain loyalty. Anything that heightens the boundaries between insiders and outsiders can do the trick. One of the more interesting strategies is deprecating the audience. Team members can enhance their solidarity by making nasty comments about the bodies of patients or the preferences of diners.

If the whole team participates in deprecating the audience, it heightens team loyalty and ensures a more effective performance.

Deprecating the audience will obviously backfire if it is done in their presence; it must occur out of view. This suggests another part of everyday performances. In the theater, we know that performances happen front stage while being assembled and supported backstage. We also know that audiences aren't supposed to go backstage, because it will undermine the illusion of the front-stage performance.

The same is true of social life and its performances. Front regions are places where performances occur, and back regions are places where they are prepared. Sometimes the distinction has more to do with time than space. When a band sets up and sound-checks their instruments before the club opens, it is a back region; when the doors open and the music begins, the same physical space is now a front region.

However defined, front regions are where performers and audiences interact, and back regions are where performers can retreat from the audience and drop out of their roles. But it's all relative. If the set designer also has designs on the lead actress, a second performance is occurring in the back region of the main performance.

As noted earlier, people are aware of the dramaturgical aspect of social life. At some level, we know people are engaged in performances. Consider how audiences typically support performances through tactfulness. Take an extreme case of audience support: the grade-school play. When the play inevitably goes awry, the audience will go out of its way to ignore the mishaps and maintain the illusion the play is trying to create. Such audience tact applies to a much broader range of performances.

Audiences exercise tact when they respect boundaries between front and back regions. If they must enter a back region, they announce their intention by knocking on a door, coughing loudly, or otherwise alerting performers so they can reassemble their fronts. Audiences also exercise tact when they symbolically isolate themselves from intimate performances not meant for them; if we are trapped on a long elevator ride with a bickering couple, we signal detachment and disinterest (while secretly listening in). Audiences are tactful whenever they overlook or excuse mistakes that could otherwise undermine a performance.

Audiences thus recognize that it is crucial for people to save face and maintain integrity. Because a discredited performance undermines integrity, audiences can be surprisingly supportive and gentle in their reception of flawed performances. Even though we routinely monitor authenticity, we seem inclined to support performances within rather broad limits. In accepting even flawed performances, we help construct a social world that we take to be orderly and meaningful.

THE SELF AS PROJECT, COMMODITY, AND STORY

Selves involve phenomenological and dramaturgical elements, but they also exist in sociohistorical contexts. For instance, societies like the United States have been described as late modernity, advanced capitalism, or postmodern societies. Each description poses distinct challenges to the self.

Anthony Giddens (1991) has described a late modern age that alters the nature of personal identity. As modern institutions undercut traditional customs, "self-identity becomes a reflexively organized endeavor" and "the notion of lifestyle takes on a particular significance" (Giddens 1991, 5). People now select lifestyles in a self-consciously deliberate way. The notion of "choosing" a lifestyle would strike most people throughout human history as bizarre. For better and worse, their identity was determined by birth, whereas ours is increasingly a matter of choice. The expansion of such choices typifies the self in late modern society.

The terms *ontological security* and *existential anxiety* refer to our degree of certainty about who we are and how we cope with life's uncertainties. Traditional societies relied upon myth, religion, and custom to establish ontological security and manage existential anxiety. Late modern societies undermine traditional knowledge and replace it with uncertainty, risk, and relativism. This leaves many people less certain about who they are or how to cope with life's unknowns. The "good news" is that modern selves have more options for dealing with these issues; the "bad news" is that the burden falls on us as individuals to find solutions, as custom and tradition lose their relevance.

These dynamics enlarge "space" for the self in modern life and turn us into self-therapists. We see the self as having a certain trajectory. We plan this trajectory from a menu of life options that might include going to a particular college, starting a certain career, moving to a new city, finding a partner, beginning a family, having children, and achieving particular goals by certain stages in the life cycle. To see the self as a reflexive project means we design our life out of the choices before us. Such lifestyle planning extends to the body as well. In making choices about nutrition, exercise, muscle toning, bodybuilding, or cosmetic surgery, we construct a physical self as part of a chosen lifestyle.

Late modern selves also experience a new type of relationship. A "pure relationship" is one whose only rationale is the satisfactions or rewards that are generic to the relationship itself. It contrasts with more traditional societies where relationships served broader social purposes. Thus, marriage was historically an economic, political, or kinship exchange, in which the partners were less individuals than representatives of larger groups and interests.

The rise of "romantic love" began to detach marriage from larger social purposes and reframe it as an individual choice based on an emotional connection. "Pure relationships" extend this pattern. Whether marriage or friendship, a pure relationship exists for intrinsic satisfactions as opposed to larger social obligations. Such relationships are double-edged. On the one hand, people have more choices about relationships and can enter into them based on what they (not others) see as fulfilling. On the other hand, such relations are fragile; when the parties no longer experience them as fulfilling, the relationship has no further justification and is likely to end. Given how we invest our modern selves in such relationships, their fragility can undermine ontological security and increase existential anxiety.

The reflexive self also involves "life politics." Where emancipatory politics meant fighting oppression as members of groups, life politics is more personalized. In life politics, daily activities become politicized. At the same time, late modernity has collapsed distinctions between the global and the personal, so that life politics involves planetary questions. Whether the issues are biology, sexuality, and reproduction or food, consumption, and environment, life politics has global implications.

This view of the late modern self as a reflexive project emphasizes choices. This emphasis, however, can be overdone. Another view of the self accentuates the power of large social forces over relatively defenseless individuals.

The commodified self has been a theme in both classical and contemporary sociology. Recall Marx's theory of alienation, whose starting premise is that labor is central to human beings. Labor means self-directed, creative, productive activity. When people do such labor, they create a material world through externalization (Berger and Luckmann 1966). Equally important, labor creates the person, because productive activity engages our senses, reveals our aptitudes, develops our skills, and fosters our humanity. We build a world but also become human through labor.

This, at least, is the ideal. Alienation means people cannot direct their own labor. The most basic way this occurs is through commodification. Capitalism reduces people to the commodity of labor-power, because it is only interested in how labor creates profits. As people are reduced to commodities, they are forced to sell themselves—or at least their labor-power—to the highest bidder. Marx likened wage-labor to prostitution. In both cases, a human capacity for self-expression (labor and sexuality) becomes a commodity sold to someone else. In both cases, people are valued only as means to ends defined by the purchaser.

Once labor becomes a commodity, people become alienated from the process and the product of their labor, as both are dictated by the boss. People become alienated from what makes them human in the first place. Labor's potential is denied and used for others' benefit. Alienation means that rather than living to work, we must work to live. As a final result, people become alienated from each other.

Contemporary commodified selves involve consumption more than production. In an advanced capitalist society shaped by compulsive consumerism and relentless advertising, meaning and identity become intertwined with the consumption of commodities. The philosopher René Descartes once said "I think, therefore I am"; bumper stickers now proclaim "I shop, therefore I am." A self that becomes real through consumption perfectly symbolizes a consumer culture in which public spaces are displaced by shopping malls.

Perhaps the pleasures of consumption compensate for the alienation of labor. Perhaps the modern bargain is that if we can't realize ourselves through producing things, we'll do it through consuming things. Despite rising consumer debt and personal bankruptcies, we seem cheerfully resigned to these circumstances, as expressed in another bumper sticker: "I owe, I owe, so off to work I go." Or maybe not. The image of a treadmill also comes to mind, and how many people have you seen on a treadmill who looked really happy?

Advertisers know they are not selling products as much as lifestyles and identities. The seemingly simple act of buying a product symbolically means identifying with a lifestyle and identity. Advanced capitalism provides do-it-yourself identity kits consumers can use for a customized self. "The advantage of market-promoted identities is that they come complete with elements of social approval ... [which] does not need to be negotiated for it has been, so to speak, built into the marketed product from the start" (Bauman and May 2001, 88).

The built-in approval of market-tested identities might explain their seductive appeal, but there is a downside. Planned obsolescence and fashion cycles guarantee that this year's hot product (and identity) will be painfully out of fashion next year. In entering the marketplace of identity, we commit to continually buying new or trading up to maintain the social approval such identities provide. It sounds like we're back on that treadmill again.

In Marx's day, labor-power became a commodity. Now the self and the body become commodities. To fetch the highest price in the marketplace of bodies, women (and now men) must approximate impossibly narrow standards of how their bodies should look. If we "choose" to pursue this goal, however, there are multibillion-dollar industries waiting to "serve" our "needs." One might question whether the benefits of the body industry outweigh its costs and risks to consumers, but there is no doubt about its profitability for those who control it.

Anthony Giddens's (1991) reflexive self emphasizes agency, control, and self-direction. The commodified self reminds us that in a consumer society, powerful forces colonize how this reflexive project of the self is carried out. When successful, the self is less a reflexive project than just another site of social control.

For still others, selves now exist in a postmodern world that undermines the very idea of a self. Imagine a continuum with modernism at one end. It has always emphasized a core self. Even modernism recognized dangers to the self. Other-directedness could become overconformity, organizational identification could lead to selling out, and emotional control could promote the commercialization of feeling. Although recognizing such dangers, modernism still assumes that a core self develops.

An intermediate position on the continuum retains the possibility of an integrated self, although acknowledging it has become more problematic. With the compression of time and space and a flood of media images, the self becomes saturated (Gergen 1991) by forces that make an integrated self more difficult to sustain.

At the postmodern end of the continuum, the very idea of an integrated self is abandoned. Postmodernism questions whether things have a clear existence apart from how they are represented. Put differently, postmodernism collapses the distance between reality and images to the point where we can no longer tell which is which. Applied to the self, this implies that core selves and integrated identities are no longer possible.

An alternative is the "narrative self" (Holstein and Gubrium 2000). This arises out of people's subjectivity, their situational circumstances, and others' influence. In contrast to the modern, unitary self, the postmodern, narrative self contains multiple identities in different locations and circumstances. Each one is "authentic" in context, but none is the "real" self, because none transcend particular situations. To use dramaturgical language, it's as if we play many supporting roles in different scenes, but there is no leading role that gives our self a single, clear meaning.

This self is still a social construction, but the building relies heavily on language to construct selves through narratives we tell about who we are. These stories don't represent a "real" self as much as they create a situational self in the telling. Because we tell different stories about ourselves in different times and places, we create many "self-stories" rather than a singular identity. Our stories and our selves are different for diverse audiences or when viewed from different angles.

The materials for building a narrative self are found in everyday conversation. As we tell our stories and narrate our selves, we are like editors. We continually revise, modify, add, and delete pieces from our stories. Stories are also set in circumstances we neither choose nor control that inevitably shape them. It is within those limits that we talk ourselves into existence as narrative selves.

Consider the construction of an alcoholic self in the context of the support group Alcoholics Anonymous (Denzin 1987). The context provides a standard script of how people introduce themselves to the group and proceed to construct a narrative self as an alcoholic. In the telling of their lives, people revise, edit, and modify their story to arrange the elements in ways that tell the story of an alcoholic self. But these same people narrate different stories and selves in other circumstances. Although other examples are not as transparent, we are all engaged in constructing narrative selves through the stories we tell about who we are.

When the self is located in a specific historical context—whether late modernity, advanced capitalism, or postmodernism—we get new insights into how identities are socially shaped. These accounts build on phenomenological and dramaturgical approaches, interactionist theory, and the premise that we are social before we are individual. Durkhiem demonstrated that individuals only emerged with modern society. These accounts of individuals, selves, and identities are thus crucial to understanding modern society and its postmodern trajectories.

PART FIVE
PATTERNS OF CHANGE

Chapter 13

The Challenge of Globalization

In our day, the shrinking of time and space links the personal and the global. Our lives are now intertwined with peoples and processes across the planet. So we move from identity questions to global issues.

There are many global connections. Here's one. Baseball is "America's game." Although played elsewhere, it originated here and is distinctly "American" in the same way as jazz music. Whereas only a few thousand make it to the big leagues, millions of kids play in Little Leagues every year. Participation provides important lessons about team dynamics, personal identity, and competitive pressures.

Playing baseball requires little equipment. Most obviously, it requires a baseball. Here's where the globe shrinks and America's game rests on a global connection. Every baseball used in the major leagues is made by hand in a baseball factory in Turrialba, Costa Rica. It takes a skilled baseball maker about fifteen minutes to hand-sew 108 stitches along the seams of the ball. It's the seams that give the ball its action. Along with grip, speed, and rotation, the seams turn pitches into the curveballs, sliders, and sinkers that almost magically elude even the best hitters. But without the workers of Turrialba, there would be no baseballs, and no game.

A closer look reveals a familiar globalization story. The factory is owned by Rawlings Sporting Goods, which has an exclusive contract to supply baseballs to the major leagues. Rawlings came to Costa Rica in 1988 when it was awarded free trade zone status by the Costa Rican government. This means Rawlings pays no taxes and can import cores, yarn, and cowhide duty free. The labor isn't free, but it's very cheap. The baseball workers earn less than $3,000 a year. An experienced worker who has been there thirteen years makes a little more than $50 a week, barely above the Costa Rican minimum wage. It costs about 30 cents to produce a baseball, and Rawlings sells them for $14.99 each. The steady supply and high quality of baseballs made by people earning less than $3,000 a year sustains a professional sport in which the average player earns more than $2 million.

The owners and managers of the baseball factory are satisfied. They say that the workplace is a good one and that the work is not very demanding. They have high praise for the workers and refer to them as a team or a family. They deny that there are any problems at the plant or that workers are harmed by the work they do.

The workers see it differently. They acknowledge that without the plant, their economic opportunities might be even worse. They acknowledge that although their wages have not increased in sixteen years, the plant has made improvements in workplace safety and brought in a less abusive manager. But they also speak of the difficulty of the work. A typical workday runs from 6 a.m. to 5 p.m. In summer, the temperature inside the plant approaches 100 degrees. One worker claims, "It is hard work, and sometimes it messes up your hands, warps your fingers, and hurts your shoulders." In contrast to management claims, a third of the workforce has developed carpal tunnel syndrome and up to 90 percent of the workers experience chronic pain from the exacting detail, precise standards, and rapid pace of the work.

The workers are also aware of the economic disparities. One notes that during a week in which he might produce 250 baseballs, the retail price of the first two or three balls pays his salary for the week; the return on the other 247 or 248 baseballs goes to the company. Another worker notes that "[w]e sacrifice a lot so they can play. It's an injustice that we kill ourselves to make these balls perfect, and with one home run, they're gone" (all information and quotes from Weiner 2004).

Even if you are a player or a fan, you were probably unaware of these global connections. Few of us are, because it's not in the interest of the large institutions that benefit to publicize them. They would prefer that we not connect these dots. But critical sociology is all about connecting such dots. By looking beyond appearances and asking who benefits, critical sociology is tailor-made for analyzing a globalizing world.

THE RISE AND FALL OF MODERNIZATION THEORY

Sociology is not always critical. Like any form of knowledge, it sees the world from a certain standpoint. Before discussing globalization directly, an overview of modernization theory will show how unexamined assumptions distort understanding.

As we saw in the first chapter, sociology emerged with modernization in Europe. Although classical sociologists had differences, they had three similarities. First, they shared a broadly European identity. Second, they focused on rapid changes occurring in their own societies. Third, they brought a Eurocentric standpoint to their understanding of the modernization process.

Such Eurocentrism is evident in the typologies these sociologists created to capture the differences between modernizing and traditional societies. They described traditional societies as preindustrial ones, in which most people worked in horticulture or agriculture for survival. Such societies had small populations and low population density. People had ascribed statuses; their position in life was largely determined by birth and not subject to much change. Mythical, magical, or religious belief systems prevailed, and science and technology were minimally developed. There was also little development of social institutions. Instead, the kinship system fulfilled social, economic, and political as well as family functions.

In contrast, European societies were seen as modern (or at least modernizing). Modern societies have industrial rather than agricultural economies. They experience rapid growth, high population density, and urban development. People in modern societies occupy more achieved statuses; their position in life depends on their own efforts or experiences rather than being determined by birth. Scientific and secular worldviews displace mythical and religious ones. Most important for social structure, the multifunctional kinship system shrinks to the nuclear family, and separate institutions emerge to fulfill economic, political, educational, and social functions.

These contrasts were the basis of much classical sociology. Durkheim traced how traditional societies with mechanical solidarity and little differentiation developed into modern ones with organic solidarity and a complex division of labor. Marx traced the transition from feudalism to capitalism in which the cash nexus of capital tore apart the motley threads that bound traditional societies. Weber revealed how the Protestant ethic and the spirit of capitalism overcame traditional barriers to profit making and launched the modern world of rational-calculative capitalism, rational-legal authority, and the disenchantment that results when science displaces myth.

Such studies revealed how modernity emerged on the European continent. They also reinforced biases about the backwardness of people in traditional societies while Europe was modernizing. There were deeper problems as well.

During the first half of the twentieth century, questions of modernization were on the back burner. At mid-century, the conclusion of World War II, the Marshall Plan to rebuild Europe, the founding of the United Nations, the rise of national independence movements, and the beginning of the Cold War brought questions of modernization back to a full boil. But the focus shifted from Europe's past to the Third World's future.

This spurred a new version of modernization theory that revived the distinction between traditional and modern societies (Apter 1967; Bernstein 1971; Kuznets 1965; Lerner 1958). But now, "traditional society" referred not to predecessors of modern Europe but rather to societies in Africa, Asia, and Latin America. Modernization theory thus transposed Europe's modernization in the past into a model of how the rest of the world might do so in the future.

Most simply, the theory understood modernization as moving from a traditional society with its interrelated characteristics to a modern society with a different set of characteristics. Modernization was seen as a holistic, universal process of societal evolution and development (Bernstein 1971, 141). The West had already done it, and now it was time for the rest to catch up. The fact that they had not yet done so supported unflattering judgments that these societies and the people in them were primitive, backward, and underdeveloped.

Some versions of the theory identified institutional barriers to economic growth. Others cited Weber's work to suggest that the impediments were primarily cultural. Underdeveloped societies were seen as trapped in traditional orientations to the world that did not provide much stimulus for achievement. In this view, they needed cultural transfusions of competitive individualism and an achievement ethic to overturn tradition and foster modernization (McClelland 1973). If not the Protestant ethic or the spirit of capitalism, some similar cultural impetus was required for these societies to "take off" on the path of modernization.

This theory was plausible to its advocates, but this had less to do with its validity than with its standpoint. After all, modernization theory presented Western-style development as the only game in town (and it implied that others would be crazy not to want to be like us anyway). When ideas portray their advocates in a flattering light, it is important to look for the flaws behind the flattery.

The flaws quickly emerged, as critics of modernization theory found multiple targets. One was the goal of modernization. By taking their own societies as the point of reference, these theorists implied that the only logical goal of modernization was a carbon copy of already developed societies. Given their highly disproportionate use of the world's resources, this goal now appears economically dubious and ecologically disastrous. Moreover, this logic denied any voice to people in "underdeveloped" societies about whether and what type of modernization they might want.

A second target of critics concerned methods of modernization. Advocacy of competitive individualism and an achievement orientation implied that there was only one way to develop. Like the goal, it just happened to be the way of the West, so once again a theory of past development in Europe was repackaged into a normative model of future development elsewhere. Such prescriptions didn't recognize how the remedies clashed with prevailing cultural practices in traditional societies.

A third target of the critics involved historical context. When the West modernized, it was the first to do so. There were no predecessors. The context is different now. Underdeveloped societies face a world of already developed societies. The unspoken assumption of modernization theory was that developed societies would provide capital investment, technology transfers, and foreign aid to spur development across the globe. Critics turned this assumption on its head. They argued that the developed world was an obstacle to global development, because developed nations benefited from ongoing underdevelopment elsewhere.

These are serious flaws, but there was a more basic problem. It was implicit in the classical typologies and became explicit in modernization theory. Consider an alternative story: Human societies have always been more diverse than the rigid dichotomy of "traditional" vs. "modern" recognizes. In addition, there have always been important connections among societies. External relations are often more critical for development (or underdevelopment) than internal factors. And finally, power has always shaped relations among societies. Where power differences exist, some societies benefit at the expense of others.

This alternative story adds a crucial insight absent from modernization theory. It is this. European modernization was made possible by domination of other societies. Colonialism, imperialism, and the exploitation of raw materials, agricultural products, and cheap labor from other places were essential to European modernization.

This alternative story downplays internal factors and emphasizes external ones. There is certainly a place for both. Weber could be right that the Protestant ethic and spirit of capitalism were necessary to make profit making an ethical duty rather than a greedy undertaking. But internal, cultural meanings were accompanied by external, economic relations that produced the actual profits that fueled Europe's development. Western modernization was underwritten by exploitation of non-European societies. If Europe was the beneficiary, the colonies were the victims. Colonial peoples saw their resources depleted, their labor exploited, their cultures oppressed, and their societies reshaped to serve colonial powers.

Recognizing colonialism drives the last nail in the coffin of modernization theory. "Underdevelopment" is not a natural, initial condition of all societies; it is a set of disadvantages *created* by colonialism. When Andre Gunder Frank (1969) spoke of "the development of underdevelopment," he meant that underdevelopment is a socially created condition arising from colonial exploitation (Chew and Denemark 1996).

The development of the West and the underdevelopment of the rest are thus two sides of the same coin; both derive from a single process that benefited some at the expense of others. The resulting underdevelopment of much of the world persists in the postcolonial era. The problem is not traditionalism, backwardness, or underdevelopment; it is rather the dependency that has been created between underdeveloped societies and former colonizers. As long as that dependency benefits Western powers, they will pose obstacles to global development.

There is a major irony here. If "underdeveloped" societies were to follow the *real* history of Europe, they would colonize others to fuel *their* development (at the expense of *their* colonies). Something like this has happened in some regions of the globe, but it is hardly the lesson modernization theorists had in mind. Modernization theory illustrates how certain standpoints and assumptions can generate plausible but seriously flawed understandings of the social world.

It is a further irony that even though modernization theory has been widely discredited in academic circles, it still provides rhetoric and imagery for politicians and policy makers. When discredited ideas live on, it often means they are serving powerful interests. Modernization theory does so by obscuring the colonialism that fueled Western development and the neocolonialism that still inhibits global progress.

THE GLOBAL WORLD SYSTEM

The greatest flaw of modernization theory was that it ignored relations *among* societies and their impact on development or underdevelopment. The greatest strength of world system theory is that this insight is its starting premise.

World system theorists assume that a cohesive, global, economic system transcending national boundaries has existed for several centuries (Hall 2000; Shannon 1989; Wallerstein 1974, 1980, 1989). This system relies on a global division of labor incorporating numerous cultures and nation-states. This capitalist economy organizes global activities through the institution of private property, the process of commodification, and the practice of exploitation. Although global, this system has distinct economic zones. Core states are economically and politically dominant nations and leaders of the world system. They use sophisticated technologies in capital-intensive, high-wage economic production. Peripheral states are weaker economically and politically, and they use less-advanced technologies in labor-intensive, low-wage production. Semi-peripheral countries are located between core and periphery and exhibit some combination of both elements.

These economic zones also differ in their conditions of labor. In core countries, most workers are "free" to seek the best wages and working conditions the market has to offer. In peripheral countries, they are more likely to be coerced into providing labor, whether this involves outright slavery, indentured servitude, or other restrictive forms of labor. The differences between free and coerced labor creates another challenge to working-class organization on a global scale, because workers in different zones confront very different working conditions, political rights, and economic opportunities.

Although the world system is economically unified, it is politically fragmented into competing nation-states. Like capitalism, the nation-state system now encompasses every region of the globe. Not surprisingly, core states are more powerful than peripheral ones, and this political power is often a tool by which the core maintains control over peripheral regions.

If capitalism is a world system, it follows that its classes are international. Hence, class analysis must recognize the global dimensions of class interest, organization, consciousness, and struggle. In terms of class formation, the capitalist class is rapidly becoming an international network without regard to nationality.

The working class is also an international class whose labor-power is sold on a global market. In terms of class formation, however, there are national, cultural, and linguistic barriers obstructing international working-class mobilization. Even so, organization within a single country is not enough, because capitalists can play workers of different nations against one another. As a world system, capitalism thus combines a global economy and class structure with diverse nation-states and status groups based on culture, language, and citizenship.

The system is driven by capital accumulation, as owners of private property seek to maximize profits through the exploitation of labor and the extraction of surplus value. These processes are increasingly acted out on a global stage, resulting in a flow of wealth from periphery to core. Historically, this exploitation underwrote development of the core and retarded modernization of the periphery. These economically driven processes are paralleled by political ones, as states compete for predominance in a global interstate system. The result is a symbiotic relationship between state managers and national capitalists where each group pursues its interests by facilitating those of the other.

This system has existed for approximately five hundred years, with different regions playing different roles over time. In the contemporary period, the core includes the United States, Western Europe, and Japan. As advanced capitalist societies, these regions are economically wealthy, politically dominant, and relatively stable. The periphery includes much of Africa and South Asia as well as parts of Latin America. Peripheral states are still dominated by a legacy of colonialism and forms of neocolonialism that constrict their economic and political options. Peripheral areas exhibit extreme economic inequality and less-stable states.

The remainder of the globe composes the semi-periphery, including much of Latin America, some of Africa and the Middle East, parts of East Asia, and the former Soviet Union and its satellites. The semi-periphery is perhaps the most diverse zone of the world system, with newly industrializing countries experiencing rapid growth rates standing alongside relatively stagnant economies. The semi-periphery resembles the periphery more than the core, but these states do establish their own exploitative relations with peripheral countries, even as they remain exploited by core countries.

The world system has cycles of economic expansion and decline that are loosely correlated with turnover in core states known as cycles of hegemony. During rare periods of full hegemony, a single core state will monopolize advantages over others in production, commerce, and finance. World system theorists generally recognize three such periods of full hegemony by a single country: Holland in the mid-1600s, Britain in the mid-1800s, and the United States in the mid-1900s. More often, no one state monopolizes power; it is rather shared among core states that nevertheless maintain their dominance over the world system.

In the ascending phase of a hegemonic cycle, a rising state takes advantage of economic opportunities for which it is better positioned than any of its rivals. Building on new technologies or forms of organization, it achieves a productive advantage, accumulates multiple resources, and acquires commercial and financial power. Such rising powers often benefit from strong states and military power.

The decline of a hegemonic power follows a similar sequence. It loses its productive advantage first, creating a downward spiral in which commercial, financial, and military power also erode. The initial loss of productive advantage occurs when competitors copy manufacturing techniques, when dominant producers lose their competitive edge, and when militarism drains off productive resources. Although there have been long periods without a single hegemonic power, sooner or later a new ascending core state attains dominance and follows the same cycle.

Different points in the cycle have different effects on domestic stability. During prosperous periods of hegemonic maturity, economic growth can blunt class conflict and encourage moderate reform. In a relatively open political climate, diverse viewpoints might be heard and popular struggles for rights and resources might succeed. In a context of domestic prosperity and global dominance, a consensus on foreign policy is often relatively easy to forge, and nationalism can become a potent force.

This political climate changes with the transition from hegemonic maturity to hegemonic decline. The latter typically fosters economic and political inequality, greater state repression, and stagnant or declining economic resources. Political options narrow to sustain a beleaguered national capitalist class. The state is likely to cut expenditures that do not serve these interests, undermining the living standards of many people.

The United States has experienced at least three stages of the rise and fall of a hegemonic power. During ascending hegemony (1897–1913/1920), there was ongoing conflict between rival powers, as the United States challenged previously hegemonic states. In the phase of hegemonic victory (1913/1920–1945), the United States consolidated productive and military advantages over rival core states and became the newly hegemonic power. In the phase of hegemonic maturity (1945–1970), the United States exercised full control in all major spheres of economic, political, and military power, and there were no comparable rival powers within the world system. In the final stage of declining hegemony (since the 1970s), the United States has seen partial erosion of its economic advantages and the appearance of strong challengers for hegemony.

Recent conditions in the United States typify a hegemonic power struggling against decline. Consider the political climate of the past thirty years. Since the mid-1970s, the U.S. economy has undergone domestic crises alongside challenges to its international predominance as well. This resulted in increasing inequality and poverty, accelerated concentration of capital assets, attacks on the wages and living standards of workers and welfare recipients, and pressure on government to cut expenditures and reduce corporate taxes. The long-term erosion of social capital investments in education and research further weakens the competitive position of the United States. These events suggest that even powerful core countries are strongly affected by their relationships with other nations.

If even the most powerful nations are affected by external pressures, imagine their impact in the rest of the world system. Remember the baseball makers of Turrialba? Their situation exemplifies world system theory quite nicely. Although belonging to a distinct nation, culture, and status group, their labor is part of a global economy. The low cost of their labor also reflects their position in the world system. Paying workers 30 cents for a product that sells for $15 suggests the degree of exploitation at the heart of the world system. The products have changed, but the economics of baseball making in Turrialba have been part of the world system for five centuries.

GLOBALIZATION: WHAT'S NEW?

World system theory was the dominant sociological perspective on global development from the mid-1970s to the mid-1990s. Its focus on relations among nations corrected the major flaw of modernization theory. It also provided a powerful explanation for the development of core countries and the underdevelopment of peripheral countries within a single theory. Finally, it offered a compelling explanation for persisting global inequality.

Since the mid-1990s, references to "globalization" have been increasingly frequent. Some argue that globalization has made world system theory outdated. Such discussions see globalization as an inevitable, technologically driven process beyond human control. Such claims need to be carefully evaluated through the lens of critical sociology.

At least three changes are central in the debate over whether globalization is creating an alternative to the world system. The first is the dissolution of the socialist bloc and its incorporation into the global economy. During the Cold War, the Soviet Union, its Eastern European satellites, and other socialist countries resembled the semi-periphery of the world system, but they were also disconnected from it. They were not open to foreign investment, and their production and trade were dictated more by political bureaucracies than market forces. With the breakup of the socialist bloc, these nations became more integrated into the semi-periphery as foreign investment increased, public goods were privatized, markets emerged, and trade expanded.

A second change involves the relative decline of (some) nation-states in the face of growing transnational corporate power. Historically, core nation-states were dominant or equal partners with national corporations in the world system. Corporations needed governments to make rules, stabilize currencies, negotiate treaties, and maintain order. With the rise of transnational corporations that dwarf many governments, nation-states have lost some of their ability to constrain corporate behavior. Core states still have considerable political and military power, but even here transnational corporate mobility gives them leverage. In the periphery and semi-periphery, former colonies have only recently become independent nation-states at precisely the time when the power of nation-states is declining relative to global corporate entities that can often dictate national policy and development options.

The third change involves new information and communication technologies. The ability to communicate instantaneously around the globe certainly appears to shrink the world and create a global village. The same technologies make it possible for financial transactions to occur instantaneously. The newfound ability to rapidly move currency around the global economy can enhance profits for some at the same time that it can potentially destabilize national and regional economies.

There is no denying that things have changed with globalization. Economically, globalization means a tighter integration of the world into a single market. Politically, it means the rise of supranational organizations that have partly displaced some functions of national governments. Culturally, globalization means the standardization and homogenization of world cultures, as mass media supplant indigenous cultures with Western consumer capitalism. Some conclude that globalization is replacing hierarchy with a world that is interconnected, leveled, flattened, or equalized—at least in comparison with the past. Such conclusions require critical scrutiny.

Rather than vague metaphors of leveling or equalizing, globalization is better seen as a tighter integration of social spaces into a hierarchical structure in which the center still dominates the periphery. This hierarchical relation between center and periphery has always characterized the world system, and globalization has done more to enhance than to undermine these dynamics. Seen this way, the undeniable facts of globalization are better seen as an intensification of dynamics that have been part of the world system for centuries. Put differently, globalization is the latest stage in the evolution of the world economic system rather than a departure from it.

There are several reasons for interpreting globalization in this way. Consider the changes cited as responsible for creating a supposedly new globalized world. The demise of socialism was among the most dramatic geopolitical events of the twentieth century, but it hardly counts against world system theory. If anything, the socialist bloc was an anomaly for world system theory, because it meant that a vast portion of the globe was only loosely linked to the world system while trying to create an alternative to it. The integration of the former "second world" into the world system is more a confirmation than a refutation of world system theory. More broadly, the integration of all regions of the globe into a world market is less a departure than an intensification of world system patterns. By this standard "globalization" has been occurring since the origins of the world system in the 1500s.

The relative decline of national power does not necessarily undermine world system theory either. This system did not begin with powerful nation-states but rather in a stew of city-states, feudal principalities, and disputed regimes. In many cases, colonial exploitation fueled the consolidation of the nation-state system we take for granted today. Powerful economic interests have always sought to manipulate state power to advance their interests. In the past, this promoted state power. Today those same interests are embodied in transnational corporations that seek to limit state power. These developments might signify a relative shift in the power of states and corporations, but not the demise of the world system itself. It emerged and survived alongside weak and strong states in different historical periods, and there is every reason to believe that it will continue in an era of shifting state powers.

The third indicator of globalization is cultural homogenization in the form of Western consumer capitalism. Once again, these developments are better seen as an intensification of world system dynamics than a departure from them. Marx himself noted that capitalism creates a world in its own image. Moreover, the world system of the past five centuries has always included cultural imperialism alongside economic exploitation and political domination. The technical capacity for cultural control might have changed, but these new technologies should not blind us to older patterns of cultural domination in the world system.

The point is not to deny that globalization has recently accelerated. The point is to challenge an interpretation that says these changes constitute a qualitative break from the operation of the world system over the past five centuries. Such changes are better seen as an intensification or new stage of world system dynamics than as a departure from them.

RECENT WORLD SYSTEM DYNAMICS

Recent developments in the world system provide the best evidence for its continuity. In 1944, the United States hosted an international conference in Bretton Woods, New Hampshire, "that more or less invented globalization" (Derber 2002, 98). Bretton Woods established the International Monetary Fund (IMF) and the World Bank (WB). More broadly, it promoted new understandings of world finance, trade rules, and open markets as cornerstones of the global economy. Despite the international veneer, the conference was an assertion of U.S. power on a global scale.

Under traditional colonialism, core countries exercised complete control over colonies. As colonies gained independence, the empire system of explicit, coercive control was replaced with an "umpire system" (Derber 2002), in which the United States created rules ensuring that the world system worked in its favor. It also created international institutions firmly under its control to establish policy and settle disputes. Bretton Woods was thus a transition from control by the British Empire to control by the U.S. "umpire." It can be described as the beginning of modern globalization, but it was really a new phase in the long-standing exercise of power by the core over the periphery.

The system was refined in the 1950s, with trade rules known as the General Agreement on Tariffs and Trade (GATT) that further entrenched U.S. power. GATT created a highly regulated global economy serving the economic and political interests of core states. In the periphery, it was another story. With few exceptions, peripheral nations did not benefit from these trade arrangements, and some saw declines in standard measures of national development and well-being. Thus, at the very time that academics were promoting modernization via the Western model, new global institutions were creating "underdevelopment" in the periphery.

Under these arrangements, investment in the Third World increased and the world economy became more densely intertwined. Core countries profited from the same dynamics that caused problems in the periphery. The development advice offered by the IMF and the World Bank often contributed to the problem. The advice went something like this. Third World nations with stagnant economies were advised to identify some raw material, resource, or type of production where they had a competitive advantage. They were urged to reorient their economies to maximize production of this commodity. Through this strategy, peripheral nations were expected to sell lots of their commodity to the world market and earn back enough revenue to fund development.

This advice sounds logical in the abstract; in reality, it was less so. The advice promoted export economies specializing in one crop or product. Such a strategy of "putting all your eggs in one basket" was risky; it violated another standard piece of economic wisdom to diversify investment and production for long-term stability. The strategy backfired in several ways. If internal problems hampered production, or if global demand declined, or if new competitors appeared, the country was in serious trouble. The strategy benefited core countries that could sample a rich supply of global commodities, but it was often destructive for poor nations struggling to develop. Such conflicts of interest and outcome between core and periphery are precisely what world system theory would predict.

This development strategy also undermined customary means of subsistence. In many regions, people survived through traditional agricultural methods that required access to land. When countries implemented IMF-style development plans, people were displaced and land was devoted to export crops or livestock. Many formerly self-sufficient people lost their means of economic survival. This created a brutal irony. Many countries with severe problems of hunger and malnutrition are actually exporting significant amounts of food to the world market in keeping with a dubious development strategy. Such instances illustrate how "underdevelopment" is less an initial state of backwardness than an emergent problem created by relations between different parts of the world system.

By the late 1970s, the periphery was in crisis. While old problems of poverty, hunger, and disease persisted or worsened in many places, new problems of massive debt owed to First World lenders were added to the mix. In yet another irony, the IMF and the World Bank that helped create the problems were now enlisted to solve them. Once again, there was a standard prescription, but it was backed up with more explicit coercion. To get assistance with debt relief, Third World countries had to adopt "structural adjustment programs" that imposed austerity measures and slashed social spending to save money to repay debts. Such programs cut (already inadequate) spending on health, education, and welfare. They also undermined workers' rights and environmental protections as further strategies to cut costs and reduce debt.

Just when formally independent governments were emerging in much of the Third World, these developments undercut any real national independence. "As the world's designated loaner of last resort, the IMF became a 'government within the government' in more than seventy-five desperately indebted poor countries...." Harvard economist Jeffrey Sachs called the IMF a "permanent 'neocolonial' force in scores of countries, drastically eroding their sovereignty" (Derber 2002, 116). The mechanisms changed from empire-driven colonialism to umpire-regulated neocolonialism, but the basic dynamic of core states benefiting from exploitation of peripheral states remained.

The economic instability of the 1970s was a catastrophe for many poor nations, but it also destabilized core countries and the larger world system. Led by the United States, core countries responded with deregulation, privatization, and relentless promotion of global "free" markets. These strategies intensified practices dating from the Bretton Woods conference and subsequent refinements through GATT, the IMF, and the World Bank. In the name of "deregulation," older constraints on trade and capital flows were overthrown, and new rules and regulations were carefully crafted to once again favor the strongest players in the world system.

These developments created the World Trade Organization (WTO) at the conclusion of the 1994 GATT negotiations. The WTO is explicitly dedicated to defending property rights, expanding investment options, and privatizing global resources. It is the latest institutional expression of the interests of core countries and transnational corporations in the world system.

Such interests frequently conflict with popular interests at home and abroad. Hence, they must be cloaked in ideologically acceptable language. The advocacy of "free trade" and the equation of capitalist markets with "democracy" are two standard methods. The "language of free trade ... [is] largely rhetorical, because the United States, Japan, and Europe all remain selectively protectionist" (Derber 2002, 121). Put differently, "free" trade is a politically constructed outcome of years of negotiations and thousands of pages of regulations; it is anything but "free." It is the U.S. umpire (and other core countries) who define "free" trade.

These efforts led to international trade agreements such as the North America Free Trade Agreement (NAFTA), the Central American Free Trade Agreement (CAFTA), and the proposed Free Trade Area of the Americas (FTAA). Alongside the WTO, such agreements have consolidated the power of international trade bodies and transnational corporations at the expense of national governments. In yet another irony, conservatives who have always feared a "world government" in the guise of a more powerful United Nations have largely welcomed the economic equivalent of a world government in the WTO.

The WTO not only makes rules about international trade; it also has the power to enforce them and impose sanctions. One example is the NAFTA provision "that sets up a court allowing corporations to sue governments for passing environmental or labor laws that 'infringe' on property rights and profits" (Derber 2002, 125). The WTO has created similar judicial tribunals to defend property rights.

With such mechanisms, transnational corporations can undermine national standards protecting workers or the environment. The strategy uses the less-rigorous standards of some nations against the stronger standards of other nations. The weakest protections to be found anywhere thus become the baseline for attacking stronger protections everywhere else. Even core states have been disciplined in this fashion. The long-term prospect is thus that the WTO will enable transnational corporations to impose Third World labor and environmental standards on First World nations in the name of defending property rights and profits (Derber 2002).

GLOBALIZATION: AN ASSESSMENT

Proponents of globalization claim that it will level the playing field, equalize competition, and create "win-win" situations. The bulk of the evidence to date suggests otherwise. It supports world system theory's claim that conflicting interests and exploitative practices remain central to the world system. Globalization intensifies these dynamics, so that heightened conflict and exploitation produce bigger winners and bigger losers in a more globalized world system.

Consider the startling admission by James Wolfensohn, a former World Bank president, that while globalization has greatly enriched powerful interests, it has been a failure "at the level of people" (cited in Brown 2004, 202). By "people," Wolfensohn presumably means the great majority of the world's population who are victims rather than beneficiaries of globalization. Indeed, a summary of recent evidence on the neoliberal policies of globalization concludes that, "the poorest people on Earth are poorer than before, everyday workers of the developed world have lost ground, and a small cadre of the rich have grown phenomenally richer" (Brown 2004, 202).

Although this assessment might sound extreme, the evidence is compelling. Globalization has sparked a race to the bottom that pits poor nations against one another to see who can lower workers' wages, dismantle safety nets, outlaw labor unions, and scrap environmental protections fast enough to attract capital investment. It is not surprising that global poverty has increased during the past two decades. Moreover, nations that used to be good at attracting foreign investment (like Mexico) are now losing the race to others (like China) who are playing the game even more effectively. As investors moved from Mexico's cheap labor to even cheaper labor elsewhere, and as Mexico has been fully integrated into the North American Free Trade zone, its poverty rate increased from 49 percent to 75 percent in a mere twenty years (Brown 2004, 202–203).

In much of the world, increased poverty stems from the debt Third World nations owe First World lenders. These debts now dwarf other economic indicators. Third World debt has more than doubled since 1980, and some poor countries spend five times more on debt payments than they have received in new loans over the past two decades. In some poor nations, debt payments exceed all other national spending on health, education, and welfare. In the most dire cases, total debt per capita exceeds gross domestic product per capita (Brown 2004, 203). Far from a "win-win" situation, globalization has been a failure for a great many of the world's people.

"People" also includes workers in core countries whose position has deteriorated with globalization. When the United States was the undisputed hegemonic power in the world economic system, benefits flowed to both capitalists and workers. Unions successfully fought for well-paying jobs with significant benefits, including health care and generous pensions. As global competition from other core countries challenged U.S. economic hegemony in the 1970s, the benefits workers derived from living in a core country began to evaporate.

The capitalist response is now familiar. Deindustrialization, runaway shops, capital flight, and downsizing combined to eliminate many well-paying manufacturing jobs and replace them with service jobs, lower wages, and fewer benefits. As jobs changed, so did government policies. For the past thirty years, U.S. domestic policy has resembled a softer version of the structural adjustment programs imposed on Third World countries. Social spending on health, education, and welfare has come under attack, leading to caps, cuts, and the complete elimination of some programs (ending "welfare as we know it"). In the name of privatization, Social Security has come under attack, and many workers have been moved from secure, "defined benefit" pensions to risky "defined contribution" accounts. Broader attacks on unions and environmental protections also follow the logic of structural adjustment programs.

The "race to the bottom" is not just a Third World sport. In industries that play on a global stage, lower standards abroad are used to undercut domestic wages, fringe benefits, worker safety, union status, health care, retirement security, and environmental protections. This amounts to the "deterritorialization" of the periphery of the world economy (Derber 2002). After centuries when the periphery was geographically separate from the core, we are now seeing "peripheral" zones within core countries in chronically depressed urban areas and pockets of extreme rural poverty. Given this, it is little wonder that "in the United States, 75 percent of the workers are worse off economically now than in 1980" (Brown 2004, 202).

So much for the evidence about who loses in a globalized economy. The evidence about who wins is even more dramatic. Corporate profits are at record levels in many industries. The gap between the pay of CEOs and ordinary workers is at an all-time high. The distribution of wealth and income in the United States is more unequal than it has been in almost a hundred years (Perrucci and Wysong 2003). Such inequality has been enhanced by government policies that subsidize profitable industries and cut taxes for wealthy interests. The problem with globalization is not that there are no winners. It is rather that such a small proportion of the world's population derives such massive benefits, while the vast majority who do the work that creates the profits reap so little. Recall, one more time, the baseball makers of Turrialba, who earn less than 30 cents producing baseballs that sell for $15.

Mainstream rhetoric speaks of globalization as inevitable, unstoppable, and irreversible. The implication is that globalization is a genie that has gotten out of a bottle and can't be put back. We're told that the new technologies driving globalization have an intrinsic momentum that cannot be stopped. The further implication is that resistance is futile. In this rhetoric, opponents of globalization are sadly misguided folks who mistakenly think you can turn back the clock and reverse history.

Like many problematic ideas, this one has grains of truth. Barring a major nuclear, ecological, or economic catastrophe, many aspects of globalization are surely here to stay. But there are two assumptions behind this view of globalization that make it deeply flawed and politically dangerous. One is that there is only one way to carry out globalization (like the older, and equally flawed, image of "development" in modernization theory). The second is that this process has so much momentum that no one is, or could be, in charge of it.

The sociological term for these flawed assumptions is *reification*. It means seeing a socially constructed process as if it were a naturally determined inevitability. It means depicting one alternative as the only game in town. It means seeing trends or tendencies as predestined to unfold. A reified view further benefits those who already benefit from globalization by making it appear inevitable.

Critical sociology offers two correctives to this reified view. First, it insists on identifying agency behind globalization. That is, globalization is happening in a particular way because certain powerful groups are acting on their interests to ensure it happens in this way and not other ways. They are using their resources to create a kind of globalization that maximizes their profits and enhances their power, even if it comes at the expense of other people and their interests.

Put differently, there is someone in the driver's seat, and they are taking us to places that aren't good for most passengers on the bus. This does not mean that elites are in complete control or that there aren't unanticipated consequences that backfire on them. But it does mean that someone is responsible for the kind of globalization that is unfolding, including its negative impacts on ordinary people.

Second, critical sociology insists that there are alternatives to the prevailing model of globalization. The issue is not whether to globalize or turn back the clock. The issue is what kind of globalization is preferable. The current model is a top-down, elite-driven, profoundly authoritarian process imposed on people against their interests and without their consent. This description suggests alternative forms of globalization that could be bottom-up, people-driven, and democratically implemented. Such alternatives are actively supported by millions around the world.

Correcting the reified view of globalization requires recognizing which interests have orchestrated it and the existence of alternatives that would serve broader interests. We return to these issues in the next chapter.

Chapter 14

The Role of Social Movements

Social movements have a major impact on our world. Often for better and sometimes for worse, movements vent frustration, express dissent, articulate grievances, transform politics, organize groups, mobilize resources, institute reform, create culture, provoke revolutions, exercise power, establish identities, change society, and more. Although movements are among the most important topics in sociology, the discipline paid little attention to them until recently.

Movements are especially important for critical sociology. People drawn to its analysis of problems are often frustrated by its lack of solutions. Whether critical sociology should prescribe solutions is debatable. What it can do is describe how ordinary people have used movements to solve problems and study the circumstances under which they have succeeded. For these reasons, movements deserve a central place in both mainstream and critical sociology.

SOCIOLOGY AND SOCIAL MOVEMENTS: SIBLINGS OF MODERNITY

Sociology began with modernity and the Enlightenment's promotion of science and reason to understand the world. The analysis of modernity has always been at the core of sociological inquiry. Modernity made sociology possible by advocating a scientific approach to all things, including social things. The modernizing world also gave sociology a wealth of social things to interpret.

The most basic premise of the sociological perspective is that the world is a social construction. Enlightenment-inspired sociology did not see society as God given, naturally ordered, or biologically determined. It was rather a social product resulting from the conscious intentions of people as well as the unintended and unanticipated consequences of those actions. If society is a social construction, then sociology has a lot of explaining to do. The broadest questions involve how and why one kind of social order gets created rather than another.

227

Sociology is thus a child of modernity, but modernity has many children and sociology has many siblings. One of its closest siblings is the social movement. Their common ancestor is the premise that the world is a social construction. Without that premise, there would be no sociology, because there would be nothing to explain in sociological terms. And without that premise, there would be no social movements, because society would appear beyond human intervention. Sociology and social movements are thus closely linked by the common premise that the world is a social construction (Buechler 2000).

The claim that social movements are distinctly modern might sound odd, because people have challenged authority throughout history. By the same token, there have always been social thinkers who pondered the world around them. But just as sociology became a distinct discipline only in the modern era, collective action only became the social movement in the same era.

The ways we refer to this period have unfortunate side effects. Terms like *modernization, development,* and *rationalization* imply a smooth, gradual process of change with a clear direction. In reality, "modernization" was experienced by most people as chaotic, unpredictable, and deeply threatening to traditional ways of life.

The disruptions created by modernization were pervasive. Economically, the transition from feudalism to capitalism and then industrialization fundamentally changed people's connections to land and livelihood. The fancy word is *proletarianization,* which means the transformation of rural peasants who survived through subsistence agriculture into urban workers who had to sell their labor. Alongside proletarianization, rapid urbanization and overcrowding created new conflicts.

Politically, modernization brought a new political organization known as the nation-state. The boundaries of newly formed nations were contested and ultimately established through political and military conflicts. The resulting governments used centralized political power to privatize property, impose taxes, conscript citizens, and coercively control problematic populations.

The speed and extent of these changes demonstrated that society was a social construction because one society was dismantled and another was created right before people's eyes. These changes also provoked collective resistance. Some actions—bread riots, peasant uprisings, and conscription protests—defended traditional ways of life against intrusions by market capitalism and state power. Other actions—labor movements, urban rebellions, slave revolts—challenged arrangements that harmed ordinary people. Still other actions—independence struggles, suffrage movements, democratization efforts—sought a political voice for ordinary citizens.

Through such actions, the modern social movement was invented. The "idea of conscious collective action having the capacity to change society as a whole came only with the era of enlightenment" (Neidhardt and Rucht 1991, 449). Put differently, "[s]ocial movements are genuinely modern phenomena. Only in modern society have social movements played a constitutive role in social development" (Eder 1993, 108). Modern social movements are self-conscious about constructing society.

They are advocates for how society should be organized. They engage in deliberate efforts to promote a certain kind of future.

Consider the role of ideology in the modern age. Ideologies envision how society should be organized; they can provide legitimacy to existing authority or challenge it through opposing visions and social movements. Whether advocating liberalism, conservatism, socialism, anarchism, authoritarianism, or communism, the flowering of ideologies only occurs when society is seen as a social construction and people are seen as having the capacity to reconstruct it through social movements.

These circumstances facilitated "the birth of what we now call the social movement—the sustained, organized challenge to existing authority in the name of a deprived, excluded or wronged population" (Tilly 1995, 144). Emerging in Great Britain and elsewhere in Europe by the 1790s, the social movement was a new way for ordinary people to make claims by repeatedly intervening in national affairs through coordinated, large-scale action. Previous forms of collective action were defensive and localized, involving revenge or resistance. The modern social movement greatly expanded the tactics ordinary people could use to pursue their interests.

This new repertoire of contention was cosmopolitan rather than parochial, meaning it was not confined to one community but rather oriented to multiple centers of power. The new repertoire was modular rather than particular, meaning that new forms of protest could be adapted to many different causes. And it was autonomous, because it allowed movement leaders to communicate directly with national centers of power. This new repertoire of contention also fostered special purpose organizations for pursuing group interests by articulating a national agenda and promoting mass mobilization to support it (Tarrow 1994; Tilly 1995).

The rise of social movements was thus intertwined with modernity itself. The growth of cities, expansion of literacy, and democratization of culture were crucial to the flow of ideas that motivated people to act collectively. The rise of the national state was also crucial, because it provided the target of grievances and the repository of resources for social movement challenges.

As siblings of modernity, sociology and social movements both saw society as a social construction. Whereas sociology sought to explain it, social movements tried to change it. The connections became even closer, as movements challenged the very society that sociology sought to understand, thereby provoking new understandings.

The link was already there in sociology's response to modernization. Many of sociology's core ideas reasserted the conservative worldview that was undermined by the Enlightenment and its political challenges. These included the ideas that society is an organic unity, that it antedates the individual, that it consists of interdependent parts, that social customs and institutions are positively functional, that small groups are essential to social order, and that status and hierarchy are also essential to social order (Zeitlin 1987, 47–48).

Some of sociology's central insights were thus provoked by social movement challenges to existing social order. The pattern continued. Capitalism was criticized by radical thinkers and opposed by socialist movements. Sociology was enriched by these conflicts, as some of the best work done by classical theorists like Weber and Durkheim emerged through a debate with "Marx's ghost" about the correct diagnosis for modern social ills.

The pattern replayed again. By the 1950s, mainstream sociology had settled into a static functionalist approach that denied conflict and ignored change. The social movements of the next decade—and the world they created—demolished these assumptions. This activism established movements themselves as a legitimate focus of sociological analysis. Moreover, these movements transformed the sociological study of power, conflict, race, gender, sexuality, ecology, and globalization.

In all these ways, sociology and social movements continue to have a close relationship. Their common premise that the world is a social construction has inspired social movements to remake the world while enriching sociology's efforts to explain how social worlds get constructed, deconstructed, and reconstructed.

UNDERSTANDING SOCIAL MOVEMENTS

For much of its history, sociology ignored its social movement sibling. When acknowledged, movements were often seen as the black sheep of the family, and people who engaged in them were sometimes viewed as disreputable and deviant.

Marx had offered a more promising start with his analysis of working-class formation. What he showed was that solidarity *within* groups was intimately tied to conflict *between* them. Over time, such solidarity should promote a collective identity or "we-feeling," a consciousness about group interests, and a commitment to act politically to advance those interests. This logic should fit any chronic group conflict; we should expect collective identity, group consciousness, and political mobilization in all such cases. These are the logical result of social conflict and the rational expression of group interests.

Durkheim provided an alternative view. He was concerned about social integration, because it provides social control and normative regulation. When integration undergoes strain or breakdown, control is weakened or destroyed. This fosters anomie, as people lose their social bearings and cultural guidelines. This in turn promotes spontaneous, unstructured, and potentially dangerous collective behavior. For Durkheim, collective behavior is less an expression of group interests than a sign of social breakdown.

Sociology followed Durkheim's lead, and the collective behavior approach prevailed for much of the twentieth century. The general idea is that social stress, strain, or breakdown spark psychological discontent or anxiety in individuals, who respond with collective behavior, ranging from panics, crazes, and crowds to social movements. Such behavior tends to be formless, unpatterned, and unpredictable; its noninstitutionalized quality separates collective from conventional behavior.

These assumptions spawned several versions of collective behavior theory. The symbolic interactionist approach focused on circular reaction, contagion, and excitability as provoking social unrest (Blumer 1951). The structural-functionalist approach outlined a stage model of collective behavior as "short-circuiting" normal channels of social action (Smelser 1962). A social-psychological version identified relative deprivation as the catalyst that spurred people into collective behavior (Geschwender 1968).

These variants all see collective behavior as spontaneous, unstructured, and sometimes irrational or deviant. Grouping social movements with panics, crazes, and fads obscured the politics, the organization, the rationality, and the longevity of at least some social movements.

A major shift occurred after the social movements of the 1960s. The civil rights movement was critical, but it was also the catalyst for student, antiwar, ethnic, feminist, and environmental movements. Such movements were hard to explain through the logic of collective behavior theory. As a result, sociologists developed a paradigm that reversed many collective behavior premises.

The new approach was resource mobilization theory. It sees social movements as a form of political struggle (McCarthy and Zald 1973, 1977; Oberschall 1973; Tilly 1978). In contrast to the collective behavior tradition, resource mobilization theory views movements as normal, rational, institutionally rooted, political challenges by aggrieved groups. The theory redefined collective action from an example of deviance and disorganization to a topic for political and organizational sociology.

Resource mobilization theory argues that people join movements based on conscious decisions rather than spontaneous impulses. Individuals are seen as rational actors who join movements when the potential benefits outweigh the anticipated costs (McCarthy and Zald 1977). The emphasis on rational calculation meant that grievances were not enough; movements only emerge when resources become available that allow groups to act on their grievances.

Resource mobilization theory developed two versions. The entrepreneurial model equates movements with small businesses trying to survive in a competitive environment (McCarthy and Zald 1973, 1977). This model explicitly downplays grievances and emphasizes resources. When groups can accumulate resources—money, people, organization, commitment, communication, and the like—movements follow. The role of leaders is especially important; they are like entrepreneurs who gather the resources needed to launch movements.

The political version of the theory sees a world divided between political insiders and outsiders. The insiders have routine, low-cost access to decision making, so they don't have to resort to social movements to achieve their objectives. Political outsiders without institutional power must create movements to achieve their objectives. This requires groups to identify collective interests, create effective organization, and mobilize available resources. When this state of readiness finds opportunities to act, movements emerge (Tilly 1978).

Both versions emphasize resources, but the entrepreneurial model stresses movement leaders and top-down strategies, whereas the political one emphasizes mass support and bottom-up strategies. The political version also stresses "cognitive liberation" whereby people come to believe that change is possible and that their action will make a difference. Finally, opportunity remains crucial. It arises whenever the power gap between elites and movements is reduced. If movements act when their opportunities are greatest, they are most likely to succeed (McAdam 1982).

This theory fundamentally reoriented the study of social movements. Where collective behavior theory equated movements with fads, panics, crazes, and riots, resource mobilization theory saw them as serious, organized, political struggles. Before long, however, this theory also attracted critics.

Some said it went too far in dismissing grievances. They argued that grievances must be socially constructed through "framing," which imparts meaning to elements within a frame and sets them apart from what is outside the frame. Framing thus assigns meanings to movement claims. Framing underscores how grievances only emerge through social interaction.

Grievances are framed in several ways (Snow and Benford 1988). Diagnostic framing identifies a problem and assigns blame or causality, so the movement has a target for its actions. Prognostic framing suggests solutions and remedies, including tactics and strategies that are likely to work against the opposition. Together, these frames create movement sympathizers. Recruiting them requires motivational framing or a "call to arms" and a rationale for action (Benford 1993). Successful framing thus translates vague dissatisfactions into well-defined grievances and compels people to join a movement to act on them.

Movements also engage in frame alignment to recruit people (Snow et al. 1986). Frame bridging happens when movements publicize their views and recruit those who already agree with them. Frame amplification appeals to values and beliefs in the general population and links them to movement issues; in this way, people's preexisting values entice them into the movement. Frame extension enlarges an initial frame to include issues important to potential recruits, making the movement a logical response to preexisting concerns. Finally, frame transformation creates new values, beliefs, and meanings to recruit people. In these ways, movements actively work to identify, create, and connect people's beliefs with grievances and participation.

Framing also defines the sides in a conflict (Hunt et al. 1994). Protagonist framing identifies members and allies of a movement. Antagonist framing identifies enemies, by specifying the source of the problem and villainizing those responsible for it. Audience framing identifies bystanders and clarifies strategies for recruiting support or neutralizing opposition. Framing is thus crucial in defining grievances, recruiting participants, and shaping identities in social activism.

This approach also describes "master frames" that broadly define grievances in terms of oppression, injustice, or exploitation and solutions in terms of liberation, fairness, or equity (Snow and Benford 1992). Their generality allows master frames to be adopted by many movements. Because of this, master frames often accompany cycles of protest that include many aggrieved groups. Thus, the 1960s protest cycle had master frames of emancipation or liberation that began with the civil rights movement and became organizing frames for many other movements.

The social constructionist approach does not deny the importance of resources, but argues that they are not enough. Movements also involve grievances, participants, and identities that must be framed to promote participation. Without such framing, movements are unlikely to emerge or to succeed.

Alongside resource mobilization and framing approaches, a third contemporary approach is new social movement theory (Cohen 1985; Klandermans 1991; Klandermans and Tarrow 1988; Larana, Johnston, and Gusfield 1994; Pichardo 1997). This European import links certain kinds of societies with certain kinds of movements. Thus, industrial societies promoted an "old" movement on behalf of working-class interests. With the coming of postindustrial society, new social movements displace the labor movement, just as postindustrial society has displaced industrial society.

New social movements respond to specific conditions of contemporary society. These include markets and bureaucracies that breed alienation, anomie, and dehumanization. New social movements, by contrast, provide personal, meaningful, human-scale relationships for participants. In addition, whereas the old labor movement revolved around materialist demands, new social movements often have postmaterialist goals. They are less about economic gain and more about winning recognition, acceptance, and participation for previously excluded groups.

Issues of identity are central in new social movements. In industrial society, social class was the most important identity, and the labor movement was central. In a postindustrial society, identities are less anchored in social class. Collective identity becomes more fluid and changeable across different situations and groups of people.

This means that collective identities are often constructed through movement activity. In fact, the major accomplishment of such a movement might be to nurture a collective identity that gains newfound recognition and acceptance. This is why (in contrast to the old class movements) new social movements might be organized around race, ethnicity, nationality, gender, age, sexual orientation, or religion.

New social movements also emphasize cultural aspects of social life. They challenge symbols and identities that marginalize certain groups and promote alternative symbols and identities that foster acceptance and legitimation. Such struggles often seek not to vanquish opponents as much as to create tolerance and peaceful coexistence. Some new social movements thereby resemble subcultures or countercultures that carve out alternative social worlds alongside mainstream society.

This cultural emphasis also means that participants in new social movements see close connections between movement goals and everyday life. The politics of new social movements is often expressed in routine decisions and actions. For new social movements, "the personal is political," and personal life becomes a major site of movement activism.

One example of a new social movement is gay and lesbian activism, where identity questions have been a major battleground. For much of the twentieth century, homosexuality was seen as a stigmatized, deviant identity and a form of mental illness. The gay and lesbian movement challenged these negative definitions by promoting gay pride, gaining acceptance, and changing discriminatory customs and laws. The focus on identity, culture, and personal life nicely exemplifies new social movements.

Sociology has thus developed many useful tools for understanding movements. The collective behavior tradition analyzes spontaneity, contagion, and group dynamics. Resource mobilization theory underscores resources, organization, mobilization, and opportunity. Social constructionism reveals how grievances, members, and identities must be framed as meaningful if movements are to arise. And finally, new social movement theory illuminates struggles around collective identities, cultural politics, and everyday life. These approaches collectively illuminate how social movements have pursued their goals and shaped the modern world in the process.

SOCIAL MOVEMENTS AND PROGRESSIVE POLITICS

The study of social movements reveals many lessons. For critical sociology, the most important is the link between social movements and progressive politics. Such politics empower ordinary people and narrow the gap between them and elites who otherwise dominate political decision making. Struggles for emancipation, liberation, or justice are examples. Campaigns to gain, extend, or preserve civil, social, political, or economic rights are other examples. They contrast sharply with reactionary politics that strengthen elites at the expense of ordinary people. They also contrast with normal, institutional politics whose distribution of power heavily favors elites.

The most important lesson here is that progressive politics have always been driven by social movements. Progressive politics can also include political parties (or wings of political parties), activist subcultures, and even some elite individuals or institutions. But what drives them are social movements. When progressive change occurs, it is largely a result of social movements.

This does not mean that all social movements are progressive. Some movements support reactionary politics. The Ku Klux Klan, neo-Nazi movements, and anti-immigrant groups are ugly movements promoting hatred, discrimination, and injustice. So we must keep our logic clear. Not all social movements are progressive. But progressive politics are always rooted in social movements.

This link is evident both analytically and historically. Analytically, society is an arena of conflict in which elite individuals and organizations pursue their interests. In a few cases, this benefits everyone. More often, however, pursuit of elite interests serves them at the expense of ordinary people and their interests.

Elites control the political arena. This means that normal, institutional politics exercised through major parties, campaigns, and elections mainly serve elite interests. The issues in institutional politics typically involve differences among elites; this is why the "choices" offered in elections are not much of a choice at all. The institutional organization of society and politics leaves little room for popular interests.

This is what links social movements and progressive politics. Movements are almost a prerequisite for getting the interests of ordinary people into the political process. By working under, over, around, and sometimes through normal channels, social movements have been the most effective way to achieve progressive change. When such change happens, it is because ordinary people have used social activism to pursue equality, overcome political inertia, and institutionalize progressive goals.

The link between social movements and progressive politics is also evident historically—and right from the beginning in the United States. Firmly rooted in the Enlightenment, the American Revolution was a form of progressive politics that overthrew British domination and created a new nation. The Revolution also inspired important statements of progressive politics in the Declaration of Independence, the Bill of Rights, and the Constitution itself. The British rulers of the American colonies largely opposed this effort, and it eventually required not just a movement but a war to achieve the progressive agenda of the American Revolution.

At the same time, these events revealed the complexity of movements, politics, and change. The Revolution was a cross-class movement that temporarily united wealthy, middling, and poor colonists against a common, external oppressor. But even as it was unfolding, elites were crafting a form of government that would preserve their wealth, defend their property, and entrench their power. Once the common enemy was defeated, preexisting class cleavages resurfaced and entrenched a new elite that pursued their interests in the new nation (Zinn 1980).

Many elite interests were tied to Southern plantation agriculture and the slave labor that made it profitable. Although the planter class was powerful and racist justifications of slavery were ubiquitous, slave resistance was also common. By the early nineteenth century, a powerful abolitionist movement added its voice to the progressive cause of ending slavery and extending political rights to African Americans. This was not just a regional or national movement. The World Anti-Slavery Convention held in London in 1840 illustrates how transnational social movements have been around for some time.

With abolitionism on the rise, chattel slavery became impossible to defend. Many abolitionist arguments were based on rhetoric and rights established by the progressive politics of the American Revolution itself. By extending the definitions of "humans" and "people" to slaves and former slaves, powerful ideological challenges to the ownership of people as property were mounted.

Like the American Revolution, the Civil War was a complex conflict of group interests. In many respects, it was another battle between competing elites (Northern industrialists vs. Southern planters) to see who would control the country. So although it is too simplistic to say that the Civil War was fought to free the slaves, the North could not have won it without freeing the slaves. The Civil War thus provided the abolitionist movement with the opportunity to achieve perhaps the greatest victory for progressive politics in U.S. history: the abolition of slavery and the extension of civil, political, and social rights to newly freed slaves.

Whereas abolitionists challenged chattel slavery, the labor movement challenged "wage slavery." In a culture that prized independence, autonomy, and self-sufficiency, "free laborers" fiercely resisted wage labor, just as slaves resisted their subordination. Although "wage slavery" persisted, this campaign initiated a labor movement that would defend the dignity of labor and the livelihood of workers for decades to come.

Whereas abolitionism attacked slavery and labor opposed capitalism, the women's rights movement challenged male domination. Abolitionism and women's rights were closely linked, because many women arrived at women's rights through antislavery work. Abolitionism provided its own provocations as well; when the delegation of the American Anti-Slavery Association arrived in London for the 1840 convention, its female members were denied participation. Such unequal treatment convinced many female abolitionists that they needed a movement of their own. It emerged at the Seneca Falls Convention of 1848, one among a series of women's rights conventions that met up to the eve of the Civil War.

One of the founding documents of this movement was a Declaration of Sentiments and Principles deliberately modeled on the Declaration of Independence. Where the latter document referred to the British or King George as the oppressor of the colonies, the former referred to men as the oppressors of women. Once again, the progressive political rhetoric of the American Revolution was strategically used to make powerful arguments on behalf of a previously excluded category of people.

The progressive politics of the women's rights movement were evident in its agenda and its alliances with abolitionism and labor (Buechler 1986). The political fallout of these entanglements was complex. After the North won the Civil War, the abolitionists were poised to solidify their victory. Women's rights activists argued that progressive reforms should include women as well as slaves. The abolitionists disagreed. They declared it the "Negro's Hour" and ignored the women's rights agenda. The decision divided women's rights advocates, and it would not be the last time that divisive politics undermined a progressive coalition.

After the Civil War, normalcy returned in the North. After Reconstruction, white supremacy returned in the South. But new groups advanced progressive politics in the last quarter of the nineteenth century. The Knights of Labor revived the labor movement and defended the status and living standards of workers. Farmers organized to protect their livelihood in a system increasingly dominated by railroads and middlemen.

Farmer's alliances were eventually undermined by an old problem for social movements: They often were cross-class organizations dominated by larger farmers who advanced their distinct interests at the expense of smaller farmers and ordinary citizens (Schwartz 1976). Such populist movements posed other dangers. Their political frustrations could be misdirected, and scapegoating sometimes diverted these movements from their real targets. But at their best, the populist movements of the late nineteenth century advanced progressive politics by seeking greater equality and better lives for ordinary Americans.

At the dawn of the twentieth century, these politics were advanced in cities by the Progressive movement. In response to the corporate excesses and governmental corruption of the Gilded Age, the Progressive movement sought to regulate corporations, dismantle monopolies, reform government, promote education, naturalize immigrants, and mediate class conflict through rational, scientific, and democratic decision making. Corporate capitalism also provoked more radical challenges. In

Western states, the International Workers of the World ("Wobblies") sought to organize "one big union" to advance the cause of labor. In many cities, states, and even at the federal level, the Socialist Party offered progressive solutions to the economic and social problems confronting working people.

The Progressive era also revived women's efforts to win the vote. They could only succeed by amending the U.S. Constitution. To do so, the movement sought the broadest possible support, recruiting rural, working, immigrant, and elite women with customized arguments about why they needed the vote. The movement developed new strategies to gain public support from men as well as women. It built on state successes and kept relentless pressure on Congress and the executive branch. It broadened its tactics to include intensive lobbying, militant demonstrations, civil disobedience, and hunger strikes.

These efforts changed the political calculus so that even opponents concluded that it was less trouble to grant the vote than continue withholding it. When the measure finally passed Congress by razor-thin margins, the movement fought the ratification battle in the states. This victory also came by the thinnest of margins in 1920. The nineteenth amendment culminated eighty years of social movement activism and progressive politics that dramatically expanded the boundaries of citizenship in the United States (Buechler 1986).

Within a decade, the stock market crash plunged the country into the Great Depression. Progressive forces responded, as the mainstream labor movement became more diverse and militant. Unemployed workers organized and pressured the government to provide work or some form of welfare in the absence of work. The Communist Party was especially effective in organizing African American workers, who had historically been shunned by the labor movement. With newfound militancy in a time of economic crisis, these movements won the right to organize unions and established the eight-hour workday. The labor movement then became a major force when wartime production reinvigorated the economy and brought the relative prosperity of the 1950s.

The progressive social movements of the 1930s also played an important role in shaping the New Deal. Some actions were temporary but important, like public works programs that put people to work when the market could not. Other responses were more lasting and fundamental. They include, most obviously, the Social Security system and unemployment compensation insurance that provide economic support for broad segments of the population. The New Deal showed that government could be responsive to ordinary citizens, but it also showed that progressive social movements were needed to ensure that it met such obligations.

Progressive politics then revived the neglected issue of race relations with the civil rights movement. After the abolitionist movement had helped to end slavery, racism took new forms with Jim Crow laws, legal and de facto segregation, and white supremacy. The civil rights movement emerged in the 1950s in the Southern United States to challenge the most egregious forms of segregation and discrimination by seeking integration. Pursuit of this modest goal produced a racist backlash, which led to federal intervention to maintain civil order. Once again, a progressive movement was required to provoke the government into protecting the fundamental rights of citizens (McAdam 1982; Morris 1984).

The civil rights movement ended legal segregation, challenged racial discrimination, reduced terrorist violence against blacks, and advanced voting and other civil rights for racial minorities. These reforms inspired the Great Society programs of the Kennedy and Johnson administrations, including new federal antipoverty efforts and the establishment of Medicare. Once again, progressive social change occurred only in the wake of a powerful social movement.

The civil rights movement also spawned a new cycle of progressive movements in the 1960s and 1970s. As the movement came north and developed more militant strategies of black power, other racial and ethnic movements borrowed this master frame on behalf of migrants, farmworkers, Latino/a groups, and Native Americans. Race-conscious movements also injected new militancy into a labor movement that had become bureaucratic and top-heavy during the complacent 1950s.

The new left also took inspiration from the civil rights movement as it promoted participatory democracy. Many student activists had participated in the civil rights movement, and they took its lessons back to campuses and communities to broaden citizenship and political participation across both class and racial lines. This also meant defending free speech to cultivate more participatory solutions to social problems.

As U.S. military involvement in Southeast Asia escalated, these movements were fertile ground for antiwar activism. Politicized students found a new target in the war, and the draft in particular. Government repression of dissent illustrated just how limited democracy really was. The antiwar movement contributed to changing U.S. policy in Southeast Asia, by dividing elites between "hawks" and "doves" and weakening support for the war. The movement also radicalized a generation of activists who took up other political causes (Gitlin 1993).

Alongside the civil rights, new left, and antiwar movements, there was a parallel and intersecting counterculture. Exemplifying a new social movement, this counterculture challenged mainstream values of authority, materialism, consumerism, competition, and success. By encouraging young people to "tune in, turn on, and drop out," the counterculture sparked critical analysis of the dominant culture (Roszak 1969).

Among the most important movements to emerge out of this cycle of protest was second-wave feminism. Recruiting professional and college women, the women's rights and women's liberation wings became a mass movement by the early 1970s. The movement overturned many public forms of sex segregation and gender discrimination, while revealing the more subtle politics behind supposedly private issues like sexuality, the body, and personal life. It is difficult to overstate the impact of contemporary feminism. Its simultaneous relevance to personal, public, political, cultural, private, global, spiritual, economic, and psychological issues speaks volumes about the role of gender in the social order (Buechler 1990; Ferree and Hess 2000).

The modern environmental movement also emerged out of this cycle of protest. Although it had predecessors in older conservation and preservation efforts, the environmental movement of the 1970s brought a qualitative shift in how people saw their relationship to the natural world. It is striking that large majorities of people now readily identify themselves as supporters of environmental causes. Although institutional practices and personal behaviors still deviate from these proclaimed values, this movement created an important foundation for future gains.

This brief summary requires some caveats. Not all movements are progressive. Not all movements succeed. Movements sometimes create new problems. And even with success, progressive victories are often overturned by reactionary forces. Having acknowledged all this, the basic conclusion still stands. Every major progressive social change in the United States has been driven by social movements that have made the world a better place for millions of ordinary people. Critical sociologists often see the glass as half empty, but the only reason it is half full is because of social movements seeking more just and equitable worlds.

A NOTE ON GLOBALIZATION AND RESISTANCE

Progressive social movements have continued around issues of sexuality and AIDS, nuclear energy and weapons, peace and justice, foreign intervention, apartheid, "third-wave" feminism, and various campus-based causes. Although the earlier protest cycle received much attention, there are significant continuities between that cycle and more recent activism.

Having said that, the most noteworthy feature of recent activism has been its transnational character (Della Porta and Tarrow 2005; Smith and Johnston 2002). This is not entirely new; abolitionism and women's rights were transnational movements in the nineteenth century. But current transnational movements are qualitatively different. Activists around the world are now routinely exchanging information, trading strategies, and coordinating protests on a daily basis. Globalization itself has made this possible through new information technologies and the shrinking of time and space that have allowed many causes to "go global."

This poses challenges for social movement theory. As noted before, social movements and the nation-state emerged together and shaped each other as modern society developed. From the beginning, the most common target of social movements has been the nation-state. Governments were often framed as the cause of problems and almost always as part of the solution. Transnational movements often have more complex targets and potential solutions.

At the same time, much transnational activism feels familiar. It still requires resources, organization, mobilization, and opportunity; it still depends on effective framing of problems, solutions, identities, and motivations; and it still involves building collective identities and deploying cultural symbols. In all these ways, sociology remains well equipped to study these newest social movements.

One form of transnational activism grows out of older causes that have historically been pursued in national contexts. In this case, globalization has simply allowed these movements to become transnational in scope. As they have done so, their organization, framing, and identities involve multiple societies and governments. This includes movements challenging apartheid, opposing wars, promoting human rights, or fighting environmental degradation.

For another form of transnational activism, globalization itself is the problem and the target. This is sometimes called the *antiglobalization movement,* but the term is problematic. It implies that only one kind of globalization is possible, and that the movement is against it. Such unqualified opposition allows activists to be painted as backward or naive for resisting the inevitable. As noted earlier, the real battle is not whether globalization will happen; it is rather what kind of globalization will happen, and who its victims and beneficiaries will be.

For social constructionism, this is a framing battle. Proponents of globalization to date portray it as the only game in town. Opponents counter-frame it as "corporate" or "top-down" globalization in contrast to "bottom-up" globalization. For resource mobilization, this is an organizational battle. Whereas elites confer at the World *Economic* Forum, popular forces organize themselves through the World *Social* Forum (and many other organizations, coalitions, and alliances). For new social movement theory, this is about collective identity. Proponents urge people to identify with national interests that supposedly benefit from globalization. Opponents challenge such identities and offer global citizenship as a more inclusive way to think. Transnational resistance to top-down globalization thereby involves many familiar dimensions of social movement theory.

Movements resisting top-down globalization offer several alternatives. One is contestation and reform, which challenges corporate prerogatives and calls on states to regulate corporate activity and punish abuses. Another is globalization from below, which builds upon social movements to create an international form of populism that will gradually supersede existing forms of government. Yet another is delinking, in which localities break away from global market forces to focus on regional development and local resources (Starr 2000, xi).

Another framing of alternatives to globalization distinguishes two views. In one camp, people promote globalization from below shaped by United Nations–style organizations and principles for establishing a genuinely new world order. This vision anticipates the gradual erosion of national sovereignty in favor of a world government that would be democratic in all the ways that the WTO is autocratic. In the other camp, people seek a locally driven version of globalization in which popular decision making in small-scale settings determines whether and how such regions will participate in broader economic and political arrangements (Derber 2002, 132–135).

Mainstream ideology about globalization says "there is no alternative." These analyses illustrate that there are actually several alternatives. Despite variations, they share one thing. Every vision of "globalization from below" rests on more participatory and democratic decision making than the current form of globalization.

The link between progressive politics and social movements applies on a global stage. If and when a more just and egalitarian form of globalization emerges, it will be largely owing to social movements challenging autocratic globalization.

Chapter 15

The Case for Democracy

Critical sociology advocates democracy. The problems identified by critical sociology have complex causes, but a lack of democracy is central to their persistence. Solving them requires extending and enriching democratic decision making. It is thereby fitting to conclude with a look at democracy.

This chapter examines how a limited form of democracy emerged in advanced capitalist society. It then explores what a richer vision of democracy might look like. It then revisits social movements as carriers of democracy. It concludes by considering how sociological consciousness can foster a more democratic society.

THE LIMITS ON DEMOCRACY

To question the democracy of the United States might seem odd. Mainstream opinion portrays the United States as the model for democracy. Here's a telling example. The United States launched an unprovoked, preemptive war against Iraq in 2003. Justification for the war had many rationales involving terrorism, weapons of mass destruction, and the like. Every one proved false. So the final rationale was that the United States was at war to bring democracy to Iraq. Although some criticized the war, few questioned that the United States is the model of democracy. For most, this self-evident fact justified imposing "democracy" on another country through warfare and occupation.

Critical sociology specializes in identifying and questioning such taken-for-granted assumptions. Consider democracy's history. Ancient Greece is lauded as the birthplace of democracy, where citizens could participate in discussion, debate, and deliberation. Less often mentioned is that democratic Greece rested on a slave economy that denied any vestige of citizenship to many who made its civilization possible. Praise of those who articulated democratic ideals must be tempered with consideration of how they put them into practice.

The democratic heritage of the United States derives from the Enlightenment. We return again to that big family parented by Enlightenment and modernity, whose children include sociology, social movements, the nation-state, and now democracy. As the Founding Fathers crafted the U.S. government, they incorporated some democratic elements seasoned with much democratic rhetoric.

What the Founders really created was not a democracy but a republic. In this government, people's voices would be heard through their representatives (if at all). In establishing institutions with checks and balances, the Founders were responding to two potential dangers. On the one hand, they wanted to prevent government from becoming too centralized and absolutist. On the other hand, they wanted to prevent direct, popular input. Through elected representatives and institutional filters, they ensured that governmental power would remain in elite hands. In limiting both absolutist tendencies and popular participation, they fashioned a government that was well suited to preserving private property and minimizing state interference. Put differently, economic property interests trumped democratic political ideals.

The equation of the United States and democracy was thus dubious from the beginning. The government was not designed to promote democracy but rather to protect elite interests and legitimate them through democratic rhetoric. More substantively—like ancient Greece—the United States rested on a slave economy that persisted for decades after the republic's founding. Reconciling slavery with republican government required elaborate legislative contortions in which fractions of slave populations were counted for purposes of representation, although slaves themselves were denied the vote and every other political right.

This suggests that democracy is not a structure or a set of institutions but rather a contested process. There *are* important links between U.S. history and real democracy, but they are less about formal institutions and more about popular struggles. We have seen how social movements advanced progressive politics, and this includes democracy. Before returning to this story, however, we must consider how democracy has been restricted and confined within the United States. It turns out that without popular pressure, the United States is not a very democratic society after all.

At least four factors have limited the extent and exercise of genuine democracy in the United States. The first is the structure of prevailing economic and political institutions. Capitalism and bureaucracy thrive in the United States, and both are profoundly antidemocratic forms of social organization. Both use instrumental rationality to maximize economic profits and centralize political power. Both concentrate resources in few hands. Both reinforce hierarchy. Both expand elite influence. Both are highly resistant to popular input. The logic of capitalism and bureaucracy is deeply antithetical to meaningful democracy.

This is obscured by the frequent equation of "capitalism" and "democracy" or the term *capitalist democracy* in mainstream discourse. Such rhetoric reduces democracy to property rights and entrepreneurial freedoms. It implies that this is the only viable type of democracy. By sheer repetition, it further implies that a capitalist economy and a democratic polity are naturally suited to each other. In fact, their underlying logics are diametrically opposed. There is a fundamental contradiction between capitalism and democracy. In the absence of popular pressure on social institutions, that contradiction severely restricts democratic decision making.

A second factor limiting democracy is the actions taken by elites to promote capitalism at the expense of democracy. These actions built walls around democracy that limit its scope (Piven and Cloward 1982). Thus, for much of our history, the doctrine of laissez-faire prevented democratic decision making in the political sphere from influencing capitalist priorities in the economic sphere. Put differently, there never was a politics of property that allowed democracy to intrude on economic activity. There might, at times, have been a vibrant democratic political culture, but it was walled off from economics.

This remained true until the Great Depression necessitated the New Deal, which broke down the walls between democratic decision making and economic priorities. This was a historically rare moment when popular, political pressure limited profit making and forced government to promote the general welfare. In the past three decades, however, the capitalist defense of property has renewed its attacks on democracy. The strategies to rebuild the walls around democracy include stigmatizing government itself, limiting its power, and reducing its revenue. The cumulative effect undermines the state's ability to sustain the public good.

A third factor limiting democracy has been its equation with formal, electoral politics; democracy has been reduced to voting for candidates. "Winner-take-all" electoral rules all but guarantee a two-party system that marginalizes many and narrows the political spectrum. The reduction of politics to elections between two parties makes it much easier for elites to control such politics. On many issues, mainstream parties merely represent differences among elites, with little voice for popular interests. Under these conditions, electoral politics is more about policing public sentiments than expressing popular interests.

These realities lead to low voter turnout. Although many decry it, low turnout is less about "apathy" than the fact that electoral politics rarely speak to people's needs in meaningful ways. As elections become elite-controlled, money-dominated, poll-driven, media spectacles that deliberately use negative advertising to suppress voter turnout, *not* voting becomes a rational response. As politics are reduced to elections, elections are reduced to spectacles, and citizens are reduced to spectators, proclamations of "democracy" ring ever more hollow.

A final factor limiting democracy is the gap between making history and everyday life (Flacks 1988). Because of their institutional positions, elites make history through their everyday activities. For most people, everyday life distances them from institutional power and the capacity to make history. The gap narrows only in rare circumstances of political crisis and popular mobilization.

The apolitical nature of everyday life involves more than apathy. It also reflects a libertarian bargain whereby people accept public alienation in exchange for private satisfactions (even though many such private satisfactions have only been made possible by prior public struggles). The tacit bargain is this: The masses will leave elites alone as long as elites maintain material conditions that support satisfying private lives. The outcome is a quasi withdrawal from democratic politics by ordinary people. If elites don't maintain their end of the bargain, or if people have new reasons to reject the bargain, then a more meaningful democracy might emerge (Flacks 1988).

TOWARD A RICHER DEMOCRACY

All these factors limit democratic politics in the United States. They reveal how democracy only flowers through popular mobilization. Because critical sociology advocates for a more democratic society, it becomes important to envision what that might look like. There are alternatives to the impoverished democracy that typically prevails in advanced capitalist societies.

Having identified four limits on democracy, let's counterpose four images of a richer democracy. One is found in the history of the public sphere. In early modern society, the public sphere developed with the spread of literacy, the emergence of a free press, the creation of public spaces, and an ethic that discussion and debate are vital to a democratic culture and society (Habermas 1989). A viable public sphere is essential to sustaining meaningful democracy through popular participation.

The danger to the public sphere has always been commercialization. Public sphere debates are too often displaced by public relations manipulations. But just as earlier technologies like daily newspapers were vital to creating a democratic public sphere, newer technologies like the Internet could revive the public sphere and sustain some crucial elements of democratic politics.

A second image of democracy is the ideal speech situation (Habermas 1975). As we saw in chapter three, this is a counterfactual set of conditions that would lead to democratic decision making and the formulation of a rational political will. In this hypothetical situation, everyone is allowed to participate in discussions to endorse a value, establish a norm, or select an action. Preexisting power differences between participants are set aside and not allowed to influence the course or the outcome of the debate. The only "force" allowed is the force of the better argument. The goal is to establish a consensus in all areas that involve generalizable interests.

The ideal speech situation is neither a utopian dream nor a concrete proposal. It is rather a benchmark for judging other systems of decision making. The farther such systems depart from the ideal speech situation (because not all can speak, because power distorts the dialogue, because rationality does not decide disputes, etc.), the less democratic they are. Moreover, the ideal speech situation provides a positive model for democratic decision making. It might never be accomplished, but the more it can be approximated, the more democratic our decision making will become.

Another positive image is participatory democracy. In the 1960s, the New Left advocated this form of democracy as an alternative to mainstream politics. Whereas electoral democracy marginalizes citizens and reduces them to spectators, participatory democracy empowers them as active members of a broader political community engaged in collaborative decision making. The goal is to narrow the gap between everyday life and making history, so that ordinary citizens and popular masses can influence the course of historical events.

Participatory democracy emphasizes that "the personal is political." The slogan suggests that politics is not a narrow set of distant issues decided by others but rather a broad canvas of daily choices and actions with inevitably political consequences. If everyday life is political, then people already are political actors. What remains is to raise consciousness about the politics implicit in personal lives and thereby foster a political community in the form of participatory democracy.

A fourth vision is deliberative democracy (Della Porta 2005, 74). This begins with preference formation. Rather than simply tabulating preexisting preferences, deliberative democracy involves discussion during which preferences can be revised and transformed on the basis of information presented through such discussion. A further goal of deliberative democracy is to set aside self- or group-interest to focus explicitly on the public good.

Following Habermas's ideal speech situation, deliberative democracy promotes discussion based on rational argument. People must present defensible reasons for positions they advocate and consider the reasons of others in a rational manner. The goal of such discussion is not to win a vote but to create a consensus. If all reasons are heard and all positions are considered, such a consensus should be the outcome.

In order to be effective, deliberative democracy requires equality. The discourse must be a horizontal one between equals rather than a vertical one between unequals. It must include all citizens who might be affected by a decision and have a stake in the outcome. Such discussion must also be transparent, meaning that the motives and reasons that shape the discourse are continually accessible to all. In short, "we have deliberative democracy when, under conditions of equality, inclusiveness, and transparency, a communicative process based on reason (the strength of the argument) transforms individual preferences into consensual decision making oriented to the public good" (Della Porta 2005, 74–75).

These hypothetical visions of a full, rich participatory democracy contrast sharply with the institutional realities of a thin, impoverished electoral democracy. The next question is whether and how the former might begin to replace the latter.

SOCIAL MOVEMENTS AS INCUBATORS OF DEMOCRATIC POLITICS

Enriching democracy requires political struggle. Social institutions are inherently conservative. They persist, in part, because they serve the interests of powerful groups in society. These conservative institutions include the mainstream political system. Democratization will not arise from the status quo. It can only arise when social movements advocating progressive politics begin to succeed. The history of social movements and progressive politics reviewed earlier is also a history of how social movements have pushed society in more democratic directions.

This is why there is an element of truth in claims about the United States and democracy. Whatever democracy exists in the United States has arisen from popular pressure that has forced elites and institutions to become more democratic than they would like to be. When social movements and progressive politics are strong, we are at our most democratic. When they are weak, we are at our least democratic.

Free spaces are an important link between social movements and democratic politics. A free space is an environment "in which people are able to learn a new self-respect, a deeper and more assertive group identity, public skills, and values of cooperation and civic virtue" (Evans and Boyte 1992, 17). Such spaces reside between the micro level of personal life and the macro level of public institutions. They are big enough to create connections with others but small enough to invite meaningful, individual participation.

Free spaces emerge in social settings like churches, neighborhoods, and voluntary organizations. They grow from communal roots that link people together, provide autonomy from larger, coercive powers, and nurture a focus on the common good (Evans and Boyte 1992, 24). The value of such spaces to meaningful democracy cannot be overestimated. "Democratic action depends upon these free spaces, where people experience a schooling in citizenship and learn a vision of the common good in the course of struggling for change" (Evans and Boyte 1992, 18).

The concept of free spaces suggests several associations. It is the kind of setting that would support an ideal speech situation or deliberative democracy. It sounds like our (somewhat romanticized) image of a New England town hall meeting. It calls to mind a public sphere in which the promotion of literacy, the free flow of information, and the principle of rational debate hold sway. Free spaces are places where we are likely to see meaningful democracy in action.

The problem is that for all our technological and material advances, free spaces have become scarce in late modern society. Our schools, workplaces, institutions, media, and communities are increasingly shaped by distant powers that do not welcome our participation. Consider the commercialization of daily life. As genuine public squares disappear, some claim that shopping malls are the new public spaces. Unfortunately, the courts have largely disagreed, ruling that malls are private property whose owners can restrict speech within their boundaries. If meaningful democracy requires free spaces, then the scarcity of these spaces threatens democracy.

As free spaces become scarce, social movements become more valuable as one of the few remaining free spaces that can incubate democratic politics. Once again, we must be clear about the logic here. Some movements are hierarchical and authoritarian; there is no necessary link between social movements and democratic politics. But many movements *are* explicitly dedicated to this principle, and that makes progressive movements important defenders of free spaces and democratic politics.

An important example is the Free Speech movement of the 1960s. The initial issue was the seemingly small one of whether students had the right to set up tables and distribute political pamphlets on a plaza at the University of California campus at Berkeley. When campus administrators denied this right, it became a symbolically charged issue about defending a free space in which to debate ideas. The movement didn't support any particular political position as much as it supported the right to debate all political positions. In defending the free space necessary to democratic politics, the Free Speech movement was one of the most important progressive movements of the 1960s.

Progressive social movements have other traits that link them to the practice of democracy. As noted previously, deliberative democracy means that discussion or experience can transform initial preferences. Social movements often revise their agendas, goals, strategies, and tactics on the basis of such discussion. They also do it on the basis of experience and the trial-and-error lessons learned from movement failures and successes. In short, movements are learning mechanisms in which reflexive actors monitor and revise goals and actions informed by internal discussion and external experience.

This applies not only to a movement's agenda but also to its organization. Movement organization involves a basic dilemma. The most efficient way to organize a movement might be a hierarchical, centralized structure with clear divisions of labor and lines of authority between leaders and followers. This might provide efficiency, but it doesn't inspire much commitment. The other option is a decentralized, participatory, and egalitarian form of organization that elicits high commitment and loyalty, because people feel directly connected to the movement. Such organization, however, can be cumbersome and inefficient for achieving movement goals.

The reflexive quality of activism leads many progressive movements to consciously debate not just agendas or tactics but also organization. Such deliberation has led many to question the wisdom of using hierarchical organization to pursue egalitarian outcomes. In such cases, the means not only contradict the ends, but might overwhelm them and contaminate even successful outcomes by sustaining hierarchical means at the expense of egalitarian ends.

These considerations generated two principles central to many progressive movements. The first is prefigurative politics. This means that if the goal is a more democratic society, movements should "prefigure" this goal in the democratic organization of the movement itself. Even if it sacrifices efficiency, this ethic maintains that prefiguring democracy in the movement is more important than instrumental success at the expense of internal democracy.

The second, closely related notion is participatory democracy. Progressive movements are committed to maximizing participation for several reasons. It is consistent with the ethic of prefigurative politics. It allows the movement to benefit from a wide range of viewpoints. And it means that movements become a training ground for developing skills required for democratic politics. In all these ways, the goal of expanding democracy in society creates pressures to ensure that progressive movements themselves remain as democratic as possible.

Although internal democracy is laudable, the ultimate aim of progressive movements is to democratize the larger society. This occurs through several kinds of struggles. Resistance movements often arise from initially conservative impulses to defend everyday life against an external threat, though such impulses can eventually spark more radical demands for change. Liberation movements seek new rights for a subordinated group. But both resistance and liberation struggles tend to have temporary effects. They defend or alter the terms of an everyday life that remains divorced from making history (Flacks 1988).

A more basic change occurs in movements promoting democratic consciousness. They seek to permanently narrow the gap between everyday life and making history. To the extent such movements succeed, the making of history becomes a more democratic process that includes popular interests alongside elite ones. Although resistance and liberation movements are important, their greatest significance arises when they also activate a democratic consciousness that allows ordinary people to make history (Flacks 1988).

When we look at popular movements through this lens, it becomes evident that "the theme of democratization is the thread that runs through the history of each of the popular movements and that links each of them to the others" (Flacks 1988, 247). Moreover, it reveals how each of the progressive movements reviewed in the preceding chapter won partial victories whose cumulative impact has been the democratization of society. With each movement's gains, it became a little more possible for the next movement to build on previous organization, frames, rights, and resources to mount its own struggle (Flacks 1988, 247).

This historical analysis suggests that despite their limitations, "*movements are themselves the primary vehicles of democratic restructuring in America*" (Flacks 1988, 253; italics in original). In both internal organization and external impacts, progressive social movements have been our most important incubators of democratic politics.

The links between social movements and democratic politics transcend national boundaries. Consider the global justice movement. This transnational movement is really a "movement of movements" or a "network of networks" that faces daunting organizational challenges. Participants have responded by adopting deliberative democracy as their organizing principle (Della Porta 2005). This reflexive approach allows them to incorporate lessons from prior organizing to strengthen subsequent mobilization.

In practice, deliberative democracy in the global justice movement means fostering a culture of diversity and inclusiveness. It also means valuing personal experience rather than rigid obedience to organizational demands. In the same spirit, the movement consciously opts for transparency in its operations, even if this limits short-term effectiveness and goal achievement. The movement also sacrifices the efficiency of decision making through voting in favor of ongoing debates oriented to reaching a consensus. Finally, the movement is tolerant of ideological differences among participants, and it consciously avoids any dogmatism or "litmus test" as a condition of membership (Della Porta 2005).

This example illustrates two broader points about global organizing and democracy. First, movement organizing is enriched when participants bring diverse knowledge and experience to the process. Transnational organizing takes this to a new level, as activists from different national origins and protest cultures share knowledge, exchange lessons, and revise strategies. Second, the sheer diversity inherent in global movements all but requires inclusive, democratic organizing. It is difficult to envision how such movements could function without commitments to diversity and inclusiveness. The links between social movements and democratic organizing might thus be especially strong at the transnational level.

A wider analysis of resistance to current forms of globalization also finds democracy at the center of the struggle. Although this resistance takes various forms, its common denominator is a commitment to democracy. Indeed, whereas the integrating principle of current globalization is the market, the alternative integrating principle of global movements is democracy (Derber 2002, 139).

It follows that "reinventing globalization is really about reinventing democracy" (Derber 2002, 140). The reinvented democracy sought by global movements is not a procedural one that legitimates market domination but a substantive democracy that maximizes citizen participation. Such a democracy rests on three principles. Subsidiarity means that decisions are to be made at the most local level that can address a given problem. Federalism means that powers not explicitly granted to national or international bodies continue to reside with state, regional, or local governments. Globalization means that democratization must be vigorously pursued at every level of decision making. Its vitality at any one level is intimately tied to its health at all levels (Derber 2002, ch. 6).

Although these movements have distinct agendas, their common goals are to create democratically accountable world governments, to reconstruct national democracies, to democratize global business, to resurrect local community, and to create collective security (Derber 2002, 143). For obvious reasons, such a progressive agenda will not be advanced by elites who benefit from current arrangements. It depends vitally on the "people power" of popular movements.

The links between democratization and collective security deserve special emphasis. In the United States, the "war on terrorism" has been used to legitimate preemptive warfare, revive militarism, expand executive power, restrict civil liberties, and promote a climate of fear. Each has corrosive effects on national and international democracy.

For global movements, the solution is not less but more democracy. More democracy at home would enrich the range of solutions at our disposal and ensure that we don't lose our democracy in the process of "defending" it. More democracy abroad would undermine the appeal of terrorism and provide other avenues for political engagement. But to be meaningful, such democracy cannot be imposed from above through military invasion and occupation. It must develop organically as part of a broader global dynamic of substantive democratization.

Empirical research supports similar conclusions. Globalization has created a crisis of legitimacy for many governments that can no longer cope with the growing inequality produced by market forces. With the resulting erosion of democracy within nation-states, "many see transnational social movements as helping to define a global polity that is more democratic and inclusive than that preferred by either the economic globalizers or those who mobilize fundamentalist resistance to it" (Smith 2004, 2–3).

The democratic impulses of transnational activism have a longer history than is often recognized, reaching back to socialist, pacifist, world federalist, and liberal internationalist movements that predated World War II. In the 1960s and 1970s, transnational activism supported national independence movements and Third World solidarity campaigns. In the 1980s and 1990s, United Nations conferences facilitated peace movements, IMF and World Bank protests, denser transnational alliances, and nongovernmental organizations. Most recently, transnational activism has coalesced around the theme of global justice. The UN has played less of a role, as activists have increased the militancy of their opposition to corporate globalization and become more proactive in events like the World Social Forum (Smith 2004).

Although these movements have yet to fulfill the vision of global democracy, they are having an impact. The best indicator is that national governments and corporate interests can no longer ignore them and have been forced to respond. The responses have included violence against protesters and repression of dissent. Powerful interests have also moved more decision making outside of UN control and into financial institutions under their control (Smith 2004).

It is revealing that the response to demands for more democratic participation in global decision making has been to make decisions in more hidden and hierarchical ways. The historic tensions between capitalism and democracy have never been clearer than in the struggle over what kind of globalization will unfold in the twenty-first century. As capitalist elites defend property rights, progressive movements incubate democratic politics. The prospects for democratization depend heavily on their efforts.

SOCIOLOGY AND DEMOCRACY

This book began by claiming that the sociological perspective is critical to understanding and solving social problems. The sociological perspective sees society as a social construction, an emergent reality, and a historical product. It reveals the interaction between social structures and reflexive actors. It sensitizes us to the unintended and unanticipated consequences of social action.

There is a second meaning of critical sociology. The sociological perspective is inherently critical, because it assumes that the social world is not what it appears to be. Sociology examines the unintended consequences, latent functions, and hidden realities behind surface appearances. Sociology is suspicious in the face of official authority and belief, and thereby acquires its debunking quality. It is perfectly suited to asking who benefits from social arrangements and to pursuing answers that often contradict conventional truths.

A third meaning of critical sociology invokes a particular style of sociology that is explicitly based on the values of reason, freedom, equality, and democracy. Such values demand a critical analysis of our world and how it falls short of realizing them. They also pose the challenge of how to transform the social world and bring it into closer alignment with these values and the social practices that sustain them.

The multiple meanings of critical sociology coalesce in C. Wright Mills's (1959) concept of the sociological imagination. This imagination analyzes the connections among social structure, historical location, and personal biography. It reframes personal troubles as public issues. The sociological imagination embodies the classic Enlightenment values of reason, freedom, and democracy.

So a book that begins with sociology ends with democracy. The transition is no accident. Meaningful democracy requires an informed and engaged citizenry. The sociological imagination epitomizes this ideal. It exposes connections between social things. It sees behind surface appearances. It reveals who benefits from social arrangements. It encourages political engagement. It reinforces values that support democracy.

"The promise of sociology, in other words, is equivalent to the promise of democracy" (Dandaneau 2001, 194). By nurturing the sociological imagination, we cease to be objects of history made by others and begin to be subjects of our own history making. The prospects for democracy and the project of critical sociology are thus intimately connected.

References

Adelman, Larry. 2003. *Race: The Power of an Illusion.* Videodisc: California Newsreel.

Aires, Philippe. 1965. *Centuries of Childhood.* New York: Vintage Books.

Anderson, Charles. 1974. *The Political Economy of Social Class.* Englewood Cliffs, NJ: Prentice-Hall.

Apter, David. 1967. *The Politics of Modernization.* Chicago: University of Chicago Press.

Arnove, Anthony. 2000. "Publish and Perish." *In These Times* (December 25): 51–52.

Barstow, David, and Robin Stein. 2005. "Under Bush, a New Age of Prepackaged News." *New York Times* (March 13): 1, 18–19.

Baudrillard, Jean. 1983. *Simulations.* New York: Semiotext(e).

Bauman, Zygmunt, and Tim May. 2001. *Thinking Sociologically.* Malden, MA: Blackwell.

Bellah, Robert, Richard Madsen, William Sullivan, Ann Swidler, and Steven Tipton. 1985. *Habits of the Heart.* Berkeley: University of California Press.

Benford, Robert. 1993. "'You Could Be the Hundredth Monkey': Collective Action Frames and Vocabularies of Motive within the Nuclear Disarmament Movement." *The Sociological Quarterly* 34:195–216.

Berger, Peter. 1963. *Invitation to Sociology.* New York: Doubleday.

Berger, Peter, and Thomas Luckmann. 1966. *The Social Construction of Reality.* Garden City, NY: Anchor.

Bernstein, Henry. 1971. "Modernization in Theory and the Sociological Study of Development." *Journal of Development Studies* 7(2):141–160.

Black, Naomi. 1989. *Social Feminism.* Ithaca, NY: Cornell University Press.

Blau, Peter. 1964. *Exchange and Power in Social Life.* New York: Wiley.

Blau, Peter, and Otis Dudley Duncan. 1967. *The American Occupational Structure.* New York: Free Press.

Block, Fred. 1987. *Revising State Theory.* Philadelphia, PA: Temple University Press.

Blumer, Herbert. 1951. "The Field of Collective Behavior." In *Principles of Sociology,* ed. A. M. Lee, 167–222. New York: Barnes and Noble.

———. 1969. *Symbolic Interaction: Perspective and Method.* Englewood Cliffs, NJ: Prentice-Hall.

Bonilla-Silva, Eduardo. 2003. *Racism without Racists.* Lanham, MD: Rowman & Littlefield.

Bourdieu, Pierre. 1977. *Outline of a Theory of Practice.* London: Cambridge University Press.

———. 1998. *On Television.* London: Pluto Press.

Bowles, Samuel, and Herbert Gintis. 1976. *Schooling in Capitalist America.* New York: Basic Books.

Brown, David. 2004. *Social Blueprints.* New York: Oxford.

Buechler, Steven. 1986. *The Transformation of the Woman Suffrage Movement.* New Brunswick, NJ: Rutgers University Press.

———. 1990. *Women's Movements in the United States.* New Brunswick, NJ: Rutgers University Press.

———. 2000. *Social Movements in Advanced Capitalism.* New York: Oxford University Press.

Butler, Judith. 1991. *Gender Trouble.* New York: Routledge.

Chafetz, Janet Saltzman. 1984. *Sex and Advantage.* Totowa, NJ: Rowman & Allanheld.

Chew, Sing C., and Robert A. Denemark, eds. 1996. *The Underdevelopment of Development.* Thousand Oaks, CA: Sage.

Cohen, Jean. 1985. "Strategy or Identity: New Theoretical Paradigms and Contemporary Social Movements." *Social Research* 52:663–716.

Collins, Patricia Hill. 1990. *Black Feminist Thought.* Boston: Unwin Hyman.

Collins, Randall. 1975. *Conflict Sociology.* New York: Academic Press.

Cooley, Charles Horton. 1998. *On Self and Social Organization.* Chicago: University of Chicago Press.

Coser, Lewis. 1956. *The Functions of Social Conflict.* New York: Free Press.

Coser, Lewis, Charles Kadushin, and Walter W. Powell. 1982. *Books: The Culture and Commerce of Publishing.* New York: Basic.

Cross, Gary. 2000. *An All-Consuming Century.* New York: Columbia University Press.

Dahl, Robert. 1961. *Who Governs?* New Haven, CT: Yale University Press.

Dahrendorf, Ralf. 1959. *Class and Class Conflict in Industrial Society.* Stanford, CA: Stanford University Press.

Dandaneau, Steven. 2001. *Taking It Big.* Thousand Oaks, CA: Pine Forge Press.

Davis, Kingley, and Wilbert Moore. 1945. "Some Principles of Stratification." *American Sociological Review* 10:242–249.

de Tocqueville, Alexis. 1853/1969. *Democracy in America.* Garden City, NY: Doubleday.

Della Porta, Donatella. 2005. "Making the Polis: Social Forums and Democracy in the Global Justice Movement." *Mobilization* 10:73–94.

Della Porta, Donatella, and Sidney Tarrow, eds. 2005. *Transnational Protest and Global Activism.* Lanham, MD: Rowman & Littlefield.

Denzin, Norman. 1987. *The Alcoholic Self.* Newbury Park, CA: Sage.

Derber, Charles. 2002. *People before Profit.* New York: Picador.

Domhoff, G. William. 1967. *Who Rules America?* Englewood Cliffs, NJ: Prentice-Hall.

———. 2002. *Who Rules America?* 4th ed. Boston: McGraw-Hill.

Donovan, Josephine. 1985. *Feminist Theory.* New York: Ungar.

DuBois, W. E. B. 1903/1989. *The Souls of Black Folk.* New York: Bantam Books.

Durkheim, Emile. 1893/1964. *The Division of Labor in Society.* New York: Free Press.

———. 1897/1951. *Suicide.* New York: Free Press.

———. 1912/1965. *The Elementary Forms of the Religious Life.* New York: Free Press.

Eder, Klaus. 1993. *The New Politics of Class.* Newbury Park, CA: Sage.

Eissenstein, Zillah. 1979. *Capitalist Patriarchy and the Case for Socialist Feminism.* New York: Monthly Review Press.

Engels, Friedrich. 1985. *The Origin of the Family, Private Property, and the State.* Harmondsworth, Middlesex: Penguin Books.

Epstein, Cynthia Fuchs. 2007. "Great Divides: The Cultural, Cognitive, and Social Bases of the Global Subordination of Women." *American Sociological Review* 72:1–22.

Evans, Sara, and Harry Boyte. 1992. *Free Spaces*. Chicago: University of Chicago Press.

Feagin, Joe, and Clairece Booher Feagin. 1978. *Discrimination American Style*. Englewood Cliffs, NJ: Prentice-Hall.

Ferree, Myra Marx, and Beth Hess. 2000. *Controversy and Coalition*. 3rd ed. New York: Routledge.

Firestone, Shulaminth. 1970. *The Dialectic of Sex*. New York: Morrow.

Flacks, Richard. 1988. *Making History*. New York: Columbia University Press.

Foucault, Michel. 1965. *Madness and Civilization*. New York: Vintage.

———. 1966. *The Order of Things*. New York: Vintage.

———. 1969. *The Archaeology of Knowledge and the Discourse on Language*. New York: Harper Colophon.

———. 1975. *The Birth of the Clinic*. New York: Vintage.

———. 1979. *Discipline and Punish*. New York: Vintage.

———. 1980. *Power/Knowledge*. New York: Pantheon.

Frank, Andre Gunder. 1969. *Latin America: Underdevelopment or Revolution?* New York: Monthly Review Press.

Fraser, Nancy. 1989. *Unruly Practices*. Minneapolis: University of Minnesota Press.

Freedman, Estelle. 2002. *No Turning Back*. New York: Ballantine Books.

Freidan, Betty. 1963. *The Feminine Mystique*. New York: Dell.

Freud, Sigmund. 1955. *Civilization and Its Discontents*. London: Hogarth Press.

Garfinkel, Harold. 1967. *Studies in Ethnomethodology*. Englewood Cliffs, NJ: Prentice-Hall.

Gergen, Kenneth. 1991. *The Saturated Self*. New York: Basic Books.

Geschwender, James. 1968. "Exploration in the Theory of Social Movements and Revolutions." *Social Forces* 47:127–135.

———. 1978. *Racial Stratification in America*. Dubuque, IA: Wm. C. Brown.

Giddens, Anthony. 1984. *The Constitution of Society*. Berkeley: University of California Press.

———. 1991. *Modernity and Self-Identity*. Stanford, CA: Stanford University Press.

Gitlin, Todd. 1993. *The Sixties*. New York: Bantam.

Goffman, Erving. 1959. *The Presentation of Self in Everyday Life*. Garden City, NY: Anchor.

Gordon, Milton. 1964. *Assimilation in American Life*. New York: Oxford University Press.

Gramsci, Antonio. 1971. *Selections from the Prison Notebooks*. New York: International Publishers.

Habermas, Jürgen. 1969. *Knowledge and Human Interests*. Boston: Beacon.

———. 1975. *Legitimation Crisis*. Boston: Beacon.

———. 1987. *The Theory of Communicative Action, Volume 2: System and Lifeworld*. Boston: Beacon.

———. 1962/1989. *The Structural Transformation of the Public Sphere*. Cambridge, MA: MIT Press.

Hacker, Helen. 1951. "Women as a Minority Group." *Social Forces* 30:60–69.

Hall, Thomas, ed. 2000. *A World-Systems Reader*. Lanham, MD: Rowman & Littlefield.

Henslin, James. 2005. *Sociology*. 7th ed. Boston: Allyn and Bacon.

Herman, Edward, and Noam Chomsky. 1988. *Manufacturing Consent*. New York: Pantheon.

Holstein, James, and Jaber Gubrium. 2000. *The Self We Live By.* New York: Oxford University Press.

Homans, George. 1974. *Social Behavior: Its Elementary Forms.* New York: Harcourt, Brace Jovanovich.

How, Alan. 2003. *Critical Theory.* New York: Palgrave Macmillan.

Hunt, Scott, Robert D. Benford, and David A. Snow. 1994. "Identity Fields: Framing Processes and the Social Construction of Movement Identities." In *New Social Movements,* ed. Enrique Larana, Hank Johnston, and Joseph R. Gusfield, 185–208. Philadelphia, PA: Temple University Press.

Hunter, Floyd. 1953. *Community Power Structure.* New York: Anchor.

Ignatiev, Noel. 1995. *How the Irish Became White.* New York: Routledge.

Jacobson, Matthew. 1998. *Whiteness of a Different Color.* Cambridge, MA: Harvard University Press.

Jay, Martin. 1973. *The Dialectical Imagination.* Boston: Little, Brown.

Kivisto, Peter. 1998. *Key Ideas in Sociology.* Thousand Oaks, CA: Sage.

Klandermans, Bert. 1991. "New Social Movements and Resource Mobilization: The European and American Approaches Revisited." In *Research on Social Movements: The State of the Art in Western Europe and the USA,* ed. Dieter Rucht, 17–44. Boulder, CO: Westview Press.

Klandermans, Bert, and Sidney Tarrow. 1988. "Mobilization into Social Movements: Synthesizing European and American Approaches." In *International Social Movement Research, Volume 1, From Structure to Action,* ed. Bert Klandermans, Hanspeter Kriesi, and Sidney Tarrow, 1–38. New York: JAI Press.

Klein, Naomi. 1999. *No Logo.* New York: Picador.

Kuznets, Simon. 1965. *Economic Growth and Structure.* New York: Norton.

Larana, Enrique, Hank Johnston, and Joseph R. Gusfield, eds. 1994. *New Social Movements: From Ideology to Identity.* Philadelphia, PA: Temple University Press.

Lasch, Christopher. 1977. *Haven in a Heartless World.* New York: Basic Books.

———. 1979. *The Culture of Narcissism.* New York: Norton.

Lemert, Charles. 1997. *Social Things.* Lanham, MD: Rowman & Littlefield.

———. 2004. *Social Theory: The Multicultural and Classic Readings.* Boulder, CO: Westview Press.

Lerner, Daniel. 1958. *The Passing of Traditional Society.* Glencoe, IL: Free Press.

Lerner, Gerda. 1986. *The Creation of Patriarchy.* New York: Oxford University Press.

Luhman, Reid, and Stuart Gilman. 1980. *Race and Ethnic Relations.* Belmont, CA: Wadsworth.

Lyotard, Jean-François. 1979. *The Postmodern Condition.* Minneapolis: University of Minnesota Press.

Marcuse, Herbert. 1964. *One-Dimensional Man.* Boston: Beacon.

Marx, Karl, and Friedrich Engels. 1848/1948. *The Communist Manifesto.* New York: International Publishers.

McAdam, Doug. 1982. *The Political Process and the Development of Black Insurgency.* Chicago: University of Chicago Press.

McCarthy, Thomas. 1981. *The Critical Theory of Jurgen Habermas.* Cambridge, MA: MIT Press.

McCarthy, John D., and Mayer N. Zald. 1973. *The Trend of Social Movements in America: Professionalization and Resource Mobilization.* Morristown, NJ: General Learning Press.

————. 1977. "Resource Mobilization and Social Movements: A Partial Theory." *American Journal of Sociology* 82:1212–1241.

McChesney, Robert. 2000. *Rich Media, Poor Democracy.* New York: New Press.

————. 2004. *The Problem of the Media.* New York: Monthly Review Press.

McClelland, David. 1973. "Business Drive and National Achievement." In *Social Change,* ed. Eva Etzioni and Amitai Etzioni, 165–178. New York: Basic Books.

McHugh, Peter. 1968. *Defining the Situation.* Indianapolis, IN: Bobbs-Merrill.

McIntosh, Peggy. 2005. "White Privilege and Male Privilege." In *Great Divides,* ed. Thomas Shapiro, 300–307. New York: McGraw-Hill.

Mead, George Herbert. 1934/1962. *Mind, Self and Society.* Chicago: University of Chicago Press.

Merton, Robert. 1968. *Social Theory and Social Structure.* New York: Free Press.

Milgram, Stanley. 1974. *Obedience to Authority.* New York: Harper.

Miliband, Ralph. 1969. *The State in Capitalist Society.* London: Weidenfeld and Nicolson.

Mills, C. Wright. 1956. *The Power Elite.* New York: Oxford University Press.

————. 1959. *The Sociological Imagination.* New York: Oxford University Press.

Mohanty, Chandra Talpade. 2003. *Feminism without Borders: Decolonizing Theory, Practicing Solidarity.* Durham, NC: Duke University Press.

Moore, Michael. 2001. *Stupid White Men.* New York: Regan.

Moraga, Cherrie, and Gloria Anzaldua, eds. 1981. *This Bridge Called My Back.* New York: Kitchen Table Press.

Morris, Aldon. 1984. *The Origins of the Civil Rights Movement.* New York: Free Press.

Myrdal, Gunnar. 1944. *An American Dilemma.* New York: Harper and Row.

Niedhardt, Friedhelm, and Dieter Rucht. 1991. "The Analysis of Social Movements: The State of the Art and Some Perspective for Future Research." In *Research on Social Movements: The State of the Art in Western Europe and the USA,* ed. Dieter Rucht, 422–464. Boulder, CO: Westview Press.

Oberschall, Anthony. 1973. *Social Movements.* New Brunswick: Transaction.

O'Connor, James. 1973. *The Fiscal Crisis of the State.* New York: St. Martin's Press.

Offe, Claus. 1985. *Disorganized Capitalism.* Cambridge: Polity.

Omi, Michael, and Howard Winant. 1994. *Racial Formation in the United States.* 2nd ed. New York: Routledge.

Parsons, Talcott. 1937. *The Structure of Social Action.* New York: McGraw-Hill.

————. 1951. *The Social System.* Glencoe, IL: Free Press.

Perrucci, Robert, and Earl Wysong. 2003. *The New Class Society.* 2nd. ed. Lanham, MD: Rowman & Littlefield.

Pichardo, Nelson. 1997. "New Social Movements: A Critical Review." *Annual Review of Sociology* 23:411–430.

Piven, Frances Fox, and Richard A. Cloward. 1982. *The New Class War.* New York: Vintage.

————. 2004. *The War at Home.* New York: New Press.

Poulantzas, Nicos. 1975. *Political Power and Social Classes.* London: New Left Books.

Reich, Michael. 1981. *Racial Inequality.* Princeton, NJ: Princeton University Press.

Reynolds, Larry T. 2003. "Early Representatives." In *Handbook of Symbolic Interactionism,* ed. Larry T. Reynolds and Nancy J. Herman-Kinney, 59–81. Lanham, MD: AltaMira.

Ricci, David. 1971. *Community Power and Democratic Theory.* New York: Random House.

Riesman, David. 1950. *The Lonely Crowd.* New Haven, CT: Yale University Press.

Ritzer, George. 2000. *The McDonaldization of Society.* Thousand Oaks, CA: Pine Forge Press.

Roszak, Theodore. 1969. *The Making of a Counter Culture.* Garden City, NY: Anchor Books.

Rupp, Leila, and Verta Taylor. 1987. *Survival in the Doldrums.* New York: Oxford University Press.

Sadker, Myra, and David Sadker. 1994. *Failing at Fairness.* New York: Charles Scribner's Sons.

Scheff, Thomas. 2005. "Looking Glass Self: Goffman as Symbolic Interactionist." *Symbolic Interaction* 28(2):147–166.

Schiffrin, Andre. 2000. *The Business of Books: How International Conglomerates Took Over Publishing and Changed the Way We Read.* London: Verso.

Schmid, Thomas J., and Richard S. Jones. 1991. "Suspended Identity: Identity Transformation in a Maximum Security Prison." *Symbolic Interaction* 14(4):415–432.

Schor, Juliet. 2004. *Born to Buy.* New York: Scribner.

Schutz, Alfred. 1932/1967. *The Phenomenology of the Social World.* Evanston, IL: Northwestern University Press.

Schwartz, Michael. 1976. *Radical Protest and Social Structure.* New York: Academic Press.

Scott, James. 1990. *Domination and the Arts of Resistance.* New Haven, CT: Yale University Press.

Shannon, Thomas. 1989. *An Introduction to the World-System Perspective.* Boulder, CO: Westview Press.

Simmel, Georg. 1908/1955. *Conflict and the Web or Group Affiliations.* New York: Free Press.

Skocpol, Theda. 1979. *States and Social Revolutions.* Cambridge: Cambridge University Press.

Slater, Philip. 1970. *The Pursuit of Loneliness.* Boston: Beacon Press.

Smelser, Neil. 1962. *Theory of Collective Behavior.* New York: Free Press.

Smith, Dorothy. 1987. *The Everyday World as Problematic: A Feminist Sociology.* Boston: Northeastern University Press.

———. 1990. *The Conceptual Practices of Power: A Feminist Sociology of Knowledge.* Boston: Northeastern University Press.

Smith, Jackie. 2004. "Democratizing Globalization? Impacts and Limitations of Transnational Social Movements." Working Paper Series, Institute on Globalization and the Human Condition, McMaster University, Hamilton, Ontario.

Smith, Jackie, and Hank Johnston. 2002. *Globalization and Resistance.* Lanham, MD: Rowman & Littlefield.

Snow, David, and Robert Benford. 1988. "Ideology, Frame Resonance, and Participant Mobilization." In *International Social Movements Research, Volume 1, From Structure to Action,* ed. Bert Klandermans, Hanspeter Kreisi, and Sidney Tarrow, 197–217. Greenwich, CT: JAI Press.

———. 1992. "Master Frames and Cycles of Protest." In *Frontiers of Social Movement Theory,* ed. Carol Mueller and Aldon Morris, 133–155. New Haven, CT: Yale University Press.

Snow, David, E. Burke Rochford Jr., Steve K. Worden, and Robert D. Benford. 1986. "Frame Alignment Processes, Micromobilization and Movement Participation." *American Sociological Review* 51:464–481.

Spivak, Gayatri Chakravorty. 1996. *The Spivak Reader: Selected Works of Gayatri Chakravorty Spivak,* ed. Donna Landry and Gerald MacLean. New York: Routledge.

———. 1999. *A Critique of Postcolonial Reason.* Cambridge, MA: Harvard University Press.

Starr, Amory. 2000. *Naming the Enemy.* London: Zed.

Strasser, Susan. 1982. *Never Done.* New York: Pantheon Books.

Swartz, David. 1997. *Culture and Power.* Chicago: University of Chicago Press.

Tarrow, Sidney. 1994. *Power in Movement.* London: Cambridge University Press.

Thompson, John. 1990. *Ideology and Modern Culture.* Stanford, CA: Stanford University Press.

Tilly, Charles. 1978. *From Mobilization to Revolution.* Reading, MA: Addison-Wesley.

———. 1995. *Popular Contention in Great Britain, 1758–1834.* Cambridge, MA: Harvard University Press.

Trinh, T. Minh-Ha. 1989. *Woman, Native, Other: Writing Postcoloniality and Feminism.* Bloomington: Indiana University Press.

Truman, David. 1951. *The Governmental Process.* New York: Knopf.

Tumin, Melvin. 1953. "Some Principles of Stratification: A Critical Analysis." *American Sociological Review* 18:387–394.

Turner, Ralph, and Lewis, Killian. 1987. *Collective Behavior.* 3rd ed. Upper Saddle River, NJ: Prentice-Hall.

Vryan, Kevin D., Patricia A. Adler, and Peter Adler. 2003. "Identity." In *Handbook of Symbolic Interactionism,* ed. Larry T. Reynolds and Nancy J. Herman-Kinney, 367–390. Lanham, MD: AltaMira.

Wallerstein, Immanuel. 1974. *The Modern-World System.* New York: Academic Press.

———. 1980. *The Modern-World System II.* New York: Academic Press.

———. 1989. *The Modern-World System III.* New York: Academic Press.

Weber, Max. 1904/1958. *The Protestant Ethic and the Spirit of Capitalism.* New York: Scribners.

———. 1921/1968. *Economy and Society.* 3 Volumes. Totowa, NJ: Bedminster Press.

Weiner, Tim. 2004. "Low-Wage Costa Ricans Make Baseballs for Millionaires." *New York Times* (January 25): 3.

Whyte, William H. 1956. *The Organization Man.* Garden City, NY: Doubleday.

Winant, Howard. 1994. *Racial Conditions.* Minneapolis: University of Minnesota Press.

———. 2004. *The New Politics of Race.* Minneapolis: University of Minnesota Press.

Wright, Erik Olin. 1978. *Class, Crisis and the State.* London: Verso.

———. 1985. *Classes.* London: Verso.

Zeitlin, Irving. 1987. *Ideology and the Development of Sociological Theory.* Englewood Cliffs, NJ: Prentice-Hall.

Zinn, Howard. 1980. *A People's History of the United States.* New York: Harper Collins.

About the Author

Steven M. Buechler is Professor of Sociology at Minnesota State University, Mankato. He teaches social theory, social movements, and social stratification. He has researched and written extensively on women's movements and social movement theory. His publications include *The Transformation of the Woman Suffrage Movement* (Rutgers University Press, 1986), *Women's Movements in the United States* (Rutgers University Press, 1990), and *Social Movements: Perspectives and Issues* (with F. Kurt Cylke, Mayfield Press, 1997). His most recent book is *Social Movements in Advanced Capitalism*, published by Oxford University Press (2000).

Index